Classroom-Ready Activities for Teaching History and Geography in Grades 7–12

Related Titles of Interest

Teaching Thinking Skills: A Handbook for Secondary School Teachers
Barry K. Beyer
ISBN: 0-205-12797-5

Interdisciplinary High School Teaching: Strategies for Integrated Learning
John H. Clarke and Russell M. Agne
ISBN: 0-205-15710-6

Interdisciplinary Strategies for English and Social Studies Classrooms: Toward Collaborative Middle and Secondary Teaching
Joseph John Nowicki and Kerry F. Meehan
ISBN: 0-205-19839-2

The Collaborative Social Studies Classroom: A Resource for Teachers, Grades 7–12
Joseph John Nowicki and Kerry F. Meehan
ISBN: 0-205-17391-8

Literature-Based History Activities for Children, Grades 4–8
Patricia L. Roberts
ISBN: 0-205-14737-2

Teaching Social Studies in Grades K–8: Information, Ideas, and Resources for Classroom Teachers
Thomas P. Ruff
ISBN: 0-205-14606-6

The Thinking Classroom: Learning and Teaching in a Culture of Thinking
Shari Tishman, David N. Perkins, and Eileen Jay
ISBN: 0-205-16508-7

For more information or to purchase a book, please call 1-800-278-3525.

Classroom-Ready Activities for Teaching History and Geography in Grades 7–12

THOMAS P. RUFF
Washington State University

JENNIFER T. NELSON
Gonzaga University

Allyn and Bacon
Boston   London   Toronto   Sydney   Tokyo   Singapore

Copyright © 1998 by Allyn & Bacon
A Viacom Company
Needham Heights, MA 02194

Internet: www.abacon.com
America Online: keyword: College Online

Library of Congress Cataloging-in-Publication Data

Ruff, Thomas P.
    Classroom-ready activities for teaching history and geography
in grades 7–12 / Thomas P. Ruff, Jennifer T. Nelson.
        p.   cm.
    Includes bibliographical references and index.
    ISBN 0-205-26375-5
    1. History—Study and teaching (Secondary)   2. Geography—
Study and teaching (Secondary)   I. Nelson, Jennifer T.   II. Title.
D16.2.R84   1998
907.1'2—dc21   97-15531
                                                                CIP

Printed in the United States of America
10 9 8 7 6 5 4 3 2 1   01 00 99 98 97

This book is dedicated to my grandsons,
Matthew and Nicholas Squires.
May their world be a better one than ours.
—T.R.

I would like to dedicate this book
to Sheila Nelson,
to my family and high school students
in South Africa,
and to Pat and Altamae.
—J.N.

"If I had a child who wanted to be a teacher, I would bid him Godspeed as if he were going to a war. For indeed the war against prejudice, greed and ignorance is eternal, and those who dedicate themselves to it give their lives no less because they may live to see some fraction of the battle won."

—James Hilton

CONTENTS

PREFACE AND ACKNOWLEDGMENTS

A great many books are available that were written expressly to train teachers in how to teach social studies. They all tend to follow a similar format: (1) identify and define the social sciences, (2) present rationales for teaching social studies, (3) review curricular trends, and (4) illustrate some instructional options.

This is not one of those books!

As important as it is to know and understand historical and geographical content, such knowledge, by itself cannot ensure that any person will become an effective classroom teacher. This has been a myth too long accepted and practiced by the vast majority of secondary school social studies teachers—the erroneous notion that the mere acquisition of facts or mastery in the disciplines will create academic paragons serving interested, eager students who are seeking data and knowledge from them.

To the contrary, research reveals that most middle-level and high school students are bored by teachers and classes that focus mainly on the trivia of history and social studies. All too frequently, these students view social studies as a disjointed set of facts and dates, with little relevance or meaning to their lives. The traditional university model of lecture, discussion, and examinations does not work well with secondary-age students.

Teachers need concrete, classroom-tested examples of how better to teach the content they already know so well, how to interest their students in learning the content in a more dynamic way—making it more relevant, more meaningful, and certainly more fun than the more traditional ways.

As the title implies, *Classroom-Ready Activities for Teaching History and Geography in Grades 7–12* proposes to provide information, ideas, and resources for classroom teachers. The book will also offer many classroom-tested activities designed to inform, educate, and motivate students. The text clearly illustrates how history and geography, taught by themselves or integrated into other subject areas, can become an exciting and worthwhile adventure for both teachers and their students, making it a more rewarding experience for all.

During the past several years, social studies education has come under intense scrutiny by friend and critic alike. Many scholars have surveyed K–12 curriculum, analyzed standardized test scores, and interviewed teachers and students. They have all come to many of the same conclusions. Americans, they find, are functionally illiterate in history, geography, and civics. And most of those surveyed remember hating social studies, finding it boring, irrelevant, and all too frequently based on the memorization of isolated facts that had nothing to do with their lives.

The fault, as Shakespeare reminded us, is not in the stars but in ourselves. Until classroom teachers view history and geography as relevant school subjects and make them a meaningful learning experience for their students, nothing will change. The challenge is to give teachers knowledge; appropriate and usable materials; skills to integrate the subject matter into the curriculum; and the ability to make history and geography fun, interesting, and relevant for all students.

This is not a reform package that will resolve all the problems previously stated. Rather, it is intended as an information guide and resource for those who work daily to shape the minds, hearts, and futures of students—the classroom teachers. It is on their shoulders that the burden of curriculum implementation directly rests, and it is their knowledge, skills, and commitment that we must trust and rely on if history and geography are to become a valuable academic component, especially at the middle and secondary school levels.

ACKNOWLEDGMENTS

A specific thank-you to research assistants Melissa Mackay, Tariq Akmal, and Tim Cashman, who gave so generously of their time in the completion of this manuscript. Thanks also go to Lennis Larson and Norman Dale Conard for their review of the manuscript.

Classroom-Ready Activities for Teaching History and Geography in Grades 7–12

CHAPTER ONE

Perspectives

We Americans are the best informed people on earth as to the events of the last twenty-four hours; we are not the best informed as to the events of the last sixty centuries.

—Will and Ariel Durant

WHAT IS SOCIAL STUDIES?

In November 1992, the National Council for the Social Studies (NCSS) provided the first official definition for social studies:

> Social Studies is the integrated study of the social sciences and humanities to promote civic competence. Within the school program, social studies provides a co-ordinated, systematic study drawing upon such disciplines as anthropology, archeology, economics, geography, history, law, philosophy, political science, psychology, religion and sociology, as well as appropriate content from the humanities, mathematics and natural sciences. The primary purpose of social studies is to help young people develop the ability to make informed decisions for the public good as citizens of a culturally diverse, democratic society in an interdependent world. [McBride, p. 282]

Most colleges of education will be unable to prepare prospective social studies teachers to be even minimally competent to teach an integrated course in all the disciplines referred to in this definition.

History is the one discipline that could provide the catalyst for integrating the many fields of study identified in the definition. The California History/Social Science Framework (1988) and the Bradley Commission on History in the Schools (1988) envisaged placing history at the center of the social studies curriculum. Bill Honig (1987), superintendent for public instruction in California, wrote, ". . . history is what makes the past meaningful. History is the lens through which children and adults can come to understand the world in which they live and the powerful forces that make it what it is . . . history's rightful place is at the center of the social studies curriculum" (p. 3).

America 2000 singled out history and geography as core subjects. To understand history, students must also understand the characteristics of the places in which the historical events occurred. The National Council for Geographic Education (1991) has suggested approaching the teaching of geography through these five themes:

1. *Location:* Absolute and relative position on the earth's surface
2. *Place:* Physical and human characteristics

3. *Human/environment interactions:* Humans depending on, modifying, and adapting to the environment
4. *Movement:* Of people, goods, ideas, animals, water, air, and earth
5. *Regions:* Particular unifying feature or set of features that distinguishes the region from surrounding areas.

Geography combines the physical and human aspects of our world into one field of study. This combination focuses on the interdependent parts of our world to provide a practical framework for studying local, national, and global questions. Geography shows the relationship between people and the environment. It is this bridge that makes geography unique among the traditional academic disciplines.

A study of history and geography offers the perspectives of time and place. It has been said that history cannot exist without a sense of place, geography cannot exist without a sense of time, and neither would have meaning without humanity as the common denominator. Unique among subjects taught in school, history and geography are necessarily interdisciplinary, encompassing all other fields of thought. A study of these two disciplines will endow students with a broad knowledge of other times, cultures, and places.

A study of history and geography is also a study of global education, for global education as defined by Tye in 1991,

> involves learning about those problems and issues that cut across national boundaries, and about the interconnectedness of systems—ecological, cultural, economic, political and technological. Global education involves perspective-taking, seeing things through the eyes and minds of others; and it means realizing that while individuals and groups view life differently, they also have common needs and wants. (p. 163)

It is imperative that more time and better ways of teaching global issues be found if students are to emerge from secondary education programs with an intelligent global perspective.

MAJOR REPORTS

There are too many reports to discuss in this chapter, but it is important to review some of the more prominent studies and cite their respective recommendations. The reports we will review are the Bradley Commission on History in Schools, *Charting a Course: Social Studies for the Twenty-first Century* by the National Council for the Social Studies and the California History/Social Science Framework.

Although the commissions reviewed here had different members, started in different years, and probably had different agendas, all came to many of the same conclusions.

1. History and geography remain at the core of kindergarten through grade 12 (K–12) social studies curriculum.
2. History should be taught chronologically.
3. The subject matter should be taught in depth.
4. Social studies should be integrated more into existing curricula (especially in literature and literacy development).
5. Global education should be introduced early in the elementary grades.

6. Multicultural education should be integrated into the K–12 experience.
7. Non-Western history and geography should be given a more important role in the curriculum.
8. Civic education is an essential component for students who live in a participatory democracy such as ours.
9. Classroom teachers should be trained or retrained in history and geography education.
10. New and more appropriate teaching/learning materials should be developed for classroom use.

The Bradley Commission

The Bradley Commission on History in the Schools was created in 1987 in response to concern over the inadequacy in both quality and quantity of the history taught in U.S. schools. The commission set itself two goals: (1) to examine what contributes to the effective teaching of history, and (2) to make recommendations on the curricular role of history as the core of the social studies.

The commission made the following major recommendations:

1. The knowledge and habits of mind to be gained from the study of history are indispensable to the education of citizens in a democracy. Therefore, the study of history should be required of all students.
2. Such study must reach well beyond the acquisition of useful information in order to promote the development of judgment and perspective.
3. The curricular time essential to develop the genuine understanding and engagement necessary to exercising judgment must be considerably greater than that now common in U.S. school programs in history.
4. Every student should have an understanding of the world that encompasses the historical experiences of peoples of Africa, the Americas, Asia, and Europe.
5. History can best be understood when the roles of all constituent parts of society are included. Therefore, the history of women, racial and ethnic minorities, and men and women of all classes and conditions should be integrated into historical instruction.

Charting a Course: Social Studies for the Twenty-first Century

In 1985, the National Council for the Social Studies, the American Historical Association, the Carnegie Foundation for the Advancement of Teaching, and the Organization of American Historians formed a coalition and established the National Commission on Social Studies in Schools. The commission's tasks included examining the content and effectiveness of instruction in the social studies in U.S. elementary and secondary schools, determining goals for the social studies, and establishing priorities of importance in the field.

The commission's recommendations were first published in November 1989 in a publication entitled *Charting a Course: Social Studies for the Twenty-first Century*, which clearly outlined both the substance and structure of a K–12 social studies curriculum. It listed the characteristics of a social studies program, outlined the goals, and discussed specific grade-level curriculum. A summary of some of these recommendations follows:

1. Because they offer the perspectives of time and place, history and geography should provide the matrix or framework for social studies; yet concepts and understandings from political science, economics, and other social sciences must be integrated throughout all social studies courses. By the end of the twelfth grade, students would then have a firm understanding of their principles and methodologies.

2. Selective studies of geography, government, and the economic systems of the major civilizations and societies should together receive attention at least equal to the study of the history, geography, government, economics, and society of the United States. A curriculum that focuses on only one or two major civilizations or geographic areas while ignoring others is neither adequate nor complete.

3. Learning materials must incorporate a rich mix of written matter, including original sources, literature, and expository writing; a variety of audiovisual materials including films, television, and interactive media; a collection of items of material culture including artifacts, photographs, census records, and historical maps; and computer programs for writing and analyzing social, economic, and geographic data. Social studies coursework should teach students to evaluate the reliability of all such sources of information and to be aware of the ways in which various media select, shape, and constrain information.

History–Social Science Framework for California Public Schools, K–12

In 1987, the California State Board of Education adopted a framework for teaching history/social studies education for grades K–12. This was a direct and powerful response to the widespread concern and demand for a renaissance of the teaching of history and geography in the K–12 system. Like many other studies and reports, it places history and geography at the hub and establishes a sequential curriculum that allows students to understand the development of their own nation and that of other major civilizations and cultures.

The framework integrates history and geography with the humanities and social sciences; it is designed to enrich the content at the early grades and to teach civic values throughout the sequence. It involves ethical concepts and values as well as religious and secular notions and how they affected history, and it recognizes the plurality of U.S. society. Finally, it spends considerable time reviewing appropriate and responsible citizenship in a representative democracy. Specifically, the framework includes the following:

1. This framework is centered in the chronological study of history. History, placed in its geographic setting, establishes human activities in time and place. History and geography are the two great integrative studies of the field. In examining the past and present, students should recognize that events and changes occur in a specific time and place; that historical change has both causes and effects; and that life is bounded by the constraints place. Throughout this curriculum, the importance of the variables of time and place, when and where, history and geography, is stressed repeatedly.

2. This framework emphasizes the importance of history as a story well told. Whenever appropriate, history should be presented as an exciting and dramatic series of events in the past that helped to shape the pres-

ent. The teacher should endeavor to bring the past to life and to make vivid the struggles and triumphs of men and women who lived in other times and places. The story of the past should be lively and accurate as well as rich with controversies and forceful personalities. While assessing the social, economic, political, and cultural contest of events, teachers must never neglect the value of good storytelling as a source of motivation for the study of history.

3. This framework emphasizes the importance of enriching the study of history with the use of literature *of* the period and *about* the period. Teachers of history and teachers of language arts must collaborate to select representative works. Poetry, novels, plays, essays, documents, inaugural addresses, myths, legends, tall tales, biographies, and religious literature help to shed light on the life and times of the people. Such literature helps to reveal the way people saw themselves, their ideas and values, their fears and dreams, and the way they interpreted their own times.

4. The framework emphasized the importance of studying major historical events and periods in depth as opposed to superficial skimming of enormous amounts of material. The integrated and correlated approach proposed here requires time; students should not be made to feel that they are on a forced march across many centuries and continents. The courses in this framework identify specific eras and events that are to be studied in depth so that students will have time to use a variety of nontextbook materials, to think about what they are studying, and to see it in rich detail and broad scope.

5. This framework incorporates a multicultural perspective throughout the history/social science curriculum. It calls on teachers to recognize that the history of community, state, region, nation, and world must reflect the experiences of men and women and of different racial, religious, and ethnic groups.

6. This framework encourages teachers to present controversial issues honestly and accurately within their historical or contemporary context. History without controversy is not good history, nor is such history as interesting to students as an account that captures debates of the times. Students should understand that the events in history provoked controversy as do the events reported in today's headlines. Students should try to see historical controversies through the different perspectives of participants. These controversies can best be portrayed by using original documents such as newspapers, court decisions, and speeches that represent different views. Students should also recognize that historians often disagree about the interpretation of historical events and that today's textbooks, may be altered by future research. Through the study of controversial issues, both in history and in current affairs, students should learn that people in a democratic society have the right to disagree, that different perspectives have to be taken into account, and that judgments should be based on reasonable evidence and not on bias and emotion.

7. This framework supports a variety of content-appropriate teaching methods that engage students actively in the learning process. Local and oral history projects, writing projects, debates, simulations, role playing, dramatizations, and cooperative learning are encouraged, as is the use of technology to supplement reading and classroom activities

and to enrich the teaching of history and social science. Video resources such as video programs and laser discs, computer software, and newly emerging forms of educational technology can provide invaluable resources for the teaching of history, geography, economics, and other disciplines.

It is important to be aware and understand what is being proposed for the teaching of history and geography in grades 7–12. These commissions and their respective reports have had a direct impact on the curriculum, the textbooks and other teaching/learning materials, and most certainly on the pre- and inservice training given to classroom teachers.

CHAPTER TWO

The National History and Geography Standards: What They Mean for Classroom Teachers

The development of national standards in United States history, World history, and Geography presents a special challenge in deciding what human activities in time and place are the most significant for all students to acquire.

—History and Social Studies Framework

THE NATIONAL GEOGRAPHY STANDARDS, 1994

Why Standards?

The inclusion of geography as a core subject in Goals 2000: Educate America Act (Public Law 103-227) is the culmination of a decade of reform in geography education. There is now a widespread acceptance among the people of the United States that being literate in geography is essential if students are to leave school equipped to earn a decent living, enjoy the richness of life, and participate responsibly in local, national, and international affairs. In response to this desire for a geographically literate society, educators and parents, as well as members of business, professional, and civic organizations, have built a national consensus regarding the study of geography and produced *Geography for Life: National Geography Standards 1994.*

The purpose of standards for geography is to bring all students up to internationally competitive levels to meet the demands of a new age and a different world. For the United States to maintain leadership and prosper in the twenty-first century, the education system must be tailored to the needs of productive and responsible citizenship in the global economy.

The Eighteen Standards

Physical and human phenomena are spatially distributed over the earth's surface. The outcome of *Geography for Life* is a geographically informed person who (1) sees meaning in arrangement of things in space; (2) sees relations between people, places, and environments; (3) uses geographic skills; and (4) applies spatial and ecological perspectives to life situations.

The World in Spatial Terms

Geography studies the relationships between people, places, and environments by mapping information about them into a spatial context.

The geographically informed person knows and understands:

1. How to use maps and other geographic representations, tools, and technologies to acquire, process, and report information from a spatial perspective
2. How to use mental maps to organize information about people, places, and environments in a spatial context
3. How to analyze the spatial organization of people, places, and environments on the earth's surface

Places and Regions

The identities and lives of individuals and people are rooted in particular places and in those human constructs called regions.

The geographically informed person knows and understands:

4. The physical and human characteristics of places
5. That people create regions to interpret earth's complexity
6. How culture and experience influence people's perceptions of places and regions

Physical Systems

Physical processes shape the earth's surface and interact with plant and animal life to create, sustain, and modify ecosystems.

The geographically informed person knows and understands:

7. The physical processes that shape the patterns of earth's surface
8. The characteristics and spatial distribution of ecosystems on earth's surface

Human Systems

People are central to geography in that human activities help shape earth's surface, human settlements and structures are part of earth's surface, and humans compete for control of earth's surface.

The geographically informed person knows and understands:

9. The characteristics, distribution, and migration of human populations around the globe
10. The characteristics, distribution, and complexity of earth's cultural mosaics
11. The patterns and networks of economic interdependence on the earth
12. The processes, patterns, and functions of human settlement
13. How the forces of cooperation and conflict among people influence the division and control of the earth's

Environment and Society

The physical environment is modified by human activities, largely as a consequence of the ways in which human societies value and use earth's natural resources. Human activities are also influenced by earth's physical features and processes.

The geographically informed person knows and understands:

14. How human actions modify the physical environment
15. How physical systems affect human systems
16. The changes that occur in the meaning, use, distribution and importance of resources

The Uses of Geography
Knowledge of geography enables people to develop an understanding of the relationships between people, places, and environments over time—that is, on earth as it was, is, and might be.
The geographically informed person knows and understands:

17. How to apply geography to interpret the past
18. How to apply geography to interpret the present and plan for the future (*National Geographic Standards 1994*)

THE NATIONAL HISTORY STANDARDS, 1994

Definition of Standards

In history, standards are of two types:

1. *Historical thinking skills* that enable students to evaluate evidence, develop comparative and causal analyses, interpret the historical record, and construct sound historical arguments and perspectives on which informed decisions in contemporary life can be based.
2. *Historical understandings* that define what students should *know* about the history of their nation and of the world. These understandings are drawn form the record of human aspirations, strivings, accomplishments, and failures in at least five spheres of human activity: the social, political, scientific/technological, economic, and philosophical/religious/aesthetic. They also provide students with the historical perspectives required to analyze contemporary issues and problems confronting citizens today.

Criteria for the Development of Standards

The development of national standards in United States and World History presents a special challenge in deciding what, of the great storehouse of human history, is the most significant for all students to acquire. Perhaps less contentious but no less important is deciding what historical perspectives and what skills in historical reasoning, values analysis, and policy thinking are essential for all students to achieve.

The following criteria, developed and refined over the course of a broad-based national review and consensus process, were adopted by the National Council for History Standards to guide the development of history standards for grades K–12.

1. Standards should be intellectually demanding, reflect the best historical scholarship, and promote active questioning and learning rather than passive absorption of facts, dates, and names.

2. Such standards should be equally expected of *all students,* and all students should be provided equal access to the curricular opportunities necessary to achieving those standards.

3. Standards should reflect the ability of children from the earliest elementary school years to learn the meanings of history and the methods of historians.

4. Standards should be founded in chronology, an organizing approach that fosters appreciation of pattern and causation in history.

5. Standards should strike a balance between emphasizing broad themes in United States and World History and probing specific historical events, ideas, movements, persons, and documents.

6. All historical study involves selection and ordering of information in light of general ideas and values. Standards for history should reflect the principles of sound historical reasoning—careful evaluation of evidence, construction of causal relationships, balanced interpretation, and comparative analysis. The ability to detect and evaluate distortion and propaganda by omission, suppression, or invention of facts is essential.

7. Standards should include awareness of, appreciation for, and the ability to utilize a variety of sources of evidence from which historical knowledge is achieved, including written documents, oral tradition, popular culture, literature, artifacts, art and music, historical sites, photographs, and films.

8. Standards for United States History should reflect both the nation's diversity exemplified by race, ethnicity, social and economic status, gender, region, politics, religion, and the nation's commonalities. The contributions and struggles of specific groups and individuals should be included.

9. Standards in United States History should contribute to citizenship education through developing understanding of our common civic identity and shared civic values within the polity, through analyzing major policy issues in the nation's history, and through developing mutual respect among its many peoples.

10. History standards should emphasize the nature of civil society and its relationship to government and citizenship. Standards in United States History should address the historical origins of the nation's democratic political systems and the continuing development of its ideals and institution, its controversies, and the struggle to narrow the gap between its ideas and practices. Standards in World History should include different patterns of political institutions, ranging from varieties of democracy to varieties of authoritarianism, and ideas and aspirations developed by civilizations in all parts of the world.

11. Standards in United States and World History should be separately developed but interrelated in content and similar in format. Standards in United States History should reflect the global context in which the nation unfolded, and World History should treat United States History as one of its integral parts.

12. Standards should include appropriate coverage of recent events in United States and World History, including social and political developments and international relations of the post–World War II era.

13. Standards in United States History and World History should utilize regional and local history by exploring specific events and movements through case studies and historical research. Local and regional history should enhance the broader patterns of United States and World History.

14. Standards in United States History and World History should integrate fundamental facets of human culture such as religion, science and technology, politics and government, economics, interactions with the environment, intellectual and social life, literature, and the arts.

15. Standards in World History should treat the history and values of diverse civilizations, including those of the West, and should especially address the interactions among them.

DEVELOPING STANDARDS IN UNITED STATES HISTORY

Periodization

Students should understand that the periods into which the written histories of the United States or the world are divided are simply inventions of historians trying to impose some order on an inherently messy past that can be read and conceptualized in a variety of ways. In a diverse nation like the United States, no periodizing scheme will work for all groups. Native American history has benchmark eras that sometimes but not always overlap with those of European settlers in the colonial period. Iroquois history would have to be periodized differently form Sioux or Zuni history. African American history would have its own watersheds, such as the shift from white indentured servitude to black slave labor in the South, the abolition of the slave trade, the beginning of emigrationism, and so forth. So also with women's history and with Mexican American history.

Nonetheless, we believe that teachers will appreciate a periodization that attempts to blend political and social history. For this purpose, political events in U.S. history such as the American Revolution, the Constitution, the Civil War, Progressivism, the New Deal, and the Cold War, all of which have fairly definite beginning and end points, are still useful ways to provide breakpoints in the United States history curriculum. The industrial revolution, the labor movement, environmentalism, shifts in child rearing and family size, and so forth have no such precise beginning and end points and cut across eras defined by revolution, civil war, depression, and the like. In fact, none of the college texts in U.S. history that have tried in recent years to infuse social history into political and institutional history have been able to get around the general determinacy of wars and political reform movements and the indeterminacy of demographic, cultural, and social transformations.

We have tried to overcome, in part, the difficulties inherent in periodizing history by overlapping eras to demonstrate that there really is no such thing as an era's beginning or ending and that all such schemes are simply the historian's way of trying to give some structure to the course of history. The ten eras selected for periodizing United States history are as follows:

Era 1 Three Worlds Meet (Beginnings to 1620)
Era 2 Colonization and Settlement (1585–1763)
Era 3 Revolution and the New Nation (1754–1820s)
Era 4 Expansion and Reform (1801–1861)

Era 5 Civil War and Reconstruction (1850–1877)
Era 6 The Development of the Industrial United States (1870–1900)
Era 7 The Emergence of Modern America (1890–1930)
Era 8 The Great Depression and World War II (1929–1945)
Era 9 Postwar United States (1945–early 1970s)
Era 10 Contemporary United States (1969–present)

Historical Understanding

History is a broadly integrative field, recounting and analyzing human aspirations and strivings in various spheres of human activity: social, political, scientific/technological, economic, and cultural. Studying history—inquiring into families, communities, states, nations, and various peoples of the world—at once engages students in the lives, aspirations, struggles, accomplishments, and failures of real people.

Through social history, students come to deeper understandings of society: of what it means to be human, of different and changing views of family structures, of men's and women's roles, of childhood and of children's roles, of various groups and classes in society, and of relationships among all these individuals and groups. This sphere considers how economic, religious, cultural, and political changes have affected social life, and it incorporates developments shaping the destiny of millions: the history of slavery, of class conflict, and of mass migration and immigration; the human consequences of plague, war, and famine; and the longer life expectancy and rising living standards following upon medical, technological, and economic advances.

Through political history, students come to deeper understandings of the political sphere of activity as it has developed in their local community, their state, their nation, and various societies of the world. Efforts to construct governments and institutions; the drive to seize and hold power over others, the struggle to achieve and preserve basic human rights, justice, equality, law and order in societies, and the evolution of regional and world mechanisms to promote international law are all part of the central human drama to be explored and analyzed in the study of history.

Through history of science and technology, students come to deeper understanding of how the scientific quest to understand nature, the world we live in, and humanity itself is as old as recorded history. So, too, is the quest to improve ways of doing everything from producing food, caring for the ill, and transporting goods, to advancing economic security and the well-being of the group. Understanding how scientific/technological developments have propelled change and how these changes have altered all other spheres of human activity is central to the study of history.

Through economic history, students come to deeper understandings of the economic forces that have been crucial in determining the quality of people's lives, in structuring societies, and in influencing the course of events. Exchange relationships within and between cultures have had major impacts on society and politics, producing changing patterns of regions, hemispheric, and global economic dominance and permitting the emergence in the twentieth century of a truly international economy, with far-reaching consequences for all other spheres of activity.

Through cultural history, students learn how ideas, beliefs, and values have profoundly influenced human actions throughout history. Religion, philosophy, art, and popular culture have all been central to the aspirations and achievements of all societies and have been a mainspring of historical change from the earliest times. Students' explorations of this sphere of human activity, through literature, sacred writings and oral traditions, political treatises, drama, art, architecture, music, and dance of a people, deepen their understanding of the human experience.

Analyzing these five spheres of human activity requires considering them in the contexts of both *historical time* and *geographic place.* The historical record is inextricably linked to the geographic setting in which it developed. Population movements and settlements, scientific and economic activities, geopolitical agendas, and the distributions and spread of political, philosophical, religious, and aesthetic ideas are all related in some measure to geographic factors. The opportunities, limitations, and constraints within which any people have addressed the issues and challenges of their time have, to a significant degree, been influenced by the environment in which they lived or to which they had access, and by the traces on the landscape, malignant or benign, irrevocably left by those who came before.

Because these five spheres of human activity are also interwoven in the real lives of individuals and societies, essential understandings in United States history often cut across these categories. Thus, to comprehend the causes of the American Revolution, students must address the *philosophical ideas* of the Enlightenment; the competing *economic interests* of British mercantilism and colonial self-interest; the *political antecedents* defining the right of Englishmen under English common law; the English Bill of Rights; the Glorious Revolution; and the varying aspirations of different *social groups* in the colonies, defined by gender, race, economic status, and region.

Similarly, understanding the consequences of the American victory demonstrates how change in any one of these spheres of activity often has impact on some or all of the others. The many consequences of the colonists' military victory included their development of new and lasting *political institutions,* the *social and economic effects* of the American victory on the various groups who entered the war with differing aspirations and who allied themselves with different sides during the conflict, and the long-term *philosophical consequences* of the American Revolution, inspiring what has been called the Age of Democratic Revolution. Together, these consequences demonstrate the complexity of historical events and the broadly integrative nature of history itself. They also affirm, once again, the unique power of history to deepen students' understanding of the past, and the ways in which we are still affected by it.

Historical Thinking

Beyond defining what students should *know*—that is, the understandings in United States history that all students should acquire—it is essential to consider what students should be able to *do* to demonstrate their understandings and to apply their knowledge in productive ways.

The study of history involves much more than the passive absorption of facts, dates, names, and places. Real historical understanding requires students to think through cause-and-effect relationships, to reach sound historical interpretations, and to conduct historical inquires and research leading to the knowledge on which informed decisions in contemporary life can be based. These thinking skills are the processes of *active* learning.

Properly taught, history develops capacities for analysis and judgment, it reveals the ambiguity of choice, and it promotes a wariness of quick, facile solutions, which have so often brought human suffering in their wake. History fosters an understanding of paradox and a readiness to distinguish between that which is beyond and that which is within human control, between the inevitable and the contingent. It trains students to detect bias, to weigh evidence, and to evaluate arguments, thus preparing them to make sensible, independent judgments, to sniff out spurious appeals to history by partisan pleaders, to distinguish between anecdote and analysis.

To acquire these capabilities, students must develop competence in the following five types of historical thinking:

1. *Chronological thinking:* Developing a clear sense of historical time—past, present, and future—in order to identify the temporal sequence in which events occurred, measure calendar time, interpret and create time lines, and explain patterns of historical succession and duration, continuity and change.

2. *Historical comprehension:* Including the ability to read historical narratives with understanding to identify the basic elements of the narrative structure (characters, situation, sequence of events, their causes, and their outcomes), and to develop historical perspectives—that is, the ability to describe the past through the eyes and experiences of those who were there, as revealed through their literature, arts, artifacts, and the like, and to avoid "present-mindedness," judging the past solely in terms of the norms and values of today.

3. *Historical analysis and interpretation:* Including the ability to compare and contrast different experiences, beliefs, motives, traditions, hopes, and fears of people from various groups and backgrounds, and at various times in the past and present; to analyze how these differing motives, interests, beliefs, hopes and fears influenced people's behaviors; to consider multiple perspectives in the records of human experience and multiple causes in analyses of historical events, to challenge arguments of historical inevitability; and to compare and evaluate competing historical explanations of the past.

4. *Historical research:* Including the ability to formulate historical questions from encounters with historical documents, artifacts, photos, visits to historical sites, and eyewitness accounts; to determine the historical time and context in which the artifact, document, or other record was created; to judge its credibility and authority; and to construct a sound historical narrative or argument concerning it.

5. *Historical issues—analysis and decision-making:* Including the ability to identify problems that confronted people in the past, to analyze the various interests and points of view of people caught up in these situations, to evaluate alternative proposals for dealing with the problem(s), to analyze whether the decisions reached or the actions taken were good ones and why, and to bring historical perspectives to bear on informed decision making in the present.

DEVELOPING STANDARDS IN WORLD HISTORY

Approaching World History

These standards rest on the premise that our schools must teach a comprehensive history in which all students may share. That means a history that encompasses humanity. In writing the standards, a primary task was to identify those developments in the past that involved and affected relatively large numbers of people and that had broad significance for later generations. Some of these developments pertain to particular civilizations or regions, others involve patterns of human interconnection that extended across cultural and political boundaries. Within this framework, students are encouraged to explore in depth particular cases of historical change that may have had only regional or local importance but that exemplify the drama and human substance of the past.

These standards represent a forceful commitment to world-scale history. Thus far, however, no attempt has been made to address the histories of all identifiable peoples or cultural traditions. Rather, the aim is to encourage students to ask large and searching questions about the human past, to compare patterns of continuity and change in different parts of the world, and to examine the histories and achievements of particular peoples or civilizations with an eye to wider social, cultural, or economic contexts.

Periodization

Because the standards are organized chronologically, they must incorporate a system of historical periodization. Arranging the study of the past into distinct periods of time is one way of imposing a degree of order and coherence on the incessant, fragmented flow of events. Periodizing world history—that is, dividing it into distinct eras—is part of the process of making it intelligible. Historians have devised a variety of periodization designs for world history. Students should understand that every one of these designs is a creative construction reflecting the historian's particular aims, preferences, and cultural or social values.

A periodization of world history that encompasses the grand sweep of the human past can make sense only at a relatively high level of generalization. Historians have also worked out periodizations for particular civilizations, regions, and nations, and these have their own validity, their own benchmarks and turning points. The history of India, for example, would necessarily be periodized differently than would the history of China or Europe, because the major shifts in Indian history relate to the Gupta age, the Mughal empire, the postindependence era, and so on.

We believe that as teachers work toward a more integrated study of world history in their classrooms, they will appreciate having a periodization design that encourages study of those broad developments that have involved large segments of the world's population and have had lasting significance. The standards are divided into eight eras of world history. The title of each era attempts to capture the very general character of that age. Note that the time periods of some of the eras overlap in order to incorporate both the closure of certain developments and the start of others. The beginning and ending dates should be viewed as approximations representing broad shifts in the human scene.

Era 1 The Beginnings of Human Society
Era 2 Early Civilizations to 1000 B.C.
Era 3 Classical Traditions, Major Religions, and Giant Empires, 100 B.C.–A.D. 300
Era 4 Expanding Zones of Exchange and Encounter, A.D. 300–1000
Era 5 Intensified Hemispheric Interactions, A.D. 1000–1500
Era 6 Emergence of the First Global Age, 1450–1770
Era 7 The Age of Revolutions, 1750–1914
Era 8 The Twentieth Century

CHAPTER THREE

Textbook Instruction

*Resource material should present history and
geography as an exciting and fascinating story.*

—California History/Social Studies Framework

EXPANDING THE TEXTBOOK APPROACH: INFORMATION, RESOURCES, AND CLASSROOM-TESTED ACTIVITIES

Unimaginative teaching in high school history and geography courses is due, in large part, to the reliance on the textbook and the unwillingness or inability of many history teachers to use other sources to enliven their classes. The 1960s, 1970s, and 1980s saw secondary school social studies lessons follow a typical pattern of students reading four or five pages from a textbook. Classroom dialogue then went teacher–student, teacher–student, with the teacher talking most of the time. Students completed worksheets and answered questions at the end of each chapter. Some teachers interspersed the lecture with information that extended the textbook, but nearly everywhere it was the same: Directed discussion after reading the textbook was the method of teaching social studies.

According to Mehlinger (1989) the textbook is used mainly because it is the easiest way to teach: "It takes time to prepare a good lesson, to select, preview, and arrange for appropriate source materials. . . . Time is a luxury; few teachers have enough of it (p. 204). Students, too, are accustomed to the textbook; it does not make them work too hard or think too hard.

Reliance on the textbook is particularly problematic when one considers that history textbooks cannot tell the whole story. According to Cavallini (1985), "if textbooks turn the exciting story of the past into a dull recitation of facts, history loses its dynamic quality, its high drama, its intense struggle and its humanity" (p. 600). We must stop killing history with textbooks.

It must be pointed out, however, that textbooks in themselves are not the problem. Rather, teachers who misuse the textbook or allow the textbook to represent history and geography are the problem. In the best of circumstances, the textbook should be used as a reference book, supplemented with primary and secondary sources. To teach differently, teachers need a wide variety of teaching materials. They need written sources, pictorial sources, oral sources, physical sources, and audiovisual sources if history and geography are to be made living subjects and if social studies is to cease being the most boring subject in the eyes of high school students.

Primary resources are any materials that are indigenous to a particular time period—documents, newspapers, speeches, diaries, letters, photographs, cartoons, maps, and the like. *Secondary resources* are source materials that are not the original source, such as historians' interpretations of events, newspaper editorials, excerpts from literature, and reconstructed sites. Audiovisual materials such as videos, slides, tapes, and computer programs can be classified as either primary or secondary resources or a combination of both.

When students use primary and secondary resources, they acquire the skills of history and geography: locating, compiling, organizing, interpreting, and evaluating information. Reading primary sources is a more demanding and complex activity than reading information in a textbook. Without guidance, students can often flounder when using original source materials. Therefore, whenever a document is used as a teaching resource, the following guidelines should be given to students so that they can understand and interpret the document:

Read through the entire document and then answer these questions:

Who were the authors?
What was their authority?
What was their specialized knowledge or experience?
Who were the intended readers?
What was the explicit purpose of the document?
What was the place and date of the document?
Is there ambiguity in the document?
Are there striking omissions in the document?
How does this affect the meaning?
Can you detect bias in the choice of conflicting attitudes expressed in the document?
Do other sources support this document?
What other reference sources could you consult to have additional background information?

GOVERNMENT DOCUMENTS

Documents from all periods of history should be chosen for their historical value and their intrinsic interest. The documents can then be analyzed according to the guidelines just given. In addition to analyzing documents, deciphering original handwritten documents might be an interesting undertaking. Deciphering parts of original documents enables students to get an authentic sense of other times and places. Printed copies of manuscripts can be provided for further analysis and interpretation. Authentic reproductions on "antiqued" parchment of the four Documents of Freedom (the Declaration of Independence, the Constitution of the United States, Lincoln's Gettysburg Address, and the Bill of Rights) are available from the American National Park and Monument Association for less than $5.00 for the set.

The following documents are provided, with suggested student activities, as an example of the use of primary sources in the secondary school classroom.

The Emancipation Proclamation, September 22, 1862

Whereas on the 22nd day of September, A.D. 1862, a proclamation was issued by the President of the United States, containing, among other things, the following, to wit:

"That on the 1st day of January, A.D. 1863, all persons held as slaves within any State or designated part of a State the people whereof shall then be in rebellion against the United States shall be then, thenceforward, and forever free; and the executive government of the United States, including the military and naval authority thereof, will recognize and maintain the freedom of such persons and will do no act or acts to repress such persons, or any of them, in any efforts they may make for their actual freedom.

"That the executive will on the 1st day of January aforesaid, by proclamation, designate the States and parts of States, if any, in which the people thereof, respectively, shall then be in rebellion against the United States; and the fact that any State or the people thereof shall on that day be in good faith represented in the Congress of the United States by members chosen thereto at elections wherein a majority of the qualified voters of such States shall have participated shall, in the absence of strong countervailing testimony, be deemed conclusive evidence that such State and the people thereof are not then in rebellion against the United States."

Now, therefore, I, Abraham Lincoln, President of the United States, by virtue of the power in me vested as Commander-in-Chief of the Army and Navy of the United States in time of actual armed rebellion against the authority and government of the United States, and as a fit and necessary war measure for suppressing said rebellion, do, on this 1st day of January, A.D. 1863, and in accordance with my purpose so to do, publicly proclaimed for the full period of one hundred days from the first day above mentioned, order and designate as the States and parts of States wherein the people thereof, respectively, are this day in rebellion against the United States the following, to wit:

Arkansas, Texas, Louisiana (except the parishes of St. Bernard, Palquemines, Jefferson, St. John, St. Charles, St. James, Ascension, Assumption, Terrebone, Lafourche, St. Mary, St. Martin, and Orleans, including the city of New Orleans), Mississippi, Alabama, Florida, Georgia, South Carolina, North Carolina, and Virginia (except the forty-eight counties designated as West Virginia, and also the counties of Berkeley, Accomac, Morthhampton, Elizabeth City, York, Princess Anne, and Norfolk, including the cities of Norfolk and Portsmouth), and which excepted parts are for the present left precisely as if this proclamation were not issued.

And by virtue of the power and for the purpose aforesaid, I do order and declare that all persons held as slaves within said designated States and parts of States are, and henceforward shall be, free; and that the Executive Government of the United States, including the military and naval authorities thereof, will recognize and maintain the freedom of said persons.

And I hereby enjoin upon the people so declared to be free to abstain from all violence, unless in necessary self-defense; and I recommend to them that, in all case when allowed, they labor faithfully for reasonable wages.

And I further declare and make known that such persons of suitable condition will be received into the armed service of the United States to garrison forts, positions, stations, and other places, and to man vessels of all sorts in said service.

And upon this act, sincerely believed to be an act of justice, warranted by the Constitution upon military necessity, I invoke the considerate judgment of mankind and the gracious favor of Almighty God.

ACTIVITIES

1. Which states or areas were not included in this proclamation?
2. What was Abraham Lincoln's personal attitude toward slavery prior to signing this proclamation?

3. The Emancipation Proclamation did not end slavery. Which amendment (briefly describe the contents of the amendment) did bring slavery to an end?

The Declaration of the Rights of Man, 1789

Art. 1. Men are born and remain free and equal in rights. Social distinctions may be founded only on the common good.

2. The aim of all political association is the preservation of the natural and prescriptive rights of man. These rights are liberty, property, security and resistance to oppression.

3. The principle of all authority resides essentially in the nation. No body nor individuals may exercise authority which does not proceed expressly from it.

4. Liberty comprises doing anything which harms nobody, so the exercise of the natural rights of each man has no limits beyond those which assure to other members of society the enjoyment of the same rights. These limits can only be settled by the law.

* * * * * * *

6. Law is the expression of the general will. All citizens have the right to share personally, or by their representatives, in its creation. It must be the same for all, whether it protects or punishes. All citizens, being equal in its eyes, are equally eligible for all dignities, places and public posts, according to ability and without distinction except that of their virtues and talents.

7. No man may be arrested, accused or detained save in the cases determined by law and according to the forms prescribed by it. Those who request, transmit, execute or put into effect arbitrary orders shall be punished, by any citizen summoned or arrested in virtue of the law must immediately obey; he makes himself guilty if he resists.

* * * * * * *

10. No one may be molested for his opinions, including religious views, provided their manifestation does not disturb the public order established by law.

11. The free communication of ideas and opinions is one of the most precious rights of man, every citizen may, therefore, speak, write and print freely but shall answer for any abuse of this liberty as determined by law.

* * * * * * *

13. For the upkeep of the public force and the expenses of administration, a common contribution is essential. It should be shared equally by all the citizens in proportion to their means.

14. Each citizen has the right, by himself or his representatives, to decide the necessity of the public contribution, to grant it freely, to know its use and to fix the amount, incidence, duration and collection of taxes.

* * * * * * *

16. Every society in which rights are not guaranteed nor the separation of powers determined, lacks a constitution.
17. Property being an inviolable and sacred right, none may be deprived of it, unless public necessity, legally determined, clearly compels this, and then on condition that a just and agreed recompense is given.

* * * * * * *

ACTIVITIES

1. What are the five main ideas of the declaration?
2. Which two philosophers' writings influenced the declaration? Give examples.
3. Give the French word for (a) the right to imprison someone without a trial and (b) taxation according to earnings.
4. According to the declaration, why must taxes be paid?
5. It has been said that the Declaration of the Rights of Man was drawn up for the benefit of all men everywhere. Comment on this statement.

Preamble to the Charter of the United Nations, 1945[b]

WE THE PEOPLES OF THE UNITED NATIONS DETERMINED
to save succeeding generations from the scourge of war, which twice in our lifetime has brought untold sorrow to mankind, and
to reaffirm faith in fundamental human rights, in the dignity and worth of the human person, in the equal rights of men and women and of nations large and small, and
to establish conditions under which justice and respect for the obligations arising from treaties and other sources of international law can be maintained, and to promote social progress and better standards of life in larger freedom,
AND FOR THESE ENDS
to practice tolerance and live together in peace with one another as good neighbours, and to unite our strength to maintain international peace and security, and
to ensure, by the acceptance of principles and the institution of methods, that armed force shall not be used, save in the common interest, and
to employ international machinery for the promotion of the economic and social advancement of all peoples,
HAVE RESOLVED TO COMBINE OUR EFFORTS TO ACCOMPLISH THESE AIMS
Accordingly, our respective Governments, through representatives assembled in the city of San Francisco, who have exhibited their full powers found to be in good and due form, have agreed to the present Charter of the United Nations and do hereby establish an international organization to be known as the United Nations.

ACTIVITY

Following the historic act of adopting the Charter of the United Nations, the General Assembly urged all nations to publicize, disseminate, and display the text of the charter. How would you do this from a government and an educational perspective?

The Law for the Protection of German Blood and Honor, September 15, 1935

Imbued with the knowledge that the purity of German blood is the necessary prerequisite for the existence of the German nation, and inspired by an inflexible will to maintain the existence of the German nation for all future times, the *Reichstag* has unanimously adopted the following law, which is now enacted:

Article (1) Any marriages between Jews and citizens of German or kindred blood are herewith forbidden. Marriages entered into despite this law are invalid, even if they are arranged abroad as a means of circumventing the law.

(2) Annulment proceedings for marriages may be initiated only by the Public Prosecutor.

Article 2. Extramarital relations between Jews and citizens of German or kindred blood are herewith forbidden.

Article 3. Jews are forbidden to employ as servants in their households female subjects of German or kindred blood who are under the age of forty-five years.

Article 4. (1) Jews are prohibited from displaying the Reich and national flag and from showing the national colors.

(2) However, they may display the Jewish colors. The exercise of this right is under state protection.

Article 5. (1) Anyone who acts contrary to the prohibition noted in Article 1 renders himself liable to penal servitude.

(2) The man who acts contrary to the prohibition noted in Article 2 will be punished by sentence to either a jail or penitentiary.

(3) Anyone who acts contrary to the provisions of Articles 3 and 4 will be punished with a jail sentence up to a year and with a fine, or with one of these penalties.

Article 6. The Reich Minister of the Interior, in conjunction with the Deputy to the *Fuehrer* and the Reich Minister of Justice, will issue the required legal and administrative decrees for the implementation and the amplification of this law.

Article 7. This law shall go into effect on the day following its promulgation, with the exception of Article 3, which shall go into effect on January 1, 1936.

ACTIVITIES

1. Divide the articles of this document into those that protect German blood and those that protect German honor.
2. What sinister reason might be provided for including Article 4 (2)?
3. What penalty would be meted out for breaking these laws?

LETTERS, DIARIES, AND EYEWITNESS ACCOUNTS

Letters, diaries, and eyewitness accounts of events can yield evidence that is rarely available in contemporary written resources. By reading letters and diaries written by men, women, and children during a specific time period and from a specific geographical area, students can learn about fascinating personal impressions and experiences. In evaluating these resources, students should follow guidelines similar to those they use in evaluating other written resources. Letters and diaries can provide only limited information, and other resources need to be studied in conjunction with the letters or diaries.

Letters, diaries, and eyewitness accounts of events can be used in a classroom in a variety of ways: They can be read by the teacher and/or a student to create an historical and geographical atmosphere; the content of the letters or diaries or eyewitness accounts can be analyzed; letters, diaries, and eyewitness accounts can be used to complement or refute another resource; they can also be used to study an event from a different perspective, especially that of a woman or a child. A typical activity when using letters or diaries as a resource is to get students to write their own letter or diary entry regarding the event being studied. Students can also imagine they were there and write their own "eyewitness" reports.

Letters

Major Sullivan Ballou's Letter to His Wife—July 14, 1861

July 14th, 1861
Camp Clark, Washington
My very dear Sarah:

The indications are very strong that we shall move in a few days—perhaps tomorrow. Lest I should not be able to write again, I feel compelled to write a few lines that may fall under your eye when I shall be no more. . . .

I have no misgivings about, or lack of confidence in the cause in which I am engaged, and my courage does not halt or falter. I know how strongly American Civilization now leans on the triumph of the Government, and how great a debt we give to those who went before us through the blood and sufferings of the Revolution. And I am willing—perfectly willing—to lay down all my joys in this life, to help maintain this Government, and to pay that debt. . . .

Sarah my love for you is deathless, it seems to bind me with mighty cables that nothing but Omnipotence could break; and yet my love of Country comes over me like a strong wind and bears me unresistibly on with these chains to the battlefield.

The memories of the blissful moments that I have spent with you come creeping over me, and I feel most gratified to God and to you that I have enjoyed them for so long. And hard it is for me to give them up and burn to ashes the hopes of future years, when, God willing, we might still have lived and loved together, and seen our sons grown up to honorable manhood, around us. I have, I know, but few and small claims upon Divide Providence, but something whispers to me—perhaps it is the wafted prayer of my little Edgar, that I shall return to my loved ones unharmed. If I do not my dear Sarah, never forget how much I love you, and when my last breath escapes me on the battlefield, it will whisper your name.

Forgive my many faults, and many pains I have caused you. How thoughtless and foolish I have often times been! How gladly would I wash out with my tears every little spot upon your happiness. . . .

But, O Sarah! if the dead can come back to this earth and flit unseen around those they loved, I shall always be near you: in the gladdest days and in the darkest night . . . always, always, and if there be a soft breeze upon your cheek, it shall be my breath, as the cool air fans your throbbing temple, it shall be my spirit passing by. Sarah, do not mourn me dead; think I am gone and wait for thee, for we shall meet again. . . .

Sullivan Ballou was killed at the first battle of Bull Run.

ACTIVITIES

1. Do you think Major Sullivan Ballou had a premonition of his death? Support your answer with extracts from the letter.
2. What debt was Sullivan Ballou willing to pay for with his life?
3. In your own words, describe the relationship you think Sullivan Ballou might have had with his wife.

Detroit, Michigan, November 27, 1939[*]

President Roosevelt

Dear Honorable Sir:

I am living in a city that should be one of the prized possessions of these United States of America but is only to a small group of chiseling money mongers.

I and my husband are and have been Americans for three generations and are proud of what our parents did also our grandparents to help America progress. They were builders of our country not distructors [*sic*] as is now going on to make the rich man richer and the poor man poorer in factory and starve them in a land of plenty. We have six growing children that are all separated each one pining for each other and our hearts nearly broken because we cannot keep them all together.

We have tried so hard these past seven years we lost our furniture twice, lost our car, our insurance, even my engagement ring and finally the wedding ring to buy groceries and pay rent and for illness. Neither one of us are lazy. He worked in steel mills auto factories painting dish washing and anything he could get. I worked at waitress janitress selling to make a few dollars now my health is slowly ebbing. I was a widow when I married my present husband my first husband died shortly after the world war having served as a submarine chaser. I received a check for $1.00 for each day he served. He died leaving me tow lovely children. Why should descent [*sic*] American people be made to suffer in this manner living in an attic room paying $5.00 per week and if its not paid out you go on the streets. Welfare has never solved these problems as there are far too many inefficient social workers also too much political graft for it to survive or even help survive. We are only one family out of 100,000 that are in the same position right here in Detroit where the ones we labor for and help build up vast fortunes and estates do nothing but push us down farther. They cheat the government out of taxes hire foreign labor at lower rates and if we get discouraged and take some groceries to feed our family we must serve time.

They have 40 to 100 room houses with no children to make it even like a home while we are denied a small home and enough wages to provide for them. Barbara Hutton has herself exploited that she pays $650.00 to have one tooth pulled and the girls in her dime stores slave all week for $12 or $14 and must help provide for others and of it. I'll wager to say that the poor class were lucky to have roast pork @ $.13 per lb on thanksgiving Day while the rich people in this country probably throwed a lot out in their garbage cans. These so called intelligent rich men including the Congressmen and the Senators better wake up and pass some laws that will aid labor to make a living as they would have never accumulated their vast fortunes had it not been from the hard sweat that honest labor men brought them.

We read with horror of the war in Europe and of the blockade to starve the people into submission and right here in Detroit we have the same kind of blockade. Do the intelligent men of America think we are going to stand for this much longer. I alone hear a lot of viewpoints and it will be very hard to get our men to fight another war to make more wealth for men that never had to labor and never appreciated where the real source of their wealth derived from. This country was founded on Thanksgiving day to get away from the brutal treatment the British gave them and us real Americans intend keeping it so. We need men of wealth and

---

[*]From *Slaves of the Depression,* edited by R. Markowitz and R. Rosner (Ithaca, NY: Cornell University Press, 1987).

men of intelligence but we also need to make labor healthy and self supporting or our nation will balk at an injustice and we are not prisoners. God Bless all true Americans you have my permission to read this in the next session of Congress.
    A true American mother & family

                                                                                    M.Q.L.

ACTIVITIES
1. Why do you think a woman wrote this letter to President Roosevelt?
2. Why do you think Barbara Hutton was singled out in this letter?
3. Write an imaginary letter from President Roosevelt back to this "true American mother & family."

Letter from an Epileptic Patient Who Knew of the Euthanasia Program in the Asylum of Liebenau to Her Father, 1939*

Beloved father:

Sadly it had to be. And so today I must send you my words of farewell from this earthly life as I go to my eternal home. It will make you and my other loved ones very sad. But I think that I can die as a martyr which cannot happen without the will of my Redeemer for whom I have longed for years. But father, dear father, I do not want to leave this life without once more begging your forgiveness and that of all my brothers and sisters for what I have failed you in throughout my life. May God accept my illness and this sacrifice as and expiation for it. Dearest father, please do not hold anything against your child who loved you so deeply and think always that I am going to heaven where we will all meet again with God and our loved ones who have died. Father, dear father, I am going with strong courage and faith in God and never doubt His goodness to me, though here on earth we unfortunately do not understand it. We will have our reward on the Day of Judgment. God has commanded it. Please tell my brothers and sisters not to be sorrowful but rather to rejoice. I am giving you this little picture to remember me by. And so your child goes to meet her Saviour, embraces you in true love and with the firm promise, which I gave at our last farewell, that I would endure bravely.
Your child
    Helene
    Please pray for my soul. Farewell good father till we meet in heaven.

ACTIVITIES
1. How do you think Helene knew about the euthanasia program?
2. Is there anything in the letter that surprises you? Support your answer.
3. Try to find out how many people who were disabled were put to death under the Nazi regime.

Excerpt from a Letter from Florence Nightingale to Her Family, May 1855

What the horrors of war are, no one can imagine. They are not wounds and blood and fever, spotted and low, or dysentery, chronic and acute, cold and heat and famine. They are intoxication, drunken brutality, demorilization and disorder on the part of the inferior . . . jealousies, meanness, indifference, selfish brutality on the part of the superior.

---

*"Letter from Helene to Her Father" from *Nazism 1919–1945*, Volume 2, edited by J. Noalees and G. Pridhan, reproduced with permission of University of Exeter Press, Exeter, UK.

ACTIVITIES

1. Describe in your own words what Florence Nightingale thought the horrors of war really were.
2. Although Florence Nightingale could not change the horrors of war, what did she achieve for the soldiers?

Diaries

Extracts from Oregon Trail Diaries

I well remember what a hullabaloo the neighbors set up when father said we were going to Oregon. They told him his family would all be killed by the Indians, or if we escaped the Indians we could either starve to death or drown or be lost in the desert, but father was not much of a hand to draw back after he had put his hand to the plow, so he went ahead and made ready for the trip.—Benjamin Franklin Booney, 1845

The road is strewn with articles thrown away . . . I recognize the trunks of some of the passengers who had accompanied me from St. Louis to Kansas, on the Missouri, and who had there thrown away their wagons and everything they could not pack.—Captain Howard Stansbury, 1852

There was an epidemic of cholera all along the Platte River . . . all along the road was graveyard. Most anytime of the day you could see people burying their dead; some places five or six graves in a row, with board head signs with their names carved on them. It was a sad sight: no-one can realize it. . . .—Jane Davies Kellogg, 1852

I am weary of this journey. I long for the quiet of home where I can be at peace once more. . . .—Agnes Stewart, 1853

The environs of our new home, surrounded by giant fir trees, the healthful sea breezes, the strange sights and sounds were sources of continual thought. The long distance that separated us from our old home in the Mississippi valley, precluded any form of home sickness and our united efforts were wholly set upon the building of a home.

ACTIVITIES

1. After reading these extracts, how do you think women, in general, reacted to the long journey west?
2. From the extracts, what were some of the major problems facing the pioneers on their journey west?
3. Draw an outline map of the Oregon trail and fill in important geographical and historical events that are referred to in these diary extracts.

Diary Excerpts from Children

Full statistics on the tragic fate of children who died during the Holocaust will never be known. Some estimates range as high as 1.5 million murdered children. The figure includes more than 1.2 million Jewish children, tens of thousands of Gypsy children and thousands of institutionalized handicapped children. For those with access to the Internet, outstanding information on children and the

Holocaust can be found on the World Wide Web at http://www.best.com/`md-dun./cybrary/index..html#History

---

ACTIVITIES

1. Read *The Diary of Anne Frank* (New York: Pocket Books/Washington Square Press, 1958), and write a personal reaction to the thoughts, fears, and hopes expressed by this young Dutch girl in the midst of the Nazi Holocaust.
2. Zlata Filipovic was 13 years old in 1992 as she found herself caught up in the Bosnian–Serb conflict. Read extracts from *Zlata's Diary: A Child's Life in Sarajevo* (New York: Viking/Penguin Group, 1994), and then discuss what concerned Zlata most about the war.
2. In the second extract, Zlata says "We young . . . wouldn't have chosen war." What solutions might the young people of the former Yugoslavia have come up with to bring stability and equity to the area?
4. Zlata has been called "Bosnia's Anne Frank." Is this a fair comparison? State the reasons for your opinion.

The Last Will and Testament of Alfred Nobel

The whole of my remaining realizable estate shall be dealt with in the following way: the capital, invested in safe securities by my executors, shall constitute a fund, the interest on which shall be annually distributed in the form of prizes to those who, during the preceding year, shall have conferred the greatest benefit on mankind. The said interest shall be divided into five equal parts, which shall be apportioned as follows: one part to the person who shall have made the most important discovery or invention within the field of physics; one part to the person who shall have made the most important chemical discovery or improvement; one part to the person who shall have made the most important discovery or invention within the field of physics; one part to the person who shall have made the most important chemical discovery or improvement; one part to the person who shall have made the most important discovery within the domain of physiology or medicine, one part to the person who shall have produced in the field of literature the most outstanding work of an idealistic tendency; and one part to the person who shall have done the most or the best work for fraternity between nations, for the abolition or reduction of standing armies and for the holding and promotion of peace congresses. The prizes for physics and chemistry shall be awarded by the Swedish Academy of Sciences; that for physiology or medical works by the Karolinska Institute in Stockholm; that for literature by the Academy in Stockholm, and that for champions of peace by a committee of five persons to be elected by the Norwegian Storting. It is my express wish that in awarding the prizes no consideration be given to the nationality of the candidates, but that the most worthy shall receive the prize, whether he be Scandinavian or not.

ACTIVITIES

1. What kind of document is this and who is the author?
2. According to the document, in which five fields would prizes be awarded?
3. What new fields have been added since the author's death?
4. If you were going to have $8.5 million in the bank when you died, what would you like to have done with the money?

Eyewitness or Personal Accounts of Events

Eyewitness to History, edited by John Carey, is an excellent resource for authentic evidence of the past. As Carey states in his introduction, "all knowledge of the past which is not just supposition derives ultimately from people who can say 'I was there.'" The real value of using eyewitness accounts in the classroom is that they confront us with the vivid, the frightening, or the unaccustomed. Eyewitness accounts remove the varnish of interpretation so we can see people clearly, as they originally were—"gazing incredulously at what was, for that moment, the newest thing that had ever happened to them" (p. xxxii).

A Military Spokesman on Black Americans in World War I*

The racial distinctions which are recognized in civilian life naturally continue to be recognized in military life and present a formidable barrier to the existence of that feeling of comradeship which is essential to mutual confidence and esprit de corps.

With a few exceptions there is a characteristic tendency among the colored officers to neglect the welfare of their men and to perform their duties in a perfunctory manner. They are lacking in initiative also. These defects entail a constant supervision and attention to petty details by Battalion commanders and other senior officers which distract their attention from their wider duties, with harmful results.

What a wonderful sight to see those boys march up the hillsides bearing the crosses to the resting-places of the sacred dead! It reminds us of that other sacred scene in history when an African bore the cross of Christ up the little green hill far away,

It was a privilege for me to shake the hands of these boys laden with the aroma of the dead. I said to them: "Boys, I am proud of you. You have done the most sacred task of the war. What others refused to do, you have done willingly and beautifully. I promise that when I go back home I will speak to no audience that I do not tell them of what you have done. . . ."

ACTIVITIES

1. How do both these extracts reflect the attitude of white people toward black people in 1917?
2. Do you think black people would have been fooled by the second commentary?
3. What categories of black Americans were available to the army for service in France in 1917? How did the army intend to use the black American draftees?

An Editor Loses His Job in the Great Depression†

Ward James was born in Wisconsin and educated there. When the Great Depression struck, he was working at a small publishing house in New York. In 1935 he lost his job and went on relief. Forty years later he recalled his experiences.

---

* From *The Unknown Soldier: Black American Troops in World War I* by Arthur E. Barbeau and Floretti Henri, pp. 38, 128. Copyright © 1974 by Temple University Press. Reprinted by permission of Temple University Press.

† From *Slaves of the Depression,* edited by R. Markowitz and R. Rosner. (Ithaca, NY: Cornell University Press, 1987).

I was out of work for six months. I was losing my contacts as well as my energy. I kept going from one publishing house to another. I never got past the telephone operator. It was just wasted time. One of the worst things was occupying your time, sensibly. You'd go to the library. You took a magazine to the room and sat and read. I didn't have a radio. I tried to do some writing and found I couldn't concentrate. The day was long. There was nothing to do evenings. I was going around in circles, it was terrifying. So I just vegetated.

With some people I knew, there was a coldness, shunning: I'd rather not see you just now. Maybe I'll lose my job next week. On the other hand, I made some very close friends, who were merely acquaintances before. If I needed $15 for room rent or something, it was available. . . .

I finally went on relief. It's an experience I don't want anybody to go through. It comes as close to crucifixion as. . . . You sit in an auditorium and are given a number. The interview was utterly ridiculous and mortifying. In the middle of mine, a more dramatic guy than I dived from the second floor stairway, head first, to demonstrate he was gonna get on relief even if he had to go to the hospital to do it.

There were questions like: Who are your friends? Where have you been living? Where's your family? I had sent my wife and child to her folks in Ohio, where they could live more simply. Why should anybody give you money? Why should anybody give you a place to sleep? What sort of friends? This went on for half an hour. I got angry and said, "Do you happen to know what a friend is?" He changes his attitude very shortly. I did get certified some time later. I think they paid $9 a month.

I came away feeling I didn't have any business living any more. I was imposing on somebody, a great society or something like that. . . .

I feel anything can happen. There's a little fear in me that it might happen again. It does distort your outlook and your feeling. Lost time and lost faith. . . .

ACTIVITY   Some historians write about an "invisible scar" left by the Great Depression on its victims. What overall effect does the Great Depression seem to have had on Ward James? What did he mean by "lost time and lost faith"? Did he carry an "invisible scar"?

Kurt Ludecke Records His Impression on First Hearing Hitler Speak*

My critical faculty was swept away. Leaning from the rostrum as if he were trying to impact his inner self in to the consciousness of all these thousands, he was holding the masses, and me with them, under an hypnotic spell by the sheer force of his conviction. . . . I do not know how to describe the emotions that swept over me as I heard this man. His words were like a scourge. When he spoke of the disgrace of Germany, I felt ready to spring on any enemy. His appeal to German manhood was like a call to arms; the gospel he preached, a sacred truth. He seemed another Luther. I forgot everything but the man; then glancing around, I saw that his magnetism was holding these thousands as one. Of course I was ripe for this experience. I was a man of thirty-two, weary with disgust and disillusionment, a

*An eyewitness account by Kurt Ludecke on first hearing Hitler speak. Printed in *Hitler's Third Reich: A Documentary History,* edited by Louis L. Snyder. Copyright © 1981 by Nelson Hall, Inc., Chicago. Reprinted by permission.

wanderer seeking a cause, a patriot without a channel for his patriotism, a yearner after the heroic without a hero. The intense will of the man, the passion of his sincerity, seemed to flow from him into me. I experienced an exaltation that could be likened only to religious conversion.

ACTIVITIES

1. Why and how did Hitler move the masses with his speeches?
2. Comment on the last line: "I experienced an exaltation that could be likened only to religious conversion."
3. Do you know of any other great orator in history? What might that person have shared with Hitler?

SPEECHES, ANECDOTES, AND QUOTATIONS

Speeches

Great speeches should be brought into the classroom on cassette or CD so that the original voices can take the students back through time to history in the making. An excellent collection of "Great Speeches of the Twentieth Century" is available for $40.00 (to order, call toll-free 1-800-733-3369). While listening skills can be developed by hearing the great speeches on tape, printed copies of speeches can be used to create an authentic sense of the period as well as documents for analysis and evaluation.

Napoleon's Speech to the Army of England

Soldiers!

You are about to undertake a conquest, the effects of which on the civilization and commerce of the world are incalculable. You are going to deal England the most severe blow she can receive until such time as you may give her death blow. We shall make fatiguing marches; we shall wage several battles; but we will succeed in all our undertakings; the destinies are with us.

The people among whom we are going to live are Mohammedans: the first article of their faith is this: "There is no other God but Allah and Mohammed is a prophet." Do not contradict them; act towards them as we have towards the Italians . . . extend to the ceremonies prescribed by the Koran and to the Mosques the same tolerance which you showed towards the convents and the synagogues, towards the religion of Moses and of Jesus Christ. The Roman Legions protected all religions. You will find customs different from those of Europe; you must adapt yourselves to them.

ACTIVITIES

1. Which country is about to be invaded?
2. Why would this country be invaded to deal England a severe blow?
3. Name the religion for which Mohammed is a prophet.
4. Where do Jews worship? Where do Muslims worship?
5. Choose phrases from this speech that are (a) encouraging to the soldiers (b) commanding the soldiers.

Lord Nelson's Prayer before the Battle of Trafalgar

May the great God I worship, grant to my country, and for the benefit of Europe in general, a great and glorious victory; and may no misconduct in only one tarnish it: and may humiliation after victory be the predominate feature in the British fleet. For myself individually, I commit my life to him who made me, and my his blessing light on my endeavors for serving my country faithfully. To him I resign myself and the just cause which is entrusted me to defend. Amen.

ACTIVITY

Where is Trafalgar? When was the Battle of Trafalgar fought? What was the outcome of the battle? What happened to Lord Nelson during this battle? How is Lord Nelson remembered by British sailors today?

Lincoln's Gettysburg Address

Four score and seven years ago our fathers brought forth on this continent a new nation, conceived in liberty and dedicated to the proposition that all men are created equal.

Now we are engaged in a great civil war, testing whether that nation or any nation so conceived and so dedicated can long endure.

We are met on a great battle-field of that war. We have come to dedicate a portion of that field as a final resting place of those who here gave their lives that that nation might live

It is altogether fitting and proper that we should do this. But, in a larger sense, we cannot dedicate, we cannot consecrate, we cannot hallow this ground. The brave men, living and dead, who struggled here have consecrated it far above our poor power to add or detract.

The world will little note nor long remember what we say here. But it will never forget what they did here.

It is for us the living, rather, to be dedicated here to the unfinished task which they who fought here have thus far so nobly advanced. It is further for us to be here dedicated to the great task remaining before us, that from these honored dead we take increased devotion to that cause for which they gave the last full measure of devotion; that we here highly resolve that these dead shall not have died in vain; that this nation, under God, shall have a new birth of freedom, and that government of the people, by the people, and for the people shall not perish from the earth.

ACTIVITIES

1. How did the nation react to this address in November 1863?
2. Which, if any, parts of this speech had you heard of before?
3. How long is four score and seven years?

Chief Joseph's Comments to the White Man

It is cold and we have no blankets. The little children are freezing to death. My people—some of them—have run away to the hills, and have no blankets, no food. No one knows where they are perhaps freezing to death. I want to have time to look for my children, and to see how many of them I can find; maybe I shall find among the dead. Hear me my chiefs, my heart is sick and sad. From where the sun now stands, I will fight no more with the white man.

and

Let me be a free man—free to travel, free to stop, free to work, free to trade, where I chose, free to choose my own teachers, free to follow the religion of my fathers, free to think and talk and act for myself—and I will obey every other law, or submit to the penalty.

Whenever the white man treats the Indian as they treat each other, then we shall have no more wars. We shall be all alike—brothers of one father and one mother, with one sky above us and one country around us, and one government for all.

ACTIVITIES

1. We usually hear only the last line of Chief Joseph's "we shall fight no more . . ." speech. What difference does it make to your understanding to read the last sentence in context?
2. What freedoms does Chief Joseph hold the most dear? Do these freedoms differ in any way from the freedoms we hold to be "self-evident"?
3. What is Chief Joseph's method for ending war?

Lyndon B. Johnson's Address to Congress

Mr. Speaker, Mr. President, members of the Congress, I speak tonight for the dignity of man and the destiny of Democracy. I urge every member of both parties, Americans of all religions and of all colors, from every section of this country, to join me in that cause.

At times, history and fate meet at a single time in a single place to shape a turning point in man's unending search for freedom.

So it was at Lexington and Concord. So it was a century ago at Appomattox. So it was last week in Selma, Alabama.

There, long suffering men and women peacefully protested the denial of their rights as Americans. Many of them were brutally assaulted. One good man—a man of God—was killed.

There is no cause for pride in what has happened in Selma. There is no cause for self-satisfaction in the long denial of equal rights of millions of Americans. But there is cause for hope and for faith in our Democracy in what is happening here tonight.

For the cries of pain and the hymns and protests of oppressed people have summoned into convocation all the majesty of this great government—the government of the greatest nation on earth.

Our mission is at once the oldest and the most basic of this country—to right wrong, to do justice, to serve man.

In our time we have come to live with the moments of great crises. Our lives have been marked with debate about great issues, issues of war and peace, issues of prosperity and depression.

But rarely in any time does an issue lay bare the secret heart of America itself. Rarely are we met with a challenge, not to our growth or abundance, or our welfare or our security, but rather to the values and the purposes and the meaning of our beloved nation. The issue of equal rights for American Negroes is such an issue.

And should we defeat every enemy, and should we double our wealth and conquer the stars, and still be unequal to this issue, then we will have failed as a people and as a nation.

For, with a country as with a person, "what is a man profited if he shall gain the whole world, and lose his own soul?"

There is no Negro problem. There is no Southern problem. There is no Northern problem. There is only an American problem.

And we are met here tonight as Americans—not as Democrats or Republicans; we're met here as Americans to solve that problem.

This was the first nation in the history of the world to be founded with a purpose. The great phrases of that purpose still sound in every American heart, north and south:

"All men are created equal." "Government by consent of the governed." "Give me liberty or give me death."

And those are not just clever words, and those are not just empty theories.

In their name Americans have fought and died for two centuries and tonight around the world they stand there as guardians of our liberty risking their lives.

Those words are promised to every citizen that he shall share in the dignity of man. This dignity cannot be found in a man's possessions. It cannot be found in his power or in his position. It really rests on his right to be treated as a man equal in opportunity to all others.

It says that he shall share in freedom. He shall choose his leaders, educate his children, provide for his family according to his ability and his merits as a human being.

To apply any other test, to deny a man his hopes because of his color or race or his religion or the place of his birth is not only to do injustice, it is to deny Americans and to dishonor the dead who gave their lives for American freedom.

Our fathers believed that if this noble view of the right of man was to flourish it must be rooted in democracy. This most basic right of all was the right to choose your own leaders.

The history of this country in large measure is the history of expansion of the right to all of our people. Many of the issues of civil rights are very complex and most difficult. But about this there can and should be no argument: every American citizen must have an equal right to vote.

There is no reason which can excuse the denial of that right. There is no duty which weighs more heavily on us than the duty we have to insure that right. Yet the harsh fact is that in many places in this country men and women are kept from voting simply because they are Negroes.

Every device of which human ingenuity is capable has been used to deny this right. The Negro citizen may go to register only to be told that the day is wrong, or the hour is late, or the official in charge is absent.

And if he persists and, if he manages to present himself to the registrar, he may be disqualified because he did not spell out his middle name, or because he abbreviated a word on the application. And if he manages to fill out an application, he is given a test.

The registrar is the sole judge of whether he passes this test. He may be asked to recite the entire Constitution, or explain the most complex provisions of state law.

And even a college degree cannot be used to prove that he can read and write. For the fact is that the only way to pass these barriers is to show a white skin.

Experience has clearly shown that the existing process of law cannot overcome systematic and ingenious discrimination. No law that we know have on the books, and I have helped to put three of them there, can insure the right to vote when local officials are determined to deny it. In such a case, our duty must be clear to all of us.

The Constitution says that no person shall be kept from voting because of his race or his color. We have all sworn on oath before God to support and to defend that Constitution. We must now act in obedience to that oath.

Wednesday, I will send to Congress a law designed to eliminate illegal barriers to the right to vote.

The broad principles of that bill will be in the hands of the Democratic and Republican leaders tomorrow. After they have reviewed it, it will come here formally as a bill.

ACTIVITIES

1. Provide this speech with a title. Provide the date when Johnson gave this speech.
2. Briefly describe what had happened at Selma
3. Mention some devices that were used to deny the "Negroes" the right to vote.

Anecdotes

An anecdote, according to *Webster's Collegiate Dictionary,* is "a usually short narrative of an interesting, amusing or biographical incident." With many exceptions, anecdotes seem to be predominantly urban. Mountain men and pioneers produce yarns, not anecdotes; desert and peasant cultures are rarely anecdotal. It is the institutions and vocations associated with the city that favor anecdotes—the theater, the law court, the dinner party, the university, parliaments, the senate. The anecdote is a social product; it does not flourish in isolation. Certain personalities, such as Winston Churchill, are anecdotal naturals. It is interesting to note that there are few anecdotes about women. While the authenticity of many anecdotes will always be open to some questioning, anecdotes should be included in our classrooms, chiefly to entertain.

Mark Twain

After attending a service conducted by Dr. Doane, later bishop of Albany, Mark Twain congratulated him on an enjoyable service. "I welcomed it as an old friend," he went on. "I have a book at home containing every word of it." Dr. Doane bristled. "I am sure you have not," he replied huffily. "Indeed I have," Twain persisted. "Well, I'd like to have a look at it then. Could you send it over to me?" The following day Twain sent him an unabridged dictionary.

Madame Curie

An American newspaperman tracked the Curies down to the remote cottage in Brittany where they were vacationing. He found a rather dowdy woman sitting outside the door. "Are you the housekeeper?" he began.

"Yes."

"Is your mistress inside?"

"No."

"Will she be back soon?"

"I don't think so."

The reporter sat down. "Can you tell me something confidential about your mistress?" he went on.

"Madame Curie has only one message that she likes to be given to reporters," said Marie Curie. "That is: be less curious about people and more curious about ideas."

Woodrow Wilson

One afternoon during his time as governor of New Jersey, Wilson received news of the sudden death of a personal friend, a New Jersey senator. He was still recovering from the shock when the telephone rang again. It was a prominent New Jersey politician. "Governor," he said, "I would like to take the senator's place." Wilson replied, "It's perfectly agreeable to me if it's agreeable to the undertaker."

Mrs. Einstein

Albert Einstein's wife was once asked if she understood her husband's theory of relativity. "No," she replied loyally, "but I know my husband and I know he can be trusted."

Winston Churchill

During a visit to America, Churchill was invited to a buffet luncheon at which cold fried chicken was served. Returning for a second helping, he asked politely, "May I have some breast?"

"Mr. Churchill," replied his hostess, "in this country we ask for white meat or dark meat." Churchill apologized profusely.

The following morning, the lady received a magnificent orchid from her guest of honor. The accompanying card read: "I would be most obliged if you would pin this on your white meat."

J. Paul Getty

J. Paul Getty once received a request from a British magazine for a short article explaining his success. A check for £200 was enclosed. The multimillionaire obligingly wrote: "Some people find oil. Others don't."

A newspaper reporter once asked Getty if it was true that the value of his holdings at that time amounted to $1 billion. Getty was silent for a minute or two. "I suppose so," he replied thoughtfully. "But remember, a billion dollars doesn't go as far as it used to."

ACTIVITY   Anecdotes should be read to the class at an opportune moment, for the purpose of anecdotes is chiefly to entertain.

Quotations

Quotations are "voices from the past." They can be used to give a human dimension to the teaching of history/geography. In fact, the voices of the past are the tools for putting flesh on the skeleton of information provided by the textbook. Some suggestions for integrating quotations into the teaching of history/geography follow.

1. *Quotations can be used to create a visual picture of a place or a person. For example, the following quotations can be used to describe Napoleon Bonaparte:*

He was marvelously gifted. His brain was a wonderful organ, for it planned his every move in a precise manner."

His work knew no limits: "Work is the element for which I was born and fitted." He could work twenty hours every day if necessary, being able to sleep in twenty minute periods and then awaken refreshed.

He was a keen writer; 32 volumes of published correspondence and over 50,000 dictated letters.

He found the ordinary pleasures of man tedious. He rarely smiled or laughed. He was able to lie shamelessly and cheat at cards. He was superstitious and distrustful of his fellow men.

He accepted the principle of equality but detested the idea of liberty.

He divorced Josephine, not because of matrimonial unhappiness, but for political reasons. He needed an heir to the throne.
There was a sensitive side to the character of Napoleon which is revealed in letters to his wife and very close friends who were few in number.

2. *Quotations can be used to recognize the author's attitude. For example, the following quotations from Napoleon can be used to determine his attitude toward:*

    a. Power:
        "I love power as a musician loves his violin."
        "Power is my mistress."
    b. War:
        "Victory belongs to the most persevering."
        "War justifies everything."
    c. Politics:
        "So long as I rule, I shall rule as I please."
        "Of all the political questions, education deserves the most attention."
    d. Religion:
        "I was a Mohammedan in Egypt, a Catholic in France."
        "Serving the fatherland is part of religion."
    e. Liberty and equality:
        "My motto has always been a career open to talents without distinction of birth."
        "I have come to realize that men are not born to be free. We are here to guide public opinion and not to discuss it."
    f. Himself
        "When I die, the universe will heave a sigh of relief."
        "Those who blame me have never drunk of fortune's intoxicating cup."

3. *Quotations can be used as interpretive material. For example, the following quotations from Napoleon and the Duke of Wellington can be used to compare and contrast their respective attitudes toward soldiers, war, and victory:*

The Duke of Wellington
The man who enlists in the British Army is, in general, the most drunken, and probably the worst man of the trade or profession to which he belongs, or the village or town in which he lives.

I hope to God that I have fought my last battle.
Nothing but a battle lost can be half so melancholy as a battle won.

Napoleon Bonaparte

You know what words can do to soldiers.

If 50,000 men were to die for the state, I shall certainly weep for them, but political necessity comes before everything else.

My real glory is not in having won forty battles. What will never be effaced, what will endure forever, is my civil code.

4. *Quotations can be used as an introduction to a particular topic. For example, the following quotations can be used to start a discussion on terrorism:*

We say openly; yes, in Libya, volunteers from 18 Arab countries are preparing for the fight against Israel. The stagnation in the Arab world has been ended by the Libyan revolution. Now we are in the position to be able to radicalize the war. And naturally we, Libyans, will support in these phases every Palestinian commando operation. I stress: every operation.—Rashid al-Dikhya, former Libyan foreign minister

I don't think anybody has discovered an anti terrorism policy that works . . . we are facing a new kind of warfare, and we don't know how to deal with it.—Lawrence Eagleburger, former state department official

As soon as it is possible for a small group of fanatics to manufacture nuclear weapons in their own bathtubs, I am reasonably sure several of them will get together and deliberately use these weapons against the rest of the U.S., in the name of God, Jesus, Mohammed, or what you will.—Albert Ellis, U.S. clinical psychologist

We cannot and will not abstain from forcible action to prevent, preempt, and respond to terrorist acts when conditions merit the use of force.—R. McFarlane, National Security Advisor

We must reach a consensus in this country that our responses should go beyond passive defense.—G. Schultz, U.S. Secretary of State

We have the right to take deterrent measures against all capitulationist Arab regimes. . . . We are always wronged. Therefore we have the right to export terrorism to them because they have done everything to the U.S. . . . If we really want to face up to our responsibilities then Libya has no alternative but to be the base for liberation.—Gaddafi, dictator of Libya

5. *Quotations, together with questions, can be used to analyze individuals' views and philosophies. For example, the following questions based on quotes from Adolf Hitler's Mein Kampf can be posed:*

a. Which statements refer to Hitler's dictatorial ambitions?
b. Which statements define Hitler's anti-Semitic philosophy?
c. What did Hitler believe about the power of mass demonstrations and the magic power of the spoken word?
d. Which statements could lead to a political conflict in Europe in 1939?

There must be a final active reckoning with France—a last decisive struggle—only then will we be able to end the eternal and essentially so fruitless struggle between ourselves and France; presupposing of course, that Germany actually regards the destruction of France as only a means which will afterwards enable her finally to give our people the expansion made possible elsewhere.

Territorial policy cannot be fulfilled in the Cameroons, but today almost exclusively in Europe. We must hold unflinchingly to our aim—to secure for the German people the land and soil to which they are entitled—We turn our gaze toward the land in the East.

Who is prepared to make the national cause his own to such an extent that he knows no higher ideal than the welfare of his nation; whoever has understood our great national anthem, "Deutschland ueber Alles," to mean that nothing in the wide world surpasses in his eyes this Germany, people and land—that man is a Socialist.

A world where one creature feeds on the other and where the death of the weaker implies the life of the stronger. In the end only the urge for self-preservation can conquer. The stronger must dominate and not blend with the weaker, thus sacrificing his own greatness.

Blood mixture and the resultant drop in the racial level is the sole cause to the dying out of old cultures; for men do not perish as a result of lost wars, but by the loss of that force of resistance which is continued only in pure blood. All who are not of good race in this world are chaff [Jews and Slavs].

Surely every man will have advisers by his side, but the decision will be made by one man only.

From millions of men—one man must step forward who will form granite principles and take up the struggle for their [the masses'] sole correctness.

The aim of National Socialism must be to secure for the German people an extension of the space in which our people must live.

Mass demonstrations must burn into the little man's soul the proud conviction that though a little worm he is nevertheless part of the great dragon.

The pioneer which has always started the greatest religious and political avalanches in history rolling has from time immemorial been the magic power of the spoken word, and that alone. The broad masses of the people can be moved only by the power of speech.

Gradually, I began to hate them. For me this was the time of the greatest spiritual upheaval I have ever had to go through. I ceased to be a weak-kneed cosmopolitan and became an anti-Semite.

6. *When studying a topic such as the Civil War, quotations by specific people can be located by the students as an assignment. These quotes can then be displayed and analyzed as part of the learning process. For example, quotations by the following people can be located:*

An unknown Union officer	General John Gibbon
A Confederate soldier	Isham G. Harris
Frederick Douglass	General Evander Law
Ulysses S. Grant	Colonel Patrick O'Rourke
General Philip Sheridan	William Tecumseh Sherman

Harriet Tubman   Abraham Lincoln
Captain William Wheeler   General Nathaniel Lyon

7. A quotation board in the history/geography classroom can become a permanent fixture. A particular theme can be chosen and appropriate quotes can be displayed by students and/or the teacher. For example, global education could be chosen as a theme:

For the world is not to be narrowed till it will go into the understanding . . . , but the understanding is to be expanded and opened till it can take in the image of the world.—Francis Bacon

Friendship is the golden thread that ties the heart of all the world.—John Evelyn

We were born to unite with our fellowmen, and to join community with the human race.—Anonymous

There is no such thing as a little country. The greatness of a people is no more determined by their number than the greatness of a man is determined by his height.—Victor Hugo

You cannot take sides when you know the world is round.—Patricia Sun

Civilization is a method of living, an attitude of equal respect for all men.—Jane Addams

One day the people of the world will want peace so much that the governments are going to have to get out of their way and let them have it.—Dwight D. Eisenhower

8. Individual quotations can be used at any time during a lesson on any topic. The quotation can be written on the chalkboard or on an overhead transparency. Students can analyze the quotation by answering the questions: Who said? When said? Where said? What said? Why said? For example:

The Japanese may expect a rain of ruin from the air the likes of which has never been seen on this earth.

This example of changing the constitution by assembling the wise men of the state, instead of assembling armies, will be worth as much to the world as the former examples we have given it.

9. Students can be asked to be creative and complete quotations. The teacher can then provide the full quotation for comparison. For example:

If I had known that the Germans would not succeed in constructing the bomb, . . . (Albert Einstein)
(. . . I would never have lifted a finger)

I would lay down my life for America but . . . (John Paul Jones) (. . . I cannot trifle with my honor)

10. Quotations from peacekeepers can be used to encourage discussions in class regarding the nature of peace.

A frustration of peacekeeping is meeting people who are not willing to make peace with themselves.—UN peacekeeper in Croatia

As long as both sides are angry with you, you're walking the middle road.—UN peacekeeping commander to his assistant in Croatia

I did not learn much prior to my arrival in Somalia. We got the basics. However, nothing that I learned or saw on TV prepared me for what I saw there. The level of devastation, destruction, and despair in the country, at least in the Mogadishu area, was appalling.—U.S. soldier in Somalia

Peacekeeping is a shining example connected with the Canadian military. Canadians have been involved in every UN peacekeeping mission to date. It is ingrained into the Canadian fabric of life.—UN peacekeeper in Croatia

When you raise your hand to be sworn in as a UN peacekeeping soldier, don't take that responsibility lightly. It's a life and death matter out there, and you just might be coming home in a body bag.—Staff Sergeant Gloria Josey, UN peacekeeper from the United States in Somalia

In a war situation there are no innocent parties. All sides are guilty. As a peacekeeper focused on being neutral, you learn to accept nothing at face value.—Lt. Col. Glen Nordick, UN peacekeeper from Canada in Croatia

I have the advantage of not believing that the hatred between the communities is so great that reconciliation is impossible. I believe peace is possible and that those responsible must be assisted in finding the terms. While awaiting this political solution, we must do everything possible to ease the suffering of the population.—Lt. Gen. Philippe Morillo, UN commander in Bosnia-Herzegovina

The financial threats to 1994 peacekeeping operations are like a permanent Damocles sword that is hanging over the activities of the UN.—special advisor to the secretary general

To remain calm in the face of provocation, to maintain composure when under attack, the United Nations troops, officers and soldiers alike, must show a special kind of courage, one that is more difficult to come by then the ordinary kind. Our United Nations troops have been put to the test and have emerged triumphant. —UN Secretary-General Javier Perez de Cuellar accepting the Nobel Peace Prize in 1988

The international community gets a good deal when it "borrows" a nation's soldiers for peacekeeping duties. Soldiers rarely question what they are ordered to do until the job is finished. Their loyalty deserves to be repaid from the top. The UN's role and responsibilities are expanding at a dramatic rate, and peacekeeping is a growth industry. It wouldn't take a major effort for the world body to improve significantly the command, control, and logistical support of the people doing the dirty work.—*Peacekeeper: The Road to Sarajevo* by Major General Lewis MacKenzie, Canadian peacekeeper

I pray to God for the Somali people, that they will build some kind of society based on love instead of the gun. . . . If they do that, I know the lives we have lost here will not have been in vain.—Major General Thomas Montgomery, U.S. peace-keeper

UN peacekeepers are well paid. We spent a lot of money there. It's a poor country. It's obscene how well we were treated sometimes.—UN peacekeeper in Namibia

It was the highlight of my military career. I still correspond with Russians, Chinese, French, Norwegian, and other peacekeepers from the countries with whom I served.—Major Roger B. McMaster, U.S. peacekeeper serving on the Sinai Peninsula

HISTORY, GEOGRAPHY, AND LITERATURE

For thousands of years, teachers—who often were priests or parents—told stories that taught socially desired learning and transmitted the beliefs and values of their culture. These include acceptable and unacceptable actions; what to value; the proper roles of men, women, and children; religious beliefs; and the appearance and effects of bravery, cowardice, greed, humor, grief, and love. At the same time, the stories depict other cultural characteristics, including clothing, family customs, business life, foods, housing, toys, amusements, environment, and schooling.

Such topics as clothing, customs, housing, and foods resemble a table of contents for a social studies textbook precisely because folk stories functioned as a societal catalog of required learning. Unlike most textbooks, however, folktales appeal to students. Recognizing the appeal, teachers have used tales for the enjoyment and enrichment of their pupils.

Combining Geography, Imagery, Literature, and Visuals to Create an Awareness of the Rain Forests*

Every minute, 50 to 100 acres of rich tropical rain forest disappear from the earth. Over half the world's species make their home in tropical forests and millions of species may become extinct before they are even identified. The tragedy is that "the rain forests are being destroyed not out of ignorance or stupidity but largely out of poverty and greed." (Gradwohl & Greenberg, p. 10)

Gradwohl and Greenberg exhort us all to become aware that "we are facing the first human created extinction cycle that is on the same scale as the major geological events of the past, but condensed into an incomparably smaller span of time" (p. 13).

To make our students more aware of the decreasing area of the rain forests and the effects that their loss will have on the world, the following class activity is suggested.

Geography

1. a. Identify each area and name some countries where possible.
   b. List the major rivers in each area.
   c. Fill in the Equator and the Tropic of Capricorn on each map.

---

*Excerpts from "Integrating Geography, Imagery, Literature and Visuals to Create an Awareness of the Rain Forests" by Jennifer Nelson, *Social Studies Journal*, Vol. 23, Spring 1994, are used with permission of *Social Studies Journal*.

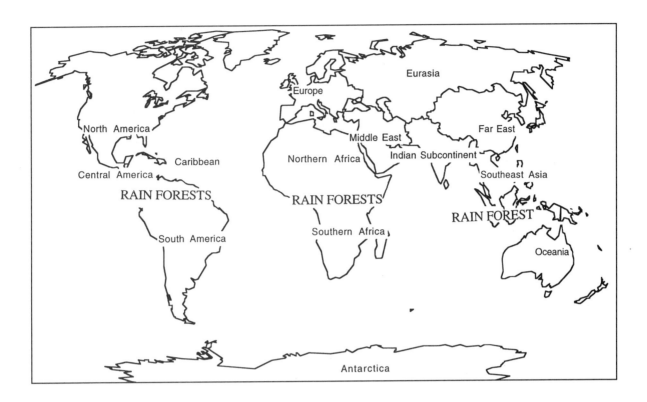

d. Under each map, list the important exports.
e. Write a paragraph on the geographical factors that help create rain forests.

Imagery

This is an enjoyable visual imagery activity that gives students a sense of scale for understanding the great diversity of species in a small area of rain forest.

Read the following instructions to your class:

Close your eyes and pretend that you are in your bathroom. Imagine that the shower has been on full blast and the bathroom is hot and steamy.

Place in the bathtub:

- 4 red-eyed frogs
- 1 anaconda snake (6 feet long) coiled across the shower curtain rod
- 2 lizards near the soap dish

Add:

- 80 different kinds of plants in various shades of green
- 1 large tree and 3 small ones
- 1 troupe of 10 spider monkeys swinging from the trees
- 8 brightly colored toucan and macaw birds, all squawking at once
- 1 three-toed sloth hanging motionless from a towel rack
- 2 piranhas in the toilet

Combine:

- 150 different species of beetles
- 16 bright blue morpho butterflies
- 42 spiders and 4 furry black tarantulas
- 12 wasps, 7 flies, and 1 swarm of mosquitoes
- 3 centipedes (at least 8 inches long)
- 1 nest of leaf-cutter ants and 1 anteater

Stir in:

- 22 different kinds of worms
- 3 brown bats hanging upside down from the towel rack
- 25 flowering plants
- 1 tree iguana
- And finally—4 pounds of bacteria and fungi

NOW THAT'S WHAT A RAIN FOREST LOOKS LIKE!!!!!! (Kay Sandmeier)

Literature

In the introduction to her delightful book, *The Great Kapok Tree,* Lynne Cherry writes:

> In the dense, green Amazon rain forest, a man is chopping down a great Kapok tree. The animals who live among its leaves and branches watch him silently. Hot and weary, the man lies down to rest at the foot of the tree and falls asleep. Then, one by one, the forest creatures emerge to whisper in his ear. They beg him not to destroy their home and tell him how important every tree is in the rain forest. . . .

Read this book to your students.

Visuals

Obtain a copy of the National Geographic video entitled *Rain Forest.* This outstanding video depicts every animal, bird, insect, tree, and plant referred to in the "Imagery" activity and in Lynne Cherry's book. Show this video to your students in parts or as a whole.

ACTIVITIES

1. Divide the class into two and debate "To save or not to save the rain forests."
2. Find articles in the newspapers over the next month that refer to the rain forests. Analyze the number of articles and their content. If no articles appear and/or you do not agree with their content, write a letter to the editor.
3. Compose a poem, a rap, or a pledge urging the global protection of the rain forests.

FOLKSONGS AND FOLKTALES

Downplay "Down Under" No Longer: Teaching about Australia[*]

Australia is very much in the news these days. Politically, Australia is seriously thinking of breaking its historic ties with the British crown. Economically, Australia finds its trading partners to be more and more in the Asian market. In the sporting world, Australia has been awarded the Olympic Games for the year 2000. Our students will be hearing more about Australia in the next four years than possibly at any other period of time.

The reemphasis on geography in the social studies curriculum provides a wonderful opportunity to study Australia from a geographic perspective. The five fundamental themes of geography suggested by the National Geographic society can be applied to a study of Australia. These five themes are as follows:

1. Location (absolute and relative position)
2. Place (physical and human characteristics)
3. Human/environment interactions
4. Movement (humans interacting with the earth)
5. Regions (how they form and change)

Over the past few years, a growing number of teachers have turned to literature to enrich the study of social studies. According to Nelli (1985), folktales can "promote the discovery of similarities, encourage the exploration of differences and foster a multicultural awareness." (p. 155) Folksongs too, can provide the "mirror of a people." Together, folktales and folksongs can add a richness to the fundamental five themes of geography.

Geography

Location
Give students an outline world map and let them locate the absolute and relative positions of the continent of Australia. Absolute location means the *site* of Australia in terms of latitude and longitude. Relative location means the *situation* of Australia, or where Australia is in relation to places around it.

Place
Give students an outline map of the continent of Australia. On the map, let them fill in the following geographical data:

> The land area in square miles
> The highest elevation
> The lowest elevation
> The four principal lakes
> The four principal rivers

---

*Excerpts from "A Note on Teaching about Australia" by Jennifer Nelson, *Canadian Social Studies*, Vol. 30, No. 2, Winter 1996, are used with permission of *Canadian Social Studies* and the Althouse Press.

The four principal mountain ranges
The four principal deserts

Human/Environment Interactions
On a second outline map of the continent of Australia, let students fill in the seven states of Australia. For each state, they should fill in the capital city and the population figures for each of those cities. They should fill in the capital city of Australia with its population figures.

Combination of Movement, Place, and Region
Provide the students with the following fact sheet:
The continent of Australia is:

- The only nation that is a continent
- The smallest continent
- The flattest
- The driest (except for Antarctica)

This explains why:

- Less than 10 percent of the land is arable
- The largest lake, Eyre, is usually bone dry
- Australians are the greatest consumers of alcohol in the English-speaking world
- Australia is also among the least populated countries, averaging only five people per square mile
- There are ten times as many sheep as there are people
- Wool production is 30 percent of the entire world's output

Elsewhere there are rocks—not just any rocks, but

- The oldest known fragments of the earth's crust from the Jack Hills, at 4.3 billion years
- 28 percent of the world's uranium, along with coal reserves that match Saudi Arabia's oil in potential energy
- Formations that supply nearly 90 percent of Australia's oil needs
- Almost all of the world's opals

Small wonder that 80 percent of Australia's 16 million people (including 200,000 Aborigines) live in cities, mainly along the fertile coast between Brisbane and Adelaide.
In statistical terms, Australians have it better than most:

- Per capita income, at $11,200 U.S., is one of the world's highest.
- Life expectancy, 76 years, is one of the world's longest.
- Literacy is virtually 100 percent.
- Workers earn from four to six weeks of annual vacation.
- Some 70 percent own their homes.
- Voting is compulsory.

. . . which may not explain why Australians spend twice as much on gambling as on national defense!! (T. Ruff, 1993, pp. 27–28)

ACTIVITY   Students can use a world almanac to compare the United States to Australia in statistical terms.

Folksong/Folktale
Obtain a copy of the folksong "Waltzing Matilda" and play it for the students. An excellent recording of "Waltzing Matilda" can be found on the cassette tape "Children's Songs Around the World" by Catherine Slonecki. Hand out a copy of the words to the folksong to each student.

Waltzing Matilda—Australia

Once a jolly swagman camped by a billabong
Under the shade of a coolibah tree
And he sang as he watched and waited till his billy boiled
"You'll come a-waltzing Matilda with me!"

Chorus
Waltzing Matilda, waltzing Matilda
You'll come a-waltzing Matilda with me
And he sang as he watched and waited till his billy boiled
"You'll come a-waltzing Matilda with me!"

Down came a jumbuck to drink at the billabong
Up jumped the swagman and grabbed him with glee
And he sang as he stowed that jumbuck in this tucker bag
"You'll come a-waltzing Matilda with me!"

Chorus
Waltzing Matilda, waltzing Matilda
You'll come a-waltzing Matilda with me
And he sang as he stowed that jumbuck in his tucker bag
"You'll come a-waltzing Matilda with me!"

Up rode the squatter, mounted on his thoroughbred
Down came the troopers one, two, three
"Where's that jolly jumbuck you've got in your tucker bag?"
"You'll come a-waltzing Matilda with me!"

Chorus
Waltzing Matilda, waltzing Matilda
You'll come a-waltzing Matilda with me
And he sang as he stowed that jumbuck in his tucker bag
"You'll come a-waltzing Matilda with me!"

Up jumped the swagman, and sprang into the billabong
"You'll never catch me alive," said he
And his ghost may be heard as you pass by that billabong
"You'll come a-waltzing Matilda with me!"

Chorus
Waltzing Matilda, waltzing Matilda
You'll come a-waltzing Matilda with me

And his ghost may be heard as you pass by that billabong
"You'll come a-waltzing Matilda with me!"

ACTIVITIES

1. The students can now do a vocabulary activity. Students locate the following Australian terms and guess or imagine what the terms might mean. Then they find out the real meanings!

Billabong	A water hole in a dried-up river bed
Billy	A tin used as a kettle
Coolibah	Eucalyptus tree
Jumbuck	Sheep
Swagman	A tramp carrying a swag which is a bundle wrapped in a blanket
Tucker	Food
Waltzing Matilda	Going on a trek carrying a bundle

2. Groups of students can choose one of the following Australian personalities and provide a "personality profile" of that person to the class in an oral report.

Evonne Goolagong Cawley	Herb Elliot
Helen Reddy	Greg Norman
Olivia Newton-John	Edmund Barton
Dame Judith Anderson	Rod Laver
Ron Clarke	Randolph Stow
Robert Hawke	Captain James Cook

3. Who are the Aborigines? What is their situation in Australia today? Are there any similarities between the Australian Aborigines and the Native Americans?

4. Using newspapers and current event magazines, make a list of the reasons that Australia is in the news.

5. Australia has been awarded the Olympic games in the year 2000. Create an emblem and a theme that Australia might adopt for this special occasion.

LEGENDS

A Legend of Multnomah Falls*

"All the cliffs and falls of the Columbia Gorge are rich in Indian legendary and enchantment," wrote one Oregon pioneer, "and each has its pretty, tragic story. There are several about Multnomah Falls."

---

*"The Legend of Multnomah Falls," from *Indian Legends of the Pacific Northwest* by Ella E. Clark. Copyright © 1953 The Regents of the University of California; © renewed 1981 Ella E. Clark. Reprinted with permission.

Multnomah is the highest of the waterfalls along the Columbia Gorge. It falls from Larch Mountain in a series of cascades.

Many years ago, the head chief of the Multomah people had a beautiful young daughter. She was especially dear to her father because he had lost all his sons in fighting, and he was now an old man. He chose her husband with great care—a young chief from his neighbors, the Clatsop people. To the wedding feast came many people from tribes along the lower Columbia and from south of it.

The wedding feast was to last for several days. There were swimming races and canoe races on the river. There would be bow-and-arrow contests, horse racing, dancing, and feasting. All the people were merry, for both the maiden and the young warrior were loved by their people.

But suddenly the happiness changed to sorrow. A sickness came over the village. Children and young people were the first to die from the plague. Then strong men became ill and died in one day. The wailing of women was heard throughout the Multnomah village and through the camps of the guests.

"The Great Spirit is angry with us, " the people said to each other. "How can we soften his anger?"

The head chief called together his old men and his warriors for counsel. "The Great Spirit is angry with us, " he told them gravely. "What can we do to please him?"

Only silence followed his question. At last one old medicine man arose. "We cannot soften such anger. If it is the will of the Great Spirit that we die, then we must meet our death like brave men. The Multnomah have ever been a brave people."

The other members of the council nodded in agreement—all except one, the oldest medicine man. He had not attended the wedding feast and games, but he came in from the mountains when he was called by the chief. He now arose and, leaning on his stick, spoke to the council. His voice was low and feeble.

"I am a very old man, my friends. I have lived a long, long time. Now you will know why. I will tell you a secret my father told me many years ago. My father was a great medicine man of the Multnomah, many summers and many snows in the past.

"When he was an old man, he told me that when I became old, the Great Spirit would send a sickness upon our people. Many would die, he said. All would die unless a sacrifice was made to the Great Spirit. It must be the life of a maiden of the tribe. Some pure and innocent maiden, the daughter of a chief, must willingly give her life for her people. Alone, she must go to a high cliff above Big River and throw herself upon the rocks below. If she does this, the sickness will leave us at once.

"I have finished," the old man said. "My father's secret is told. Now I can die in peace."

Not a word was spoken as the old medicine man sat down. At last the chief lifted his head. "Let us call in all the maidens whose fathers or grandfathers have been headmen."

Soon a dozen girls stood before him. Among them his own loved daughter. The chief told them what the old medicine man had said. "I think his words are the words of truth," he added.

Then he turned to his medicine men and his warriors. "Tell our people to meet death bravely. No maiden shall be asked to sacrifice herself. The meeting has ended."

The sickness stayed in the village, and many more people died. The daughter of the head chief sometimes wondered if she should be the one to give her life to the Great Spirit. But she loved the young warrior. She wanted to live.

A few days later she saw the sickness on the face of her lover. Then she knew what she must do. Unless she sacrificed herself, he would die. She cooled his hot face, cared for him tenderly, and left a bowl of water by his bedside. Then she slipped away, alone, without a word to anyone.

All night and all the next day she followed the trail to the great river. At sunset she reached the edge of a cliff overlooking the water. She stood there in silence for a few moments, looking at the jagged rocks far below. Then she turned her face toward the sky and lifted up her arms. She spoke aloud to the Great Spirit.

"You are angry with my people. Will you make the sickness pass away if I give you my life? Only love and peace and purity are in my heart. If you will accept me as a sacrifice for my people, let some token hang in the sky. Let me know that my death will not be in vain and that the sickness will quickly pass."

Just then she saw the man coming up over the trees across the river. It was the token. She closed her eyes and jumped from the cliff.

Next morning all the people who had expected to die that day arose from their beds, well and strong. They were full of joy. Once more there was laughter in the village and in the camps of the guests.

Suddenly someone had a thought and asked aloud, "What caused the sickness to pass away? Did one of the maidens—?"

Once more the chief asked that all the daughters and granddaughters of headmen come before him. This time one was missing.

The young Clatsop warrior hurried along the trail which leads to Big found the girl they all loved. There they buried her.

Then her father prayed to the Great Spirit, "Show us some token that my daughter's spirit has been welcomed into the land of the spirits."

Almost at once they heard the sound of water coming from above. All the people looked up to the cliff. A stream of water, silvery white, was coming over the edge of the rock. It broke into floating mist and then fell at their feet. The stream continued to float down, in a high and beautiful waterfall.

For many summers the white water has dropped from the cliff into the pool below. Sometimes in winter the spirit of the brave and beautiful maiden comes back to see the waterfall. Dressed in white, she stands among the trees at one side of Multnomah Falls. There she looks upon the place where she made her great sacrifice and thus saved her lover and her people from death.

ACTIVITY   Write your own legend about any interesting mountain, river, or waterfall in your area.

NOVELS, BIOGRAPHIES, AND AUTOBIOGRAPHIES

According to King (1990), one of the advantages of using literature in the teaching of history and geography is that literature provides a sense of time, place, and culture:

> In teaching history/geography, teachers usually race through the decades and the centuries in such great haste that students have only the vaguest notion of how other times—or places—or cultures—are both different from and similar to their own. One of the great joys of literature—and one of its great advantages to history/geography—is that it immerses the reader in the sights, the sounds, the smells, and even the tastes of other temporal and spatial settings. (p. 3)

A teaching technique especially recommended by Gagnon (1988) was this:

> Tell them a story. History offers the greatest stories ever told, full of adventure, comedy, melodrama, tragedy and mastery. The great teacher is able to take the best, most engaging stories from each area of history and set them as stepping stones through his or her course. (p. 288)

Bernard (1983) encouraged the use of literature both as a primary source and as a springboard for further research. Literature does not substitute itself for history or geography but acts as a documentary source and as a catalyst for the development of historical and geographical skills:

> Traditional study of standard primary sources can help to develop one's historical imagination and an empathy with the citizens of the past without which good history is impossible. The strength of great literature has always been its ability to extend and enrich imagination. For the sake of their students and their subject, history teachers should not neglect it. (p. 516)

ACTIVITIES

There are a number of ways in which teachers can integrate novels, biographies, and autobiographies into their teaching:

1. The class can be required to read a novel, biography, or autobiography as part of the course load. The book then can be discussed as the period being studied progresses. In the ideal scenario, the students would read the book in their English course, where its literary aspects could be discussed.
2. Students can be encouraged to read a novel, biography, or autobiography as extra credit and be asked to share their insights with the class.
3. Teachers and students can be encouraged to read novels, biographies, or autobiographies by members of an ethnic, racial, gender, or other minority group. Discussions can revolve around what surprised the students most about what they read from a different perspective.
4. Teachers can read extracts from novels at opportune moments. Extracts from books can be copied and even handed out to students for further analysis, but it is important to read from the book. Following are examples of extracts from selected novels which could be used when teaching the French Revolution.

Louis XVI

His features showed no nobility of expression. His laugh was heavy and lethargic, his face lifeless, his appearance slovenly. At the age of eleven he lost his father. His elder brother died soon after; then his mother. He was short-sighted, overgrown, shy and awkward. He liked to work with his hands. He delighted to make his own locks and keys. His only other interest was hunting and as King he spent so much time on horseback that he would fall asleep afterwards during important meetings. In 1789 when the King came to work out for himself what he had been doing since 1775 (marriage), he worked out that he had attended 400 wild boar hunts, 134 stag hunts and 324 other expeditions accounting for 1562 days devoted to the chase. He had a graceless walk, his voice at times rose to an undignified squeak and he hated dancing.

Marie Antoinette

Marie Antoinette, daughter of Maria Theresa, Empress of Austria, was chosen as a bride for Louis XVI and not by him, and as usually happened with such arranged marriages, Louis XVI faced his future with indifference. And indifference was something new for this young girl. For her slim and graceful appearance, flawless complexion, blue eyes and delicately burnished golden hair had made her the spoilt child of the Court of Vienna. She could not but be disappointed at being married to the only man at the French court who was not only disinterested in women as a sex, but incapable of concealing the fact behind a screen of elegant politeness. The young bride had never been an intellectual. She was not fond of books, or, despite having played with the young Mozart, enthusiastic about music. And so, when Louis went hunting, Marie Antoinette looked round for the more light-hearted and frivolous among those at Court with whom she could agreeably pass her time.

The Palace of Versailles

Scores of chaplains, confessors, clerics, choristers, composers and copiers of sacred music were employed in the Chapel. Forty-eight doctors including physicians, surgeons, oculists, manipulators, and bone setters supervised the King's health, 43 men tended the royal book shelves. There was never a shortage of people willing to serve at Versailles.

To serve the King as doorman or valet was a privilege for which people paid large sums. It took 198 valets of various kinds to see to the King's clothes, his armour and his washing. Men were appointed to comb the royal hair and to dry the monarch. Two noblemen were allotted the task of handling the royal perforated chair. They were paid $20,000 lires a year ($16,000) to appear every morning dressed in velvet, to examine and empty if necessary the receptacle for which they were responsible.

The King got up twice each morning. Once privately and later semi-publicly. For this ceremony five classes of people were admitted to his bed-chamber to pay their respects. In the first batch came his close relations—children, Princes, Princesses, the Chief Physician and other indispensable royal servants. The second entree included the Great Master, the Master of the Wardrobe, the First Gentleman of the Bed-Chamber and other favoured noblemen.

Court Extravagance

In 1799, the Queen's lighting bill came to $126,000, the King's lemonade F1,600 and broth for the princess F416. Marie Antoinette used up four pairs of slippers a week. Coffee and a roll for everyone at Versailles worked out at F1,600 a year per head. A single fete put on by Marie Antoinette made a loss of F320,000. The King's wine bill came to F6,000 a year.

When an outcry was made at these expenses, money was saved in Paris by doing without street lamps on moonlit nights.

Taxation

It was an indirect tax, the Gabelle, which was the most unpopular of all. This tax was levied on every grain of salt eaten by the inhabitants of France. The rate was lower in those parts of the country where salt was produced. Like other indirect taxes it was handed out to people who could pay for this privilege and was collected on the assumption that everyone over the age of 8 ate six-tenths of a gallon of salt per year. In fact they were compelled to buy their allotted ration—and treated as smugglers if they did not. Everything was done to prevent free salt from being obtained. The housewife was not allowed to use sea water for cooking and farmers were forbidden to feed their cattle on salt marshes. Drinking at salt fountains was forbidden. Some citizens rather than pay the tax let butter and meat go bad. It took 50,000 officials to enforce the Gabelle. Homes were often swooped upon and larders raided. More than 10,000 people, many of them children were arrested per year. This tax yielded F50 million a year.

The Guillotine

Only three muffled sounds could be distinguished—the first, made when the plank, with the victim bound to it, was slid into position, the second when the yoke or collar which held the victim's head was closed and the third when the knife made its swift descent. The executioner (Sanson in Paris) only had two carts of his own and had to hire others, at a high price, to be used for his traffic in blood. Other expenses included nails and wood for the maintenance of the scaffolding, ropes for binding the prisoners and wicker baskets to catch their heads. During the Reign of Terror, the executioner was deprived of his right to keep the clothes of this victims. They were sent to hospitals or prisons.

In Paris, a specially dug ditch caught the blood of the 1,500 victims dispatched there in three weeks.

"Sneezing into the sack" or "putting your head on the window-sill" was current slang for being guillotined.

5. Annotated bibliographies of good books on the topic being studied can be displayed in the classroom. An excellent resource for annotated bibliographies is the Time CD (1994) available from Compact Publishing Inc., P.O. Box 40310, Washington, DC 20016. Other excellent resources can be found by surfing the Internet, where experts in certain fields have collated the best literature. For example, literature on the Civil War can be obtained by sending e-mail to whale@leland.stanford.edu.

POETRY

Prose and poetry might be defined as a kind of language that says more and says it more intensely than does ordinary language. Prose and poetry are not primarily written to communicate information; their concern is with experience. Poetry and prose exist to bring us a sense and a perception of life, to live with greater awareness, to know the experience of others, and to better know our own experiences.

The California History/Social Science Framework (1988) recommended the use of literature in the teaching of history as a resource to demonstrate the inner life of people in other times and places: "Poetry, novels, prose, . . . help to shed light on the life and times of the people. Such literature helps to reveal the way people saw themselves, their ideas and values, their fears and their dreams, and the way they interpreted their own times." (p. 4)

Ravitch and Finn (1987) succinctly stated the reasons for integrating a study of history and literature:

We urge the study of history and literature because we believe they are important. It is not simply because they are repositories for our cultural heritage; nor is it merely that they help us understand the past. Those who study these subjects become more knowledgeable, more perceptive, and more thoughtful by doing so. They learn about the forces, individuals, trends, and events that have shaped the present; they discover from their own experience the power of novels, poems, prose, . . . to move, delight, entertain, inform, shock, and reveal us to ourselves. History and literature are the essential studies of the humanities because they interpret for us the human experience. (p. 251)

Wilfred Owen's Poetry: Integrating Poetry into the Teaching of World War I

After the slaughter at Fredericksburg (1862), Robert E. Lee commented, "It is well that war is so terrible or we should grow too fond of it." Few war poets, however, echoed these sentiments; they tended to glorify war and make heroes of those who fought in them. It was World War I (1914–1918), the most terrible war that has ever scourged humankind, that was to change the tone of war poetry.

The nightmares of war, the sights and sounds and the memories of earth and men torn asunder in the trenches of World War I, seem so remote to students sitting in our history classes today. Including a personality profile and poetry written by one of the men who lived and died in those trenches can help students better understand the change in attitude toward war. The bitter poetry of Wilfred Owen dispelled forever the power of the old lie, "Dulce et Decorum est Pro Patria Mori" ("It is good and beautiful to die for one's country").

Wilfred Owen (1893–1918)
Wilfred Owen was born in 1893. He was educated at the University of London, and had a private English tutor in Bordeaux, France, from 1913 to 1915 before enlisting in the Artists' Rifles, a unit made up of literary figures, painters, and intellectual adventures. The Great War had already started, and Owen had this to say to his mother as to why he joined:

> I don't imagine that the German War will be affected by my joining in, but I know my own future Peace will be.

Owen was involved in much of the bitterest fighting in the war. On one occasion he and 25 other men held a flooded, mud-choked, abandoned German dugout in a no-man's-land for 50 hours while the Germans shelled the position mercilessly. It was raining and they were trapped 15 feet underground by the barrage while the water and mud slowly rose over their knees inside the position. Owen related this experience in a poem:

The Sentry

> We'd found an old Boche dug-out, and he knew,
> And gave us hell; for shell on frantic shell
> Lit full on tip, but never quite burst through.
> Rain, guttering down in waterfalls of slime,
> Kept slush waist-high and rising hour by hour,
> And choked the steps too thick with clay to climb.

What murk of air remained stank old, and sour
With fumes from whizbangs, and the smell of men
Who'd lived there years, and left their curse in the den,
If not their corpses . . .
                              There we herded from the blast
Of whizbangs; but one found our door at last,—
Buffeting eyes and breath, snuffing the candles,
And thud! flump! thud! down the steep steps thumping
And splashing in the flood, deluging muck,
The sentry's body; then his rifle, handles
Of old Boche bombs, and mud in ruck on ruck.
We dredged it up, for dead, until he whined
"O sir—my eyes,—I'm blind,—I'm blind, I'm blind."
Coaxing, I held a flame against his lids
And said if he could see the least blurred light
He was not blind; in time they'd get all right.
"I can't," he sobbed. Eyeballs, huge-bulged like squids',
Watch my dreams still,—yet I forgot him there
In posting Next for duty, and sending a scout
To bag a stretcher somewhere, and flound'ring about
To other posts under the shrieking air.
Those other wretches, how they bled and spewed,
And one who would have drowned himself for good,
I try not to remember these things now.
Let Dread hark back for one word only: how,
Half-listening to that sentry's moans and jumps,
And the wild chattering of his shivered teeth,
Renewed most horribly whenever crumps
Pummeled the roof and slogged the air beneath,
Through the dense din, I say, we heard him shout
"I see your lights!"—But ours had long gone out.

Owen corresponded frequently with his mother in England and offered this description of the trenches and the experience of "Going over the top" in an attack on the enemy trench:

> The battlefield is an eternal place of gnashing teeth, the fires of Sodom and Gomorrah could not light a candle to it. . . . It is pock-marked like a body of foulest disease and its odor is the breath of cancer. . . . The sensation of going over the top is about as exhilarating as those dreams of falling over a precipice. . . . I woke up without being squashed. Some didn't.

After his unit was pulled back into reserve, Owen was diagnosed with shell-shock—severe psychological stress from combat—and was sent to a psychiatric hospital in Scotland for treatment. There he met Sigfried Sassoon, already a well-known war poet, who described Wilfred Owen as:

> Short, dark haired, and shyly hesitant . . . he spoke with a slight stammer, which was not unusual in that neurosis-pervaded hospital . . . he had a charming, honest smile, and his manners were modest and ingratiating.

Owen's attitude toward the war seemed to undergo metamorphosis as the war went on. From the nationalistic fervor and youthful curiosity that drove him to enlist, he gradually changed to the bitter irony of "Dulce et Decorum Est."

Dulce et Decorum Est Pro Patria Mori

Bent double, like old beggars under sacks,
Knock-kneed, coughing like hags, we cursed through sludge,
Till on the haunting flares we turned our backs
And towards our distant rest began to trudge.
Men marched asleep. Many had lost their boots
But limped on, blood shod. All went lame; all blind;
Drunk with fatigue; deaf even to the hoots
Of tired, outstripped shells that dropped behind.

Gas! Gas! Quick boys!—An ecstasy of fumbling,
Fitting the clumsy helmets just in time;
But someone still was yelling out and stumbling
And floundering like a man in fire or lime . . .
Dim, through the misty panes and thick green light,
As under a green sea, I saw him drowning.
In all my dreams, before my helpless sight,
He plunges at me, guttering, choking, drowning.

If in some smothering dreams you too could pace
Behind the wagon that we flung him in,
And watch the white eyes writhing in his face,
His hanging face, like a devil's sick of sin;
If you could hear, at every jolt, the blood
Come gargling from the froth-corrupted lungs,
Obscene as cancer, bitter as the cud
Of vile, incurable sores on innocent tongues,—
My friend, you would not tell with such high zest
To children ardent for some desperate glory,
The old Lie: Dulce et Decorum est
Pro Patria Mori.

Owen's experiences in the war finally moved him to write the following in a letter to his mother:

One of Christ's essential commands was: Passivity at any price! Suffer dishonour and disgrace, but never resort to arms. Be bullied, be outraged, be killed, but do not kill. . . Am I not myself a Conscientious Objector with a very seared conscience? Christ is literally in No-Man's-Land. . . . there men hear his voice. Greater love hath no man than that he lay down his life for his friends. . . . It [Christ's voice] is spoken only in French or English? I do not believe so . . . thus you see how pure Christianity will not fit in with pure nationalism.

Owen had lived a charmed life at the front—having survived (physically at least) three years of war. He was killed one week before the Armistice ending the war was signed. Found in his pack was this handwritten poem.

What passing bells for these who die as cattle?
—Only the monstrous anger of the guns
 Only the stuttering rifles rapid rattle
Can patter out their hasty orisons.
No mockeries now for them nor prayers nor bells
 Nor any voice of mourning save the choirs,
The shrill demented choirs of wailing shells;
 And bugles calling for them from sad shrires.
What candles may be held to speed them all?
 Not in the hands of boys, but in their eyes
Shall shine the holy glimmers of goodbyes.
 the pallor of girls' brows shall be their pall,
Their flowers the tenderness of silent minds,
And each slow dusk a drawing down of blinds.

ACTIVITIES

1. When discussing the use of *poisonous gas* as one of the new weapons developed during World War I, a copy of the poem "Dulce et Decorum Est Pro Patria Mori" by Wilfred Owen can be handed out to each student. The teacher can either read the poem or prepare one of the students to read the poem.

   The poem can now be analyzed with the following guidelines/questions:
   a. What gases were used during World War I?
   b. What are the effects on the human body of being caught in a gas attack? Choose five adjectives from the poem that describe these effects.
   c. Suggest some reasons why many World War I soldiers "had lost their boots." (line 6)
   d. Why do you think Wilfred Owen uses the terms "Froth-corrupted lungs," "obscene as cancer," "bitter as the cud," and "of vile, incurable sores" (lines 22–24)? What images do these terms bring to mind?
   e. Attempt to translate the last line of the poem.

2. When discussing the *human toll* of World War I, read Wilfred Owen's poem "What Passing Bells for These Who Die as Cattle."
   a. Research the human cost of life in World War I for: (a) Germany, (b) the Soviet Union, (c) Britain, (d) France, and (e) The United States of America.
   b. Write a reaction to the words of the poem and share these thoughts with the rest of the class.

3. Students can write an individual or a collaborative poem that deals with the horrors of World War I. Key events, places, people, weapons, and generalizations drawn from a study of conditions in the trenches and life on the home front can be brainstormed as a prelude to composing the poems.

4. Find other World War I poetry written by German, French, Australian, or American poets. Students can share these poetic interpretations of the war with the class.

Poetry and the Vietnam War

There are a number of ways to teach the content of the war in Vietnam—chronologically, militarily, politically, socially, thematically, geographically, and so on. Poetry from and about Vietnam might not necessarily communicate more information about the history of the war, but it can give students a different perspective on the war.

A number of outstanding anthologies contain poetry from the Vietnam War. Poems in these collections are written from a variety of perspectives—U.S. soldiers, conscientious objectors, and Vietnamese civilians, both men and women. Suggested readings include the following:

Ehrhart, W. D. (Ed). (1985). *Carrying the darkness: American Indochina: The poetry of the Vietnam War.* New York: American Book Company.

Luce, D., & Sommer, J. (1969). *Vietnam: The unheard voices.* Ithaca, NY: Cornell University Press.

McCarthy, G. (1977). *War story: Vietnam war poems.* New York: Crossing Press.

Mersmann, J. F. (1974) *Out of the Vietnam vortex: A study of poets and poetry against the war.* Lawrence: University of Kansas.

Rottman, L., Barry, J., & Pacquet, B. (Eds.). (1972). *Winning hearts and minds; War poems by Vietnam veterans.* New York: First Casualty Press.

Examples of Poems

The Dug-Out—Siegfried Sassoon

Why do you lie with your legs ungainly huddled,
And one arm bent across your sullen cold
Exhausted face? It hurts my heart to watch you,
Deep-shadow'd from the candle's guttering gold:
and you wonder why I shake you by the shoulder;
Drowsy, you mumble and sigh and shift your head . . .
You are too young to fall asleep for ever;
And when you sleep you remind me of the dead.

This poem was written during World War I, but it can be used when studying any war.

ACTIVITY   Students can write their reactions to the poem in either prose or poetry.

Lamplight—May Wedderburn Cannan

We planned to shake the world together, you and I
Being young, and very wise;
Now in the light of the green shaded lamp
Almost I see your eyes
Light with the old gay laughter; you and I
Dreamed greatly of an Empire in those days,
Setting our feet upon laborious ways,

And all you asked of fame
Was crossed swords in the Army List,
My Dear, against your name.
We planned a great Empire together, you and I
Bound only by the sea;
Now in the quiet of a chill Winter's night
Your voice comes hushed to me
Full of forgotten memories: you and I
Dreamed great dreams of our future in those days,
Setting our feet on undiscovered ways,
And all I asked of fame
A scarlet cross on my breast, my Dear,
For the swords by your name.
We shall never shake the world together, you and I,
For you gave your life away;
And I think my heart was broken by the war,
Since on a summer day
You took the road we never spoke of: you and I
Dreamed greatly of an Empire in those days;
You set your feet upon the Western ways
And I have no need of fame—
There's a scarlet cross on my breast, my Dear,
And a torn cross with your name.

ACTIVITIES

1. If you were not told the poet's name, would you think this poet was male or female? Was the poet British, American, or German? Support your answer.
2. Why do you think the poem is entitled "Lamplight"?
3. Comment on the line "You took the road we never spoke of: you and I."

Paul Revere's Ride—Henry Wadsworth Longfellow

Listen, my children, and you shall hear
Of the midnight ride of Paul Revere,
On the eighteenth of April, in Seventy-five;
Hardly a man in now alive
Who remembers that famous day and year.
He said to his friend, "If the British march
By land or sea from the town tonight,
Hang a lantern aloft in the belfry arch
Of the North Church tower as a signal light—
One, if by land, and two, if by sea;
And I on the opposite shore will be.
Ready to ride and spread the alarm
Through every Middlesex village and farm,
For the country folk to be up and to arm."
Then he said, "Good night!" and with muffled oar
Silently rowed to the Charlestown shore,
Just as the moon rose over the bay,

Where singing wide at her moorings lay
The *Somerset,* British man-of-war;
A phantom ship, with each mast and spar
Across the moon like a prison bar,
And a huge black hulk, that was magnified
By its own reflection in the tide.
Meanwhile, his friend, through alley and street,
Wanders and watches, with eager ears,
Till in the silence around him he hears
The muster of men at the barrack door,
And the measured tread of the grenadiers,
Marching down to their boats on the shore.
Then he climbed the tower of the Old North Church,
By the wooden stairs with steady tread,
To the belfry-chamber overhead,
And startled the pigeons from their perch
On the somber rafters, that round him made
Masses and moving shaped of shade
By the trembling ladder steep and tall
To the highest window in the wall,
Where he paused to listen and look down
A moment on the roofs of the town,
And the moonlight flowing over all.
Beneath in the churchyard, lay the dead,
In their night-encampment on the hill,
Wrapped in silence so deep and still
That he could hear, like a sentinel's tread,
The watchful night-wind, as it went
Creeping along from tent to tent,
And seeming to whisper, "All is well!"
A moment only he feels the spell
Of the place and the hour and the secret dread
Of the lonely belfry and the dead;
For suddenly all his thoughts are bent
On a shadowy something for away,
Where the river widens to meet the bay
A line of black that bends and floats
On the rising tide like a bridge of boats.
Meanwhile, impatient to mount and ride,
Booted and spurred, with a heavy stride
On the opposite shore walked Paul Revere.
Now he patted his horse's side,
Now he gazed at the landscape far and near,
Then, impetuous, stamped the earth,
And turned and tightened his saddle girth;
But mostly he watched with eager search
The belfry tower of the Old North Church,
As it rose above the graves on the hill,
Lonely and spectral and somber and still.
And lo! as he looks, on the belfry's height
A glimmer, and then a gleam of light!
He springs to the saddle, the bridle he turns,
But lingers and gazes, till full on his sight

A second lamp in the belfry burns!
A hurry of hoofs in a village street,
A shape in the moonlight, a bulk in the dark,
And beneath, from the pebbles, in passing, a spark
Struck out by a steed flying fearless and fleet:
That was all! And yet, through the gloom and the light,
The fate of a nation was riding that night;
And the spark struck out by that steed, in his flight,
Kindled the land into flame with its heat.
He has left the village and mounted the steep,
And beneath him, tranquil and broad and deep,
Is the Mystic, meeting the ocean tides;
And under the alders that skirt its edge,
Now soft on the sand, now loud on the ledge,
Is heard the tramp of his steed as he rides.
It was twelve by the village clock,
When he crossed the bridge into Medford town.
He heard the crowing of the cock,
And the barking of the farmer's dog,
And felt the damp of the river fog,
That rises after the sun goes down.
It was one by the village clock,
When he galloped into Lexington.
He saw the glided weathercock
Swim in the moonlight as he passed,
And the meeting-house windows, blank and bare,
Gaze at him with a spectral glare,
As if they already stood aghast
At the bloody work they would look upon.
It was two by the village clock,
When he came to the bridge in Concord town.
He heard the bleating of the flock,
And the twitter of birds among the trees,
And felt the breath of the morning breeze
Blowing over the meadows brown.
And one was safe and asleep in his bed
Who at the bridge would be first to fall,
Who that day would be lying dead,
Pierced by a British musket-ball.
You know the rest. In the books you have read
How the British Regulars fired and fled—
How the farmers gave them ball for ball,
From behind each fence and farmyard wall,
Chasing the red-coats down the lane,
Then crossing the fields to emerge again
Under the trees at the turn of the road,
And only pausing to fire and load.
So through the night rode Paul Revere;
And so through the night went his cry of alarm
To every Middlesex village and farm—
A cry of defiance and not of fear,
A voice in the darkness, a knock at the door,
And a word that shall echo forever more!

For, borne on the night-wind of the Past,
Through all our history, to the last,
In the hour of darkness and peril and need,
The people will awaken and listen to hear
The hurrying hoof-beats of that steed,
And the midnight message of Paul Revere.

ACTIVITIES

1. Draw a map of Paul Revere's midnight ride from the verbal clues given in the poem.
2. Write a paragraph (or more than one paragraph) on Paul Revere's midnight ride from the point of view of one of the following:
   a. Paul Revere's horse
   b. The "night wind"
   c. The Old North Church
   d. The farmer's dog
   e. The village clock
   f. The bridge at Concord

The Charge of the Light Brigade—Alfred Lord Tennyson

Half a league, half a league,
Half a league onward,
All in the valley of Death
        Rode the six hundred.
"Forward the Light Brigade!
Charge for the guns!" he said.
Into the valley of Death
        Rode the six hundred.

"Forward, the Light Brigade!"
Was there a man dismay'd?
Not tho' the soldier knew
        Some one had blunder'd.
Theirs not to make reply,
Theirs not to reason why,
Theirs but to do and die.
Into the valley of Death
        Rode the six hundred.

Cannon to right of them,
Cannon to left of them,
Cannon in front of them
        Volley'd and thunder'd;
Storm'd at with shot and shell,
Boldly they rode and well,
Into the jaws of Death,
Into the mouth of hell
        Rode the six hundred.

Flash'd all their sabres bare,
Flash'd as they turn'd in air

Sabring the gunners there,
Charging an army, while
    All the world wonder'd.
Plunged in the battery-smoke
Right thro' the line they broke;
Cossack and Russian
Reel'd from the sabre-stroke
    Shatter'd and dunder'd.
Then they rode back, but not,
    Not the six hundred.

Cannon to right of them,
Cannon to left of them,
Cannon behind them
    Volley'd and thunder'd;
Storm'd at with shot and shell,
While horse and hero fell,
They that had fought so well
Came thro' the jaws of Death,
Back from the mouth of hell,
All that was left of them,
    Left of six hundred.

When can their glory fade?
O the wild charge they made!
    All the world wonder'd.
Honor the charge they made!
Honor the Light Brigade,
    Noble six hundred!

ACTIVITIES

1. Locate Crimea on a world map. Name the three major powers involved in the Crimean War.
2. What is a light brigade?
3. Obtain a copy of Suppe's "Light Cavalry." One student can read the poem while another student plays the music in the background. After practicing this routine, tape the reading and the music, and play this new rendition for the whole class.

Unknown Bugle Boy of Cemetery Hill—Anonymous

There's a battlefield at Gettysburg
where swords and sabers rust
And brothers who were flesh and blood
are scattered in the dust.
But every night at Gettysburg
when everything is still,
They say a golden bugle blows
on Cemetery Hill.
Who was the unknown bugle boy
at Gettysburg that day
And was he wearing Yankee blue

or wearing Southern gray?
Why did he die? What was his motive?
That government of the people, by the people,
and for the people shall not perish from the earth.

ACTIVITIES

1. What actually happened at Cemetery Hill during the battle of Gettysburg?
2. What was the role of a bugle boy in wartime?
3. Name the source of the last two lines of this poem.

Outline for a History or Geography Poem

Not everyone can write poetry! However, if we are not given an opportunity to try our hand at writing poetry, we may never know what hidden talents we have! For those to whom writing poetry might not come easily, here is an outline to get those creative juices flowing! It can be used after discussing any poem, or it can be used as an activity after studying a particular event or place.

Line 1   Name of event or place
Line 2   What happened, or what does it offer (three items)
Line 3   What it felt or feels like (three items)
Line 4   What is interesting about it (three items)
Line 5   Who is or was there (three items)
Line 6   Where it is (three items)
Line 7   What it looks like (three items)
Line 8   Synonym for the event or place

THE NEED TO PUT PEOPLE BACK INTO HISTORY

Contrary to the impression given by most textbooks, history is not an easily summarized, two-dimensional catalog of names, dates, and events; "rather it is an immense collection of narratives all with complicated characters, plots and settings that when reconstructed and interpreted tell real life stories of people of the past" (Gundlach, 1986, p. 78).

Ravitch and Finn (1987) believed that students would not designate history as their most boring subject if they could learn about the past through exciting true stories and biographies. Their recommendation was as follows:

Enliven the study of history by the frequent use of narratives, journals, stories, biographies, and autobiographies. Students should understand that the past is not simply an unfolding of social, economic, and political trends, but it is the story of men and women whose decisions, beliefs, actions, and struggles shaped the world as we know it. (p. 211)

Problems in Putting People Back into History

It appears that one of the major reasons that history teachers do not encourage their students to research personalities in history is that students usually go to an encyclopedia, copy extensive notes on their assigned personality, almost verbatim, and then either hand in the written assignment for grading or stand up and read their information aloud in class. Paul West (1990), has created a new form for biographies: the short short or animated biographical sketch. The key words here are *short short* and *animated*. Students need definite guidelines and limits when asked to present personality sketches to the class. Personality sketches must be kept short, interesting, informative, and lively.

How to Put People Back into History

What follows is a suggestion on how to put personality sketches back into our history classes using Aaron Copland's "A Lincoln Portrait."

ACTIVITIES

1. Make a list of all the personalities that will be mentioned in the whole history course or in a certain topic area.
2. Allow students to work either in groups of two or individually. The students choose the personality they wish to research from the teachers' personality list.
3. Obtain a cassette recording of Aaron Copland's "A Lincoln Portrait."
4. Play "A Lincoln Portrait," starting with the verse that mentions where Lincoln was born and raised and continuing until the end.
5. On an overhead transparency have the following guidelines, which follow the sequence on "A Lincoln Portrait."

> BORN, RAISED, LIVED
> AND THIS IS WHAT HE (SHE) SAID . . .
> PHYSICAL ATTRIBUTES
> AND THIS IS WHAT HE (SHE) SAID/THOUGHT/DID . . .
> HIS OR HER PERSONALITY
> AND THIS IS WHAT HE (SHE) SAID/DID . . .
> POLITICAL OR OTHER POSITION
> . . . . THIS IS WHAT HE (SHE) SAID (PUNCH LINE)

6. Students research their chosen personality using this outline. It should be emphasized that direct or indirect quotations are most appropriate. The personality sketch should not be more than one or one and a half typed pages.
7. When the personality a student has researched is mentioned during the history course, the student will then be called on to present the personality portrait.
8. Students should be encouraged to add music or pictorial aids to their verbal presentation.

Examples of Personality Portraits

Ludwig van Beethoven
Born, Raised, Lived . . . Ludwig van Beethoven was born on December 15, 1770, in Bonn, Germany (fourteen years after Mozart's birth). When Ludwig was a

young child, his father began teaching him the family trade of music. It soon became clear that Ludwig had real talent. Beethoven was raised in Bonn but spent most of his life in Vienna, Austria, where he died on March 26, 1827, at the age of 56.

And this is what was said about him . . . Neefe, the court organist and one of Beethoven's teachers, remarked, "If he goes as he has begun, he will certainly become a second Mozart." Mozart himself said, "You will someday make a big noise in the world."

Physical Attributes . . . When Beethoven was about 50 years old, this description was given: "He is less than medium height, but of quite powerful, stocky build; thick-set, particularly of strong bone structure; restless, bright eyes, almost piercing when they gaze; and no movements, else quick ones . . ." "He runs with his hands behind his back, through wind and rain, paying no attention to people and events around him, erect and proud . . . Beethoven didn't smile much, though, this is the miracle—he could be happy, serene, smiling in his music."

And this is what he said . . . "For me, there can be no recreation in the society of my fellows, refined intercourse, mutual exchange of thought . . . I must live like an exile."

Personality . . . As a young man, Beethoven was neat and careful in his dress; he was said to be "an engaging dreamer, a talent erratic, unpredictable, but entirely fascinating." However, with the onset of deafness at the age of 31, he became increasingly withdrawn, with bouts of depression; and was said to be "rough, powerful, emotional, overactive, gross, uninhibited, and at times crude." Someone once remarked, "His talent amazed me; unfortunately, he is an utterly untamed personality, who is not altogether in the wrong in holding the world to be detestable, but surely does not make it any more enjoyable either for himself or others by his attitude."

And this is what he said . . . "Prince, what you are you are by accident of birth; what I am I am through myself. There have been and will still be thousands of princes; there is only one Beethoven."

Political or other position . . . Beethoven was one of the world's greatest composers. He is most famous for his Fifth and Ninth Symphonies; the latter was composed when he was completely deaf.

And this is what someone said about him . . . This is the man who brings pure joy to millions, pure spiritual joy!" (As Beethoven once wrote, "What more can be given a man than fame and praise and immortality?") One can only imagine that he would be pleased with this statement.

Thomas Edison

Born, Raised, Lived . . . Thomas Edison was born on February 11, 1847, at Milan, Ohio. At the age of 7 he moved with his parents to Port Huron, Michigan. By the age of 12, he left home and worked for the Grand Trunk Railway between Port Huron and Detroit. At 16 he became a telegraph operator and lived in Canada. He returned to the United States during the Civil War and moved to Boston. He traveled often to New York and eventually opened his first workshop in Newark, New Jersey. Later he moved to Menlo Park. He then opened a modern laboratory at West Orange, New Jersey.

And this is what he said . . . When Edison was asked why failure never disappointed him, especially when about 10,000 experiments with a storage battery failed to produce results, he said, "I have not failed. I've just found 10,000 ways that won't work."

Physical Attributes . . . As a young man, Thomas Edison had thick black hair, bright blue eyes, and a jaunty mustache. He was a hard-working, practical man who did not worry about his appearance. He would often wear the same suit for days without changing his clothes even to sleep. He could go for days without sleeping or eating, much to the frustration of his wife, who always worried about his health He began to lose his hearing as a result of an accident at an early age. His deafness progressed over the years, but Edison did not mind this because he found it easier to concentrate.

And this is what he did . . . Edison was considered the world's greatest inventor. He patented over 1,100 inventions in sixty years. These included the electric light and phonograph. He perfected motion pictures, the telephone, the electric generator, the typewriter, electric-powered trains, the stock ticker, and the mimeograph machine.

The phonograph, invented by Edison in 1877, ranks as one of the world's most original inventions. Edison considered it as his favorite invention. The electric light bulb was an ingenious idea using carbonized thread as a filament. On October 20, 1879, Edison's idea was proved successful which astounded the world. He became known as "the wizard of Menlo Park."

Personality . . . Edison was known to be a quiet, melancholy man who was always thinking about his work. He was very independent and focused on his ideas. He claimed he misunderstood only two things: women and mathematics. His youthful curiosity remained with him throughout his life. His work was by far his greatest joy.

And this is what he said . . . Edison was extremely persistent with his experiments and ideas. He never became discouraged and always hoped that a solution was just around the corner. He would always say, "I'll never give up for I may have a streak of luck before I die."

Political or other position . . . Edison's achievements were acclaimed throughout the world. In 1928, Congress awarded him a gold medal for "development and application of inventions that have revolutionized civilization in the last century."

Edison, who only had three months of formal schooling, defined genius as "1 per cent inspiration and 99 per cent perspiration."

Helen Keller

Born, Raised, Lived . . . Helen Keller was born in 1880 in Tuscumbia, Alabama.

And this is what her first word was, at the age of six months . . . WATER.

Helen was a perfectly normal child until the age of 19 months, when she developed a fever that persisted for many days. The doctors described it as "congestion of the brain and stomach." As a result, Helen lost all eyesight and hearing. As she grew older, her frustration at not being understood also grew, and she resorted to screaming and tantrums to get what she wanted. Helen was a beautiful girl with dark hair, pretty eyes, and porcelain smooth skin.

And this is what she did . . . On the recommendation of Alexander Graham Bell, Helen's parents sent for a teacher from the Perkins Institute for the Deaf and Blind in Boston. Nineteen-year-old Annie Sullivan began by teaching finger spelling to Helen so that she would learn that objects have specific manes. Next she taught Helen Braille. Within two years Helen could read and write Braille fluently. Anne also taught Helen how to speak by placing Helen's fingers on her larynx so she could "hear" the vibrations. Helen was a strong and determined student, and these characteristics helped her graduate cum laude from Radcliffe College in 1904 with a degree in communications.

And this is what she said . . . But however dark the world may seem, we have a light at our command. That light is faith.

After graduation, Helen devoted herself to increasing the country's awareness of its responsibilities toward people affected by handicapping conditions. She spent many years writing essays and articles for newspapers and magazines, writing books about her life, and traveling around the world to make public speeches, which she felt was the best way to send out her message.

During World War II, Helen became a prominent figure in Washington, D.C., by supporting American involvement in the war. She was welcomed at many military hospitals, where she supported soldiers who had become blind during combat.

Helen Keller died on June 1, 1968, at her home in Westport, Connecticut. After her death, she became known as the world's "First Lady of Courage." Today she is still viewed as a beacon of hope for many disadvantaged people, as a woman whose destiny was to show others the way.

MUSIC AND SONGS

Although much attention has been given to the inclusion of audiovisual aids to enliven the teaching of history and geography, this attention has been focused mainly on the use of videos, slides, and computer programs. Little attention has been given to the integration of music and song into the social studies curriculum.

Why should we use music in our classrooms?

1. To create an authentic period atmosphere
2. As a subject for student-based research
3. To reinforce a lesson
4. To enrich a lesson
5. To stimulate analysis and creativity
6. As background sound

Music/song aids must:

1. Be appropriate in length. The whole song or piece of music can be broken down and played in parts or played as a whole and even played more than once. Copies of song lyrics should be handed out to the students.
2. Be related academically to the topic being studied
3. Be previewed and edited if necessary
4. Have clarity
5. Have a high level of interest for students

Examples of Music and Songs

A wide variety of music and songs is available to the social studies teacher. General music subheadings are suggested next, with examples of each:

1. National anthems: Canada, Mexico, England, France, Japan, South Africa
2. Tribal/indigenous music: Maori music, African music, Indian music

3. Patriotic music: "America the Beautiful," "America," "God Bless America," "Waltzing Matilda"
4. Civil rights songs: "We Shall Overcome," "Blowin' in the Wind," "Eve of Destruction"
5. Protest songs on social/political/religious/environmental issues: "Universal Soldier," "Let Us Begin," "Where Are You Now My Son?," "Pass It On Down."
6. Country-and-Western songs: "The Ballad of Davey Crockett," "What Did Del-a-ware?," "North to Alaska"
7. Classical music: *1812 Overture,* "Land of Hope and Glory," "The Blue Danube," Beethoven's *Ninth Symphony.*
8. Military music: Civil war songs, songs from the two world wars, Sousa's military marches, songs from Vietnam
9. Popular music with a social studies theme: "We Didn't Start the Fire," "7 o'clock News/Silent Night," "Talking about a Revolution," "The Sinking of the Bismarck"

National Anthems

God Bless Africa
South Africa's turbulent history is reflected in three national anthems.

There is nothing quite like hearing or singing one's national anthem. In a way, national anthems represent all that is good in nationalism: They reflect on the history of the country, the struggles of the country, the future hopes for the country, the idealism of the country. Sung in unison, national anthems resound with the pride most people feel in belonging to a specific cultural and geographic unity.

National anthems are part of the cultural heritage of a nation. It is always difficult to disregard national heritage, but it is probably more difficult to lose that heritage entirely. For this reason, nations do not generally change their national anthems. For example, both the United States and France might think of changing their national anthems. The military overtones of these two national anthems have been criticized in recent years, and the words no longer reflect the cultural realities of their respective nations today. Yet familiarity with and respect for these anthems overrides the desire to change them.

South Africa provides a unique example of a country whose turbulent history is reflected in three national anthems in a period of less than 100 years. From "God Save the Queen" to "Die Stem" to "Nikosi Sikelel'i-Afrika."

On May 31, 1910, the two Boer Republics and the two British colonies in Southern Africa became the Union of South Africa. The Union of South Africa joined other dominions such as Canada, Australia, New Zealand, Nigeria, and India as a member of the British Commonwealth of Nations. The king of England became South Africa's official head of State, the Union Jack became the official flag, English became the official language, British sterling became the official monetary unit, and "God Save the King" became the national anthem.

On May 31, 1961, the Union of South Africa became the Republic of South Africa, and the new republic formally withdrew from the British Commonwealth of Nations. An electorate of white South Africans elected a president who replaced the Queen of England as the official head of state. The electorate also elected a prime minister, who was the leader of the majority party in parliament. A new flag, consisting of horizontal stripes of orange, white, and blue with small replicas of the Union Jack, the Boer flag of the Orange Free State, and the Transvaal Vierkleur banner in the center, became the official flag. English and Afrikaans became the two official languages. Rands and cents became the new monetary unit, and "Die Stem" or "The Call of South Africa" became the official national anthem.

On April 27, 1993, a new nation was born in South Africa, with the creation of a bill of rights; a new constitution; a new, nonracial, democratic government; new national languages; a new national flag; and a new national anthem. Nelson Mandela became the first black president. Eleven languages, including English and Afrikaans, are now official languages. Rands and cents have remained the official currency. *"Nkosi Sikelel'i-Afrika"* has become the official national anthem.

Echoes of History through the Words of the Three South African National Anthems

"God Save the King (Queen)"

> God save our gracious King
> Long live our noble King,
> God save the King.
> Send him victorious,
> happy and glorious,
> Long to reign over us;
> God save the King.

The British Commonwealth reached its peak with the addition of the Union of South Africa in 1910. From Canada to Australia, the sun never set on the British Empire. Prime ministers from the various dominions met regularly in London to discuss matters of common interest. The King of England made regular visits to all parts of the sprawling empire, and wherever he traveled he was met with resounding renditions of "God Save the King." Yet the underlying desire of nations to be independent of a mother country soon began to rear its head. India gained its independence from Britain in 1948, and many African countries gained their independence in the early 1960s. South Africa gained its independence in May 1961.

"Die Stem" "The Call of South Africa" (English Translation of "Die Stem")

Uit die blou van onse hemel,
uit die diepte van ons see,
Oor ons ewige gebergtes
waar die kranse antwoord gee,
Deur ons veer-verlate vlaaktes
met die kreun van ossewa—
Ruis die stem van ons geliefde,
van ons land Suid Afrika.
Ons sal antwoord op jou roepstem,
ons sal offer wat jy vra;
Ons sal lewe, ons sal sterwe—
ons vir jou Suid Afrika.

Ringing out from our blue heavens
from the deep seas breaking round;
Over everlasting mountains
where the echoing crags resound;
From our plains where creaking wagons
cut their trails into the earth—
Calls the spirit of our country,
of the land that gave us birth.
At thy call we shall not falter,
firm and steadfast we shall stand.
At thy will to live or perish,
O South Africa, dear land.

An Afrikaner dream was fulfilled on the May 31, 1961, when the Union of South Africa became the Republic of South Africa. The Afrikaner nation had won the general election of 1948 and had promised to implement apartheid and declare South Africa a republic. Although apartheid laws were implemented immediately, a number of constitutional steps had to be taken in order to become a republic. In 1957, for example, British symbols such as the British flag and national anthem were dropped. "Die Stem," written by C. J. Langenhoven, became the official South African national anthem. This was the first national anthem written in the Afrikaans language. "Die Stem" was translated into English, but the words reflect the ideology of the Afrikaner nation, and the song is usually sung in Afrikaans.

As recently as December 22, 1993, a group of pro-apartheid Afrikaners stood up in parliament as delegates debated the new constitution and sang South Africa's soon-to-be-replaced national anthem. The delegates, however, effectively voted the minority-ruled parliament out of existence—and with it "Die Stem."

"God Bless Africa"	*"Nkosi Sikelel'i-Afrika"*
Let her fame resound	Maluphakanyisw' udumo lwayo
Hear our prayers	Yizwa imithandazo yethu
God Bless	Nkosi sikelel
Us, your children	Woza moya
Come spirit come	(Woza moya woza)
Come spirit	Woza moya
Come spirit come	(Woza moya woza)
Come holy spirit	Woza moya oYingcwele
God bless	Nkosi sikelela
us, your children."	Thina lusapho lwayo

Neither "God Save the King (Queen) " nor "Die Stem" was inclusive of the majority of the South African population. From 1910 to 1948, the British government did very little to improve the lot of the nonwhite people of South Africa. The implementation of apartheid by the Afrikaner government ensured that the nonwhite people would be kept in a position of subjugation.

As far back as 1912, the African National Congress (ANC) began to demand liberty and equality for all the peoples of South Africa. In the 1950s, 1960s and 1970s the ANC began to resort to violence in order to bring the restrictive policies of the National party to an end, and "Nkosi Sikelel'i-Afrika" became the unofficial anthem of the majority of South Africans. This unofficial anthem was sung, in particular, at the funerals of resistance fighters.

One needs to hear African people sing "Nkosi Sikelel'i-Afrika" to begin to understand the tragedy that was apartheid and yet at the same time to recognize the hope for the future. For there is hope. In January 1991 Nelson Mandela, the imprisoned leader of the ANC, was released by the Afrikaner government. Together, President Wilhelm De Klerk, Nelson Mandela, and a myriad of other South Africans negotiated a new constitution for a nonracial and democratic government in a new South Africa.

In December 1993 Nelson Mandela said: "We start 1994 with vigor, for it is our year of freedom. The challenge before us all is to build the nonracial, democratic South Africa of our dreams." "Nkosi Sikelel'i-Afrika" epitomizes that dream— "God Bless Africa."

ACTIVITY   Research the historical background of the national anthem of whatever country is being studied at the moment.

Indigenous Music—Native American

A variety of Native American teachings, prayers, and folktales can be read to Native American music. For example, the following prayer, read to John Williams's "Buffalo Chase" from the film *Dances with Wolves* can create a wonderful atmosphere in class.

O Great Spirit—Traditional Native American Prayer

> O Great Spirit
> Whose voice I hear in the wind,
> and whose breath gives life to all the world, hear me! I am small and weak, I need
>   your strength and wisdom.
> Let me walk in beauty, and make my eyes
> ever behold the red and purple sunset.
> Make my hands respect the things
> you have made and my ears sharp to hear your voice.
> Make me wise so that I may understand the things
> you have taught my people
> Let me learn the lessons you have hidden in every
> leaf and rock.
> I seek strength, not to be greater than my brother,
> but to fight my greatest enemy—myself.
> Make me always ready to come to you with clean
> hands and straight eyes.
> So when life fades, as the fading sunset.
> my spirit may come to you without shame.

ACTIVITY   Encourage students to find their own Native American poetry and music and to read or play their selection for the class.

Patriotic Music

American patriotic music is easily obtainable on tape or CD. An example is *Celebrate Freedom* by Gary Prim (Combs Music, 1990).

America

> My country, 'tis of thee,
> Sweet land of liberty,
> Of thee I sing:
> Land where my fathers died,
> Land of the Pilgrims' pride
> From every mountainside
> Let freedom ring.

ACTIVITY   Find a copy of Martin Luther King's "I Have a Dream" speech. Locate parts of this poem that are repeated in his speech.

Classical Music

Obtain a video copy of "Ode to Joy and Freedom—The Fall of the Berlin Wall" (1990), written and directed by Beata Schubert, edited by Frank Glinski, narrated by Jerry Gerber (Rian TV, Berlin).

ACTIVITIES
1. Who conducted Beethoven's *Ninth Symphony* in Berlin in December 1989?
2. What is the significance or effectiveness of the producers using "And the wall came tumbling down" as well as Beethoven's Ninth?
3. What is the possibility that a reunited Germany might once again dominate Europe?
4. What were your emotions as you watched this dedication?

Military Music

In war, music and songs serve as a strategy for survival, as a means of bonding for a unit, as entertainment, and as a way of expressing emotion. All the traditional themes of war can be found in military songs: praise of the great leader, celebration of heroic deeds, laments for the death of comrades, epic drinking bouts, and encounters with young women. Songs provide a means of expressing protest, fear, frustration, grief, and longing for home. For these reasons, music and songs are an integral part of the history of any war. The original soundtrack recording of the PBS series *The Civil War*, coordinated by Jesse Carr, is an outstanding secondary school history music resource. *Pack Up Your Troubles—Songs of Two World Wars*, an RCA recording by Carl Tapscott male chorus is essential for teaching World War I and World War II. *Songs by Americans in the Vietnam War* is a collection of songs by the Vietnam Veterans Oral History and Folklore Project. Contact bitnet:fishlm @snybufva by e-mail for further information. Words of songs and information on artists are available on the Internet; one address is on the World Wide Web at http://www.yahoo./com/music.

*Goodnight Saigon—Billy Joel**

> We met as soul mates on Parris Island
> We left as inmates from an asylum
> and we were sharp, as sharp as knives
> And we were so gung ho to lay down our lives
> We came in spastic, like tameless horses
> We left in plastic, as numbered corpses
> And we learned fast to travel light

* Copyright 1981 JoelSongs. All Rights Reserved. Used By Permission. Available on *Greatest Hits*, Volume II, Columbia 1985.

Our arms were heavy but our bellies were tight
We had no home front, we had no soft soap
They sent us playboy, they gave us Bob Hope
We dug in deep and shot on sight
and prayed to Jesus Christ with all of our might
We had not cameras to shoot the landscape
We passed the hash pipe and played our Doors tapes
And it was dark, so dark at night
And we held on to each other like brother to brother
We promised our mothers we'd write
And we would all go down together
Yes we would all go down together
Remember Charlie, remember Baker
They left their childhood on every acre
And who was wrong? And who was right?
It didn't matter in the thick of the fight
We held the day in the palm of our hand
They ruled the night and the night
Seemed to last as long as six weeks
On Parris Island
We held the coastline, they held the highlands
And they were sharp, as sharp as knives
They heard the hum of our motors
They counted the rotors
And waited for us to arrive
And we would all go down together
We said we'd all go down together
Yes we would all go down together

ACTIVITY   React in writing or in drawing to the words and music of "Goodnight Saigon."

Popular Music

The Sinking of the Bismarck—Johnny Horton
This song, available on *American Originals* (Columbia, 1989), deals with the war at sea during World War II and the particular incidence of the sinking of the German battleship "The Bismarck." After playing the song, these activities can follow.

ACTIVITIES
1. World War II started in 1939. What aspect of the war started in May 1941?
2. What happened to the "Hood?"
3. What was the firing power in distance of the Bismarck?
4. How many days did it take the British navy to find the Bismarck?
5. Comment on the lines "We got to sink the Bismarck 'cause the world depends on us."
6. Mention two outstanding features of the Bismarck.

7. What did Churchill do to help sink the Bismarck?
8. Who was Bismarck?
9. Who was the admiral of the British fleet in 1941?
10. Where was the Bismarck sunk?

Popular Music

*Seven O'Clock News/Silent Night—Simon and Garfunkel (1966)**

This is the early edition of the news.

The recent fight in the house of Representatives was over the open housing section of the Civil Rights Bill.

Brought traditional enemies together but it left the defenders of the measure without the votes of their strongest supporters.

President Johnson originally proposed an outright ban covering discrimination by every-one for every type of housing but it had no chance from the start and everyone in Congress knew it.

A compromise was painfully worked out in the House Judiciary Committee.

In Los Angeles today comedian Lenny Bruce died of what was believed to be an overdose of narcotics.

Bruce was 42 years old.

Dr. Martin Luther King says he does not intend to cancel plans for an open housing march Sunday into the Chicago suburb of Cicero.

Cook County Sheriff Richard Ogleby asked King to call off the march and the police in Cicero said they would ask the National Guard be called to if it is held

King now in Atlanta, Georgia plans to return Chicago Tuesday.

In Chicago Richard Speck, accused murderer of nine student nurses, was brought before a grand jury today for indictment.

The nurses were found stabbed and strangled in their Chicago apartment.

In Washington the atmosphere was tense today as a special subcommittee of the House Committee on Un-American activities continued its probe into anti-Vietnam war protests.

Demonstrators were forcibly evicted from the hearings when they began chanting anti-war slogans.

Former Vice-President Richard Nixon says that unless there is a substantial increase in the present war effort in Vietnam, the U.S. should look forward to five more years of war.

In a speech before the Convention of the Veterans of Foreign Wars in New York, Nixon also said opposition to the war in this country is the greatest single weapon working against the U.S.

That's the 7 o'clock edition of the news.

ACTIVITIES

1. Brainstorm the major current events of the past two months paying special attention to:
   a. A recent debate in Congress and the outcome
   b. Death of a famous musician, artist, filmstar, sports star

---

    c. Major social issue facing the nation

    d. Murder/suicide/bombing that shocked the nation

    e. U.S. involvement in the international arena

    f. President Clinton's foreign policy statement

2. What background music would you play for your 7 o'clock edition of the news? Give a reason or reasons for your choice.

3. Select one or more readers commentators for your group's edition of the 7 o'clock news. Prepare to read the news to the class.

We Didn't Start the Fire—Billy Joel*

'49 Harry Truman, Doris Day, Red China, Johnnie Ray, South Pacific, Walter Winchell, Joe DiMaggio

'50 Joe McCarthy, Richard Nixon, Studebaker, Television, North Korea, South Korea, Marilyn Monroe

'51 Rosenbergs, H-Bomb, Sugar Ray, Panmunjom, Brando, The King and I and The Catcher in the Rye

'52 Eisenhower, Vaccine, England's Got a New Queen, Marciano, Liberace, Santayana, Goodbye

We Didn't Start the Fire

It Was Always Burning

Since the World's Been Turning

We Didn't Start the Fire

No We Didn't Light It

But We Tried to Fight It

'53 Joseph Stalin Malenkov, Nasser and Prokofiev, Rockefeller, Campanella, Communist Bloc

'54 Roy Cohn, Juan Peron, Toscanini, Dacron Dien, Bien Phu Falls, Rock Around the Clock

'55 Einstein, James Dean, Brooklyn's Got a Winning Team, Davy Crockett, Peter Pan, Elvis Presley, Disneyland

'56 Bardot, Budapest, Alabama, Khrushchev, Princess Grace, Peyton Place, Trouble in the Suez

We Didn't Start the Fire

It Was Always Burning

Since the World's Been Turning

We Didn't Start the Fire

No We Didn't Light It

But We Tried to Fight It

'57 Little Rock, Pasternak, Mickey Mantle, Kerouac, Sputnik, Chou En-Lai, Bridge on the River Kwai

'58 Lebanon, Charles DeGaulle, California Baseball, Starkweather, Homicide, Children of Thalidomide

'59 Buddy Holly, Ben Hur, Space Monkey, Mafia, Hula Hoops, Castro, Edsel Is a No-Go

'60 U-2, Syngman Rhee, Payola and Kennedy, Chubby Checker, Psycho, Belgians in the Congo

We Didn't Start the Fire

It Was Always Burning
Since the World's Been Turning
We Didn't Start the Fire
No We Didn't Light It
But We Tried to Fight It
'61 Hemingway, Eichmann, Stranger in a Strange Land, Dylan, Berlin, Bay of Pigs
    Invasion
'62 Lawrence of Arabia, British Beatlemania, Ole Miss, John Glenn, Liston Beats
    Patterson
'63 Pope Paul, Malcolm X, British Politician Sex, J.F.K. Blown Away, What Else Do
    I Have to Say
We Didn't Start the Fire
It Was Always Burning
Since the World's Been Turning
We Didn't Start the Fire
No We Didn't Light It
But We Tried to Fight It
'64 to '89 Birth Control, Ho Chi Minh, Richard Nixon Back Again, Moonshot,
    Woodstock, Watergate, Punk Rock,
Begin, Reagan, Palestine, Terror on the Airline, Ayatollah's in Iran, Russians in
    Afghanistan,
Wheel of Fortune, Sally Ride, Heavy Metal, Suicide,
Foreign Debts, Homeless Wets, AIDS, Crack, Bernie Goetz,
Hypodermics on the Shores, China's Under Martial Law, Rock and Roller Cola Wars,
I Can't Take It Anymore
We Didn't Start the Fire
It Was Always Burning
Since the World's Been Turning on Us
We Didn't Start the Fire
But When We Are Gone
Will It Still Burn On, and On, and On, and On

ACTIVITIES

1. Students can categorize the terms, events, and places mentioned in the song.
2. In groups, students can write a 1989–1996 verse for "We Didn't Start the Fire" and then share these verses with the class.
3. Students can choose one or more events to research in greater detail.

CARTOONS

The effectiveness of using cartoons as a teaching medium has been questioned in recent years. It is now necessary to review the value and the place of political cartoons in the teaching of social studies at the middle and high school level. A quote from *Cartooning Washington: 100 Years of Cartoon Art* (1990), stresses the importance of the cartoon as a primary source of evidence.

A cartoonist is a writer and artist, philosopher and punster, cynic and community conscience. He seldom tells a joke, and often tells the truth, which is funnier. In addition, the cartoonist is more that a social critic who tries to amuse, infuriate, or educate. He is also, unconsciously, a reporter and historian. Cartoons of the past leave records of their times that reveal how people lived, what they thought, how they dressed and acted, what their amusements and prejudices were, and what the issues of the day were. (p. 3)

Before students can be expected to analyze cartoons, they need to have some background on the art of cartooning. A display of a variety of cartoons can act as an introduction to analyzing cartoons. These cartoons should be carefully selected, and their message should be clear. "A good political cartoon does not treat a trite subject as trivial, has a political message that does not obviously ring false, and is not presented with trite imagery or artistry" (Press, 1981).

It must be pointed out to students that political cartoons are prejudiced; they are selective; they are controversial; they are not fair; they are ambiguous; and they do not have to justify themselves. On the other hand, they can and do speak for the silent majority. Jones (1975) points out that "political cartoons are infused with a healthy disrespect for pomposity and double-talk, indeed they thrive on them. They have an immediate impact and often a shrewd political insight."

It is imperative that students have historical background information before they can successfully analyze a political cartoon. They also need to have developed their interpretive skills. Generally, the major goal of political drawings is to acquaint the students with the opportunity to combine factual knowledge leading to the acquisition of such interpretive skills as analyzing captions, summarizing diverse view points, identifying humor and symbols, and recognizing caricatures in political cartoons.

Here are some suggestions for analyzing cartoons:

1. Teachers should select political cartoons according to the students' knowledge level.
2. Every cartoon must be placed in a historical and a geographical context—time and place.
3. All personalities represented on a cartoon must be identified.
4. Students must be taught how to interpret *symbols,* the visual clues sent out from the cartoon, as well as how to interpret *captions,* the verbal clues sent out from the cartoon.
5. Students need to pay attention to size and placement of people, objects, symbols, and writing on the cartoon.
6. Teachers should get the class to brainstorm ideas to evoke different responses. Divergent answers must be accepted. Interpretation must be open-ended.
7. Cartoon analysis can be more effective if there are lead questions asked by the teacher.
8. Cartoon analysis should end with an explanation of the gist of the cartoon.

Teachers should not expect too much from their students at first. It takes practice, over time, with a variety of cartoons, for students to recognize and then interpret symbols, caricatures, captions, humor, bias, stereotypes, historical references, and issues contained in political cartoons.

ACTIVITIES

1. Let students keep a file in which they can place:
   a. A collection of cartoon symbols
   b. A variety of cartoons drawn from a variety of resources

c. The names of well-known cartoonists
2. Let students write their own captions for cartoons. After they have created their own caption, show them the original caption.
3. Given the criteria for drawing cartoons, students can draw their own cartoon for a specific historic event.
4. Students can be provided with a page of clip art and encouraged to design their own cartoon strip with appropriate words and/or caption.
5. Instead of a written test/exam/homework question, students can be given a cartoon to analyze on their own.

Examples of Cartoons with Suggested Activities

United Nations Club

Used by permission of Cheryl Lepper.

ACTIVITIES

1. Identify the four major players as well as the country they represent.
2. Which of the Big Five is missing? Suggest a reason that this person or country is missing from the cartoon.
3. Who could the referee represent?
4. What problems might the Security Council have in the future if each country plays its own game?

The Fall of Communism

Used by permission of Cheryl Lepper.

ACTIVITIES
1. What is the domino theory?
2. To which country was the domino theory first applied?
3. To what extent has the domino theory been applied in the former Soviet Union?

Starvation in Africa

Used by permission of Cheryl Lepper.

ACTIVITIES

1. Name any four African countries in which starvation is a serious problem.
2. Which African country received military, financial, and medical aid from the United States because of the extreme poverty in that nation?
3. What are some physical signs of extreme malnutrition?
4. Provide a caption for the cartoon.

Environmental Destruction

C Lepper

Used by permission of Cheryl Lepper.

ACTIVITIES

1. What do you think of the soccer image the cartoonist uses in this cartoon?
2. Draw your own environmental destruction cartoon and provide your own caption.

PHYSICAL RESOURCES

History is too vast a subject to be confined to the classroom and too far ranging to be restricted by a timetable. History and geography contain limitless opportunities for moving out into the local community, the state, the nation, and the wider world. Field trips can vary from an excursion onto the school premises, to a morning out in the local community, to a full-day trip to places of interest, to an extended field trip that covers many days and long distances. While extended field trips are highly recommended, it is obvious that there are many stumbling blocks in organizing such educational outings. It is therefore suggested that teachers begin with a local field trip, which could be entitled "Get to Know Your School."

History is the story of people and events, and it is the record of times past. The history of a school can provide information on these two main meanings of history. Historical evidence abounds in a school building, and students can use these historical sources to learn about the people and the past events that make their school what it is today.

What follows is an outline of a field trip that can be implemented successfully at any age or grade level and at any school. This activity would be well suited to an introduction to "What is history?" and lessons following on "Where do we find historical sources?," "How do we detect bias?," and "How is history written?" Students can be involved with the historical process with hands-on experience. The lessons learned from this activity can be applied throughout the rest of the history course whenever similar questions arise.

Get to Know Your School

The following activities can incorporate cooperative learning, with each group responsible for one part of the whole. History can then be pieced together from a variety of sources in the regular classroom.

A questionnaire worksheet can be developed and given to a group of students who will have a set time to go around the school and find the answers. Examples of *who, why, where,* and *when* questions can focus on:

1. Places of interest, such as statues, plaques, foundation stones
2. Historic photographs and memorabilia on display in the school
3. Trees and/or plants planted to commemorate special occasions
4. Special gifts donated to the school
5. Sports trophies
6. School buildings—oldest, newest, architectural design, cost, and so on

Once the information has been collected, students can extend their research by validating most of the information listed through to alternative sources such as the library and/or oral sources. Critical thinking must be emphasized: deciding what information is important, looking at information from different points of view, being curious enough to look further into an event or topic, being skeptical enough to look for more than one account of an event. A written, chronological history of the school should be the end product for this group.

A second group of students can be given a Polaroid camera to take a series of photographs pertaining to the foregoing written sources or can be encouraged to find different sources to photograph. The students can be encouraged to photograph existing photographs that have been published in school yearbooks, or local newspapers, and/or placed in photographic displays in the school. Individual students in this group might wish to draw their own sketches of historical artifacts in the school. The end product for this group is to portray a pictorial, chronological history of the school.

A third group of students can conduct interviews with the following people regarding "memories" of the school. (Specific questions might be asked at each interview.)

1. The oldest faculty member
2. A member of the janitorial staff
3. The student president
4. A student in another grade or class
5. A sports captain

Interviews can be conducted with the use of a tape recorder. Each interview then will have to be transcribed. Students in this group must be critically aware of the biases and prejudices inherent in personal memories.

The end product for this group could take various forms: (1) integrating interview extracts with either the written or the pictorial history, (2) providing a "memory chapter" for the written and pictorial history of the school, or (3) using the information gathered from the interviews to validate the written or pictorial information.

A fourth group could brainstorm what their school might be like in the future. Their starting point could be to discuss what has remained the same about the school from the past to the present (this will ensure that they confer with the groups conducting the written, pictorial, and oral histories). The group can then move on to debating questions such as: What has changed? If your group could be the head of the school 30 years from now, what would you keep and what would you change based on your current school? How would you go about making the change? The end product for this group could take the form of a written and pictorial OLD versus NEW school.

Once the group projects have been collated, one final class activity could include making a historical/chronological list of important events in the school's history. Students then can use a variety of resource books to find important events, both nationally and internationally, that occurred in the same years. For example:

Year	School History	National History	World History
1950			
1965			
1972			
1980			
1994			

Pictorial sources can be added for each event or for specific events if the class so chooses.

Conclusion

"Get to Know Your School" is an ideal way to introduce students to their new school at the elementary, middle or high school levels. It is also an ideal way to introduce students to the historical method of finding information from a variety of resources. And it is an ideal way to relate school history and events to the broader national and international arena.

ARTIFACTS, ARTIFACTS, ARTIFACTS

Every family's old trunk in the attic has a collection of historical artifacts! The local community is a rich resource when it comes to artifacts. Local residents might have family heirlooms, historic artifacts of their own, military memorabilia, old clothing, travel souvenirs, and wonderful family stories. Residents of different cultures can be encouraged to visit the classroom and share both cultural and physical resources. Local travel agents and other businesses can be contacted as community resources. Teachers who use physical resources in their classrooms can involve their students in the historic process of analyzing artifacts. What follows is a guide for analyzing artifacts:

1. What might this artifact be?
   a. Is there a name on it?
   b. Are there any instructions for its use?
   c. Does it have an indoor or outdoor use?
   d. Is it for heavy or light duty?
   e. Are there any moving parts?
   f. what happens when they are moved?
2. How old is the artifact?
   a. Is there a date on it?
   b. Can you tell the age by looking at the artifact?
   c. Did it do something that was useful only during a certain historic period?
3. What is the artifact made of?
   a. Are the component parts of the artifact rare or unusual, or are they made from commonplace materials?
   b. Do the materials used to make this artifact present any special problems to the manufacturer?
4. Was the artifact manufactured with a machine or was it handmade?
   a. Would special skills have been required to make it?
   b. Did the person who made it have a good plan or just a rough idea?
   c. Is the artifact aesthetically pleasing in overall design and in its details?
5. Are there any distinguishing marks on the artifact?
   a. Are there any labels?
   b. Is there a signature?
   c. Is there a patent number?
   d. Are there any marks made through use?
   e. Are there any marks made on purpose (for example, gradations for measuring)?
6. Where was the artifact made?
   a. Is the place of manufacture identified on the artifact?
   b. Is there a trademark on the artifact?
   c. Can you contact the manufacturer?
   d. Is this type of artifact produced mainly in one locality or region?
7. Does the artifact tell us anything about the people who might have used it?
   a. What might their socioeconomic status have been?
   b. What might the artifact reveal about their culture or occupation?
   c. Would a man or woman, or an adult or child, use this object?
8. What is the value of this artifact?
   a. Consider the material it is made from and the quality of the construction.
   b. Was it made to last for an extended period of time, or was it disposable?
   c. Was it a luxury item or a necessity?
   d. Was it ornamental or functional?

e. Is this artifact more valuable because it is associated with famous people, places, or events?

f. How much would you be willing to pay for this item today, in
its present condition?

9. Is there an object comparable to this artifact available today?

a. If this artifact is no longer in use, what has replaced it?

b. Why might the artifact have fallen out of use?

c. How is today's item similar?

d. How is it different?

Combining Resources

Any primary or secondary resource can be used as a teaching aid by itself. The examples provided so far use a single resource, with suggested activities for each.
"Variety is the spice of teaching," and therefore the ideal scenario in the classroom
is to combine a variety of resources when teaching a specific lesson. For example,
an avenue for exploring assassinations in general, or a particular assassination in
more depth, can be provided by combining a variety of resources. The resources
can include charts, speeches, extracts, music, and eyewitness reports.

Assassinations

The word *assassination* is derived from an Arabic word, *hashish*, which literally
translated means "grass." Hashish, in fact, is a powerful drug. Hashish was provided to members of a secret order of Moslem extremists who would terrorize and
kill Christian crusaders. Today, the word *assassination* is defined as "a murderer, especially one who carries out a plot to kill a public official or other prominent person."

Many prominent men and women throughout history have been assassinated,
and many more have survived an assassination attempt. The murder of Julius
Caesar may well be the first recorded assassination case. On the morning of the
15th of March, the Ides of March, 44 B.C., he was assassinated by Brutus on the
steps of the Senate building in Rome. His immortal dying words were: "Et tu
Brute" ("And you, too, Brutus"). A recent assassination was that of Yitzhak Rabin,
prime minister of Israel. While the long-lasting effects of the assassination of Julius
Caesar are by now well recorded, the long-term effects of the death of Rabin are
still to be felt.

ACTIVITIES

1. Provide the following list of important assassinations. Let students
draw some generalizations from the list by looking for major similarities and differences in the assassinations.

1865—April 14, Abraham Lincoln, shot by John Wilkes Booth in
Washington, DC.

1914—June 28, Archduke Francis Ferdinand of Austria, shot by
Gavrilo Princip in Sarajevo.

1934—July 25, Austrian Chancellor E. Dolfuss shot by Nazis in Vienna.

1948—January 30, Mohandas K. Gandhi, shot by Nathuran
Vinayak Godse in New Delhi.

> 1963—November 2, Ngo Dinh Diem of the Republic of Vietnam, shot in a military coup.
>
> 1963—November 22, John F. Kennedy, shot by Lee Harvey Oswald in Dallas.
>
> 1968—April 4, Martin Luther King, shot by James Earl Ray in Memphis.
>
> 1975—February 11, King Faisal of Saudi Arabia, shot by Prince Abdel Aziz in the royal palace in Riyadh.
>
> 1979—August 27, Lord Mountbatten, killed by a bomb detonated by the Irish Republican Army off the coast of Ireland.
>
> 1984—October 31, Indira Gandhi, shot by two of her bodyguards in New Delhi.
>
> 1989—November 22, President Rene Moawad, killed by a bomb in Beirut.

2. Read the following two extracts to the students and allow for discussion. Questions of "who said," "where said," "why said," and "what said" can be asked.

   a. "We've got some difficult days ahead, but it really does not matter with me now because I have been to the mountain top. I don't mind. Like anybody, I would like to live a long life. But I am not concerned about that now. I just want to do God's will and He's allowed me to go up to the mountain and I've looked over and I've seen the Promised Land. I may not go there with you but I want you to know tonight that we as a people will get to the Promised Land. So I'm happy tonight . . . I'm not worried about anything. I don't fear any man. Mine eyes have seen the glory of the coming of the Lord."

   b. People who claim their dreams come true are seldom taken seriously. And even President Abraham Lincoln, when he experienced precognition in 1865, was not immediately believed by his associates.[*]

   Lincoln recounted his dream to a close friend, Ward Hill Lamon, who wrote down the President's words that same evening.

   "About ten days ago, I retired very late . . . I soon began to dream. There seemed to be a deathlike stillness about me. Then I heard subdued sobs, as if a number of people were weeping. I thought I left my bed and wondered downstairs.

   There, the silence was broken by the same pitiful sobbing, but the mourners were invisible. I went from room to room. No living person was in sight but the sounds of distress met me as I passed along . . . I was puzzled and alarmed . . . determined to find the cause of a state of affairs so mysterious and so shocking.

   I kept on until I arrived at the East Room, there I was met by a sickening surprise. Before me was a coffin, on which rested a corpse in funeral vestments. Around it were stationed soldiers who were acting as guards and there was a throng of people, some gazing mournfully upon the corpse, whose face was covered, others weeping pitifully.

   "Who is dead in this White House?" I demanded of one of the soldiers. "The President," was his answer. "He was killed by an assassin."

---

*Reader's Digest Book of Strange Stories, Amazing Facts, 1977, pp. 161–163.

Five days after that account, on April 15, Lincoln was shot dead by John Wilkes Booth at Ford's Theater in Washington. His body was taken to lie in state in the East Room of the White House.

3. Find a recording of "Abraham, Martin, and John." Play the song and get students to identify the people mentioned in the song and to write down their reactions to the words of the song.
4. Read the following extract to the class. In two columns, headed "Lincoln" and "Kennedy," let the students list the similarities in the assassinations of these two presidents. After listing the similarities, students can list some obvious differences that are not mentioned in this extract.

Deaths of the Presidents: How Fate Linked the Assassinations of Lincoln and Kennedy*

The assassinations of Presidents Abraham Lincoln and John Fitzgerald Kennedy were linked by an amazing series of coincidences.

Abraham Lincoln was first elected to Congress in 1846. John Kennedy followed exactly 100 years later. Lincoln was elected as the 16th President of the United States on November 6, 1860. After their deaths they were both succeeded by Southerners named Johnson. Andrew Johnson was born in 1808, Lyndon Johnson in 1908.

John Wilkes Booth, the man who killed Lincoln, was born in 1839, while Lee Harvey Oswald, Kennedy's killer, was born in 1939. Both men were Southerners, and both were themselves shot before they could come to trial.

Booth committed his crime in a theater and then ran to a warehouse. Oswald pulled the trigger on Kennedy from the window of a warehouse—and ran to a theater.

On the day he was assassinated Lincoln told a guard, William H. Crook: "I believe there are men who want to take my life . . . And I have no doubt they will do it . . . If it is to be done, it is impossible to prevent it."

And Kennedy unsuspectingly told his wife, Jackie, and his personal adviser Ken O'Donnell: "If anyone really wanted to shoot the President of the United States, it's not a hard job. All that one has to do is to get to a height building some day, with a telescopic rifle, and there is nothing anybody can do."

"Some day" proved to be that day. He was shot 2 1/2 hours later. Lincoln and Kennedy were both historic civil rights campaigners, and both were shot on a Friday, in the back of the head. Their wives were with them.

Lincoln was shot in Ford's Theater. Kennedy was shot in an automobile made by the Ford Motor Company—a Lincoln.

One final, unhappy coincidence is that Lincoln had a secretary named Kennedy, who advised him not to go to the theater in Washington on that fateful day . . . Kennedy had a secretary named Lincoln, who strongly advised him against going to Dallas.

5. Concluding activities
   a. Students can find the major similarities and differences between any two assassinations other than Lincoln and Kennedy.

Reader's Digest Book of Strange Stories, Amazing Facts, 1977, pp. 161–163.

b. Students can find tape recordings or printed copies of speeches made by people who were assassinated. The content of the speeches can be analyzed and possible reasons for their assassinations may be discovered.

c. Students can do further research on any assassination from the list or on an assassination of their own choosing.

WORLD WAR I AND THE SEVEN INTELLIGENCES: RESOURCES AND SUGGESTED ACTIVITIES

Howard Gardner's theory of the seven intelligences has had a marked influence on the teaching and learning process in the 1990s. It is evident that history and geography teachers must broaden their teaching strategies, their student activities, and their assessments to include the seven intelligences.

1. Logical/Mathematical Intelligence

This intelligence deals with inductive and deductive thinking and reasoning, numbers, and the recognition of abstract patterns.

A course on World War I might start with the logical/mathematical intelligence, as a chronology of the war is always a good starting point. What is interesting about the World War I timeline that follows is that most of the intelligences run concurrently through the period 1914–1918. As with all the intelligences, the logical/mathematical intelligence will be woven into the entire course.

World War I Timeline

1914   Archduke Franz Ferdinand is assassinated in Sarajevo, precipitating World War I.

1914   Austrian forces invade Serbia but are repulsed, with heavy losses.

1914   Black composer W. C. Handy writes the "St. Louis Blues."

1914   Charlie Chaplin develops his little tramp character in a series of slapstick films.

1914   France, Russia, and Britain (the Allies) are at war with Germany and Austria-Hungary.

1914   George Bernard Shaw's play *Pygmalion* is performed for the first time.

1914   German forces invade Belgium and France but are halted at the Marne.

1914   Japan joins the Allies and captures the German base of Tsingtao in China.

1914   President Wilson declares U.S. neutrality in World War I.

1914   Russian forces invade East Prussia but are defeated at the Battle of Tannenberg.

1914   The Panama Canal is completed, connecting the Atlantic and Pacific Oceans.

1914   Turkey declares war on the Allies; Britain annexes Turkish Cyprus.

1915   A German submarine torpedoes the British liner *Lusitania;* 124 Americans are killed.

1915   Albert Einstein formulates his General Theory of Relativity.

1915   Anglo-French forces land at Gallipoli in an attempt to force Turkey out of the war.

1915   German Zeppelin airships begin bombing attacks on Britain.

1915   Italy joins the Allies and invades Austrian territory.

1915   The Anzacs (Australian and New Zealand Army Corps) fight at Gallipoli.

1915   The Dada art and literary movement is formed.

1915   The Germans use poison gas for the first time at Ypres on the Western Front.

1915   War poet Rupert Brooke's *1914 and Other Poems* is published in the year he died.

1916   Allied forces withdraw from Gallipoli after strong Turkish opposition.

1916   American poet Carl Sandburg publishes his first book, *Chicago Poems.*

1916   British forces assault the German line at the Somme; tanks are used for the first time.

1916   German assaults at Verdun are repulsed by the French, with great loss of life.

1916   James Joyce publishes *A Portrait of the Artist as a Young Man.*

1916   Jeannette Rankin becomes the first female member of the U.S. House of Representatives.

1916   Lloyd George becomes prime minister of Britain's wartime coalition government.

1916   The British and German fleets clash at the Battle of Jutland.

1916   The Easter Rising in Dublin is suppressed within a week by the British.

1916   The Trans-Siberian railway is completed—the longest continuous rail line in the world.

1917   British forces under Allenby capture Jerusalem and Bagdad from the Turks.

1917   Germany announces the resumption of unrestricted submarine warfare.

1917   Swiss psychiatrist Carl Jung publishes *The Psychology of the Unconscious.*

1917   T. E. Lawrence (Lawrence of Arabia) leads the Arab revolt against the Turks.

1917   The Balfour Declaration endorses a Jewish national homeland in Palestine.

1917   The Germans and the Bolshevik leaders sign an armistice at Brest-Litovsk.

1917   The Germans help Lenin return to Russia from exile in Switzerland.

1917   The Jones Act gives all Puerto Ricans the right to U.S. citizenship.

1917   The Russian Revolution begins; Emperor Nicholas II abdicates.

1917   The United States declares war on Germany.

1917   The earliest jazz recordings are made in New York City.

1917   The first Pulitzer Prizes are awarded for journalism, letters, and music.

1917   The provisional Kerensky government is deposed; Bolsheviks seize power in Russia.

1918 Advances by French, British, and U.S. armies force a general German retreat.

1918 An influenza pandemic begins and kills 21 to 22 million people over the next two years.

1918 Austria, Poland, and Czechoslovakia become republics in the aftermath of World War I.

1918 German air ace Manfred von Richthofen (the Red Baron) is shot down and killed.

1918 Nicholas II, the last emperor of Russia, and his family are executed by the Bolsheviks.

1918 Revolution breaks out in Germany; Emperor William II flees to the Netherlands.

1918 The Germans renew their assault on the western front in the Ludendorff offensive.

1918 The Weimar Republic negotiates an armistice for Germany, ending World War I.

ACTIVITY   As the unit progresses, students can build up a timeline on butcher paper, which can be displayed on the walls of the classroom.

TABLE 3-1   Mobilization Chart

	Mobilized	Total Force Deaths (2)	Military Battle Military Wounded	Civilian Dead (4) ($ million)	Economic and Financial Cost
Allies					
France	8,410,000	1,357,800	4,266,000	40,000	49,877
British Empire	8,904,467	908,371	2,090,212	30,633 (5)	51,975
Russia	12,000,000	1,700,000	4,950,000	2,000,000 (6)	25,600
Italy	5,615,000	462,391	953,886	(7)	18,143
United States	4,355,000	50,585	205,690	(7)	32,320
Belgium	267,000	13,715	44,686	30,000	10,195
Serbia	707,343	45,000 (8)	133,148	650,000	2,400
Montenegro	50,000	3,000	10,000	(7)	2,400
Romania	750,000	335,706	120,000	275,000	2,601
Greece	230,000	5,000	21,000	132,000	556
Portugal	100,000	100,000	13,751	(7)	(7)
Japan	800,000	300	907	(7)	(7)
Total	42,188,810	4,888,891	12,809,280	3,157,633	193,899
Central Powers					
Germany	7,800,000	1,808,546	4,247,143	760,000	58,072
Austria-Hungary	7,800,000	922,500	3,620,000	300,000 (10)	23,706
Turkey	2,850,000	325,000	400,000	2,150,000 (11)	3,445
Bulgaria	1,200,000	75,844 (12)	152,390	275,000	1,015
Total	22,850,000	3,131,889	8,419,533	3,485,000	86,238
Neutral Nations					1,750
Grand Total	65,038,810	8,020,780	21,228,813	6,642,633	281,887

ACTIVITY   Given the mobilization chart, students can deduce similarities, differences, and generalizations from the information.

The ADFGX Cipher

	A	D	F	G	X
A	A	F	L	Q	V
D	B	G	M	R	W
F	C	H	N	S	X
G	D	I	O	T	Y
X	E	K	P	U	Z

FG	XA	FF	GA		FD	XA	AF	XF
S	E	N	D		H	E	L	P

1. ASSIGNATION

FO AX AX GG   AA DD AX FF GG   GF DG XF

DA FG GX GD   AA GG

AD FG FG DX GF DF FG FX   FF AX AA GD

AG GD FG FX AD FG XF   FD FG FF AG AA XG

AA GG   GG AX FF   FX FD

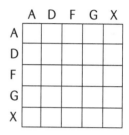

2. THEY'RE ONTO US

FX XX FF FX AX XF

XG AD GD DD FG AX GD

GF AX AX DD DG FF GG FD   GA DG DD FG .

DG FF XG DF GD GF XX FF DD   FG AX   DG FD

GX AX DG FF GG   GA XX DDFX FG AX DX

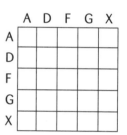

3. FLYBOYS

FX FA XA FF   DD FG

FX XX FF XX DD DG XA DD XX   XX FF XX FD AG

FA GD FF XX DG   XD AG

FX XA DG XA XF GF DA DD XX   DF DD XA FF XG

XD AG   GX FG DG   DG XA XG GD FG

DF GD GG FF XA FA

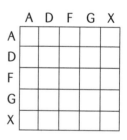

ACTIVITY There is no letter *J* in the following code. Once the code has been broken, each message has a different combination of the *ADFGX* letters. For example, the letter combination "THEY'RE ONTO US" would read

JUPKE
YTOID
XSNHC
WRMGB
VQLFA

The students can work out the letter combinations and then crack the code.

2. Verbal/Linguistic Intelligence

This intelligence deals with words and language, written and spoken.

Fiction and Nonfiction
Combining the literature of World War I with the historical facts will enliven the teaching of this period. Ideally, the English class would read Ernest Hemingway's *Farewell to Arms* and Erich Maria Remarque's *All Quiet on the Western Front* while the history class covered World War I. If that is not possible, then extracts from both of these books should be read to the class at opportune moments.

Variety of Opinion
Excerpts from speeches, letters, memoirs, and scholarly publications can be used for analysis and evaluation.

Poetry
Poetry written from different perspectives, by men and women, and by people from different cultures would be included in the teaching of World War I. Poetry written during World War I can be used to create an authentic period atmosphere, as primary sources to be analyzed, and as a catalyst for students to write their own war poetry.

3. Visual/Spatial Intelligence

This intelligence deals with the sense of sight and being able to visualize and create mental images/pictures.

Maps
Maps are basic tools of the historian. Maps provide a visual representation of the place where events took place. Every effort should be made to ensure that students have a mental picture of the historical and geographical setting of an event. While it is important to stress a sense of time in the teaching of World War I, it is equally important to try to cultivate a sense of place, a stage on which history is played out. A variety of maps should be used continually throughout the teaching of World War I.

Etchings/Paintings/Drawings
Visual aids of this nature include women, people of color, and artists' interpretations of war.

ACTIVITY   Students can be encouraged to draw their own interpretations of certain events that took place during World War I.

Cartoons

In this ink drawing, The Harvest Is Ripe, the Dutch artist Racmakers shows the Grim Reaper at work in Flanders, August 1914.

ACTIVITIES

1. Students can interpret this cartoon according to the guidelines suggested in the section on cartoons.
2. Students can draw their own cartoon of events, people, or places from World War I.

4. Bodily/Kinesthetic Intelligence

This intelligence is related to physical movement.

ACTIVITIES

1. Mime a poem.
2. Build a model.
3. Role-play a scene from *All Quiet on the Western Front* or *A Farewell to Arms.*
4. Conduct a military drill exercise.

5. Musical/Rhythmic Intelligence

This intelligence is based on the recognition of tonal patterns and on a sensitivity to rhythm and beats.

ACTIVITIES

1. Play songs from World War I, such as "Pack Up Your Troubles," "It's a Long Way to Tipperary," and "Over There" to create an authentic period atmosphere.
2. Learn and sing a song from World War I.
3. Students can write their own song.
4. Analyze the words of a World War I song.
5. Discuss the effect of music on war.
6. Combine music with other resources by reading a poem to music, drawing to music, or reenacting a scene to music.

6. Interpersonal Intelligence

This intelligence involves person-to-person relationships and communication.

ACTIVITIES

1. Students can do projects in groups.
2. Students can critique each other's work.
3. Students can debate issues related to World War I.
4. Students can interview people with a special interest in World War I. This activity involves the larger community.

7. Intrapersonal Intelligence

This intelligence involves self-reflection and awareness of spiritual realities.

ACTIVITIES

1. Students can maintain portfolios to evaluate their own learning.
2. Students can keep journals or logs in which they express their feelings about lessons as well as their insights into the content being studied.
3. Students can pursue an independent project of their own choice.
4. Students can reflect on their own learning in a variety of ways.

TECHNOLOGY

The National Task Force on Educational Technology (1986) reported that all schools should plan for a computer-managed learning environment. Unfortunately, computer technology has not been widely used in social studies classrooms. With the advent of the Internet, interactive educational history and geography CDs, encyclopedia CDs, atlas CDs, and *Time* magazine on disk, there is no longer any excuse not to use technology to enliven the teaching of history and geography, and for student research.

The major concern with the new technology available to teachers and students is that there is too much information. Naisbitt (1982), in *Megatrends*, wrote: "We have for the first time an economy based on a key resource (information) that is not only renewable, but self-generating. Running out of it is not a problem, but drowning in it is."

Collecting, selecting, collating, analyzing, and evaluating information accessible from the computer is the major task facing teachers and students as we approach the twenty-first century. The Apple Student Resource Set (Apple Computer Inc., 1994) is a set of powerful tools on a CD that will help students use the technology available to them in a more meaningful way.

Some Neat Web Sites for History and Geography

Yahoo	www.yahoo.com
History/Social Studies web site for K–12 education	http://www.ececpc.com/~dboals.html
Library of Congress	www.loc.gov
The Virtual Tourist II	wings.buffalo.edu/world/vt2
Time-Warner Pathfinder	www.pathfinder.com
The Smithsonian Institution	http://www.si.edu/
Welcome to the White House	http://www.whitehouse.gov/
Cybrary of the Holocaust	http://www.best.com/mddun/cybrary/index.html#history
American Studies web	http://pantheon.cis.yale.edu/~davidp/amstud.html
Multicultural Resources	http://www.rosauer.Gonzaga.edu
Simon Wiesenthal Center	http://www.wiesenthal.com/

To whet your appetite, here is an excerpt from one document, published in 1995 by the Simon Wiesenthal Center, 9760 West Pico Boulevard, Los Angeles, CA 90035.

Excerpts from 36 Questions about the Holocaust

1. When speaking about the Holocaust, what time period are we referring to?
   Answer: The Holocaust refers to the period from January 30, 1933, when Adolf Hitler became chancellor of Germany, to May 8, 1945 (V-E Day), the end of the war in Europe. . . .
5. How many Jews were murdered in each country and what percentage of the prewar Jewish population did they constitute?

Answer: (*Source:* Encyclopedia of the Holocaust)
          Austria 50,000—27.0%
          Italy 7,680—17.3%
          Belgium 28,900—44.0%
          Latvia 71,500—78.1%
          Bohemia/Moravia 78,150—66.1%
          Lithuania 143,000—85.1%
          Bulgaria 0—0.0%
          Luxembourg 1,950—55.7%
          Denmark 60—0.7%
          Netherlands 100,000—71.4%
          Estonia 2,000—44.4%
          Norway 762—44.8%
          Finland 7—0.3%
          Poland 3,000,000—90.0%
          France 77,320—22.1%
          Romania 287,000—47.1%
          Germany 141,500—25.0%
          Slovakia 71,000—79.8%
          Greece 67,000—86.6%
          Soviet Union 1,100,000—36.4%
          Hungary 569,000—69.0%
          Yugoslavia 63,300—81.2%

6. What is a death camp? How many were there? Where were they located?
   Answer: A death (or mass murder) camp is a concentration camp with special apparatus specifically designed for systematic murder. Six such camps existed: Auschwitz-Birkenau, Belzec, Chelmno, Majdanek, Sobibor, Treblinka. All were located in Poland. . . .

9. How did the Germans define who was Jewish?
   Answer: On November 14, 1935, the Nazis issued the following definition of a Jew: "Anyone with three Jewish grandparents; someone with two Jewish grandparents who belonged to the Jewish community on September 15, 1935, or joined thereafter; was married to a Jew or Jewess on September 15, 1935, or married one thereafter; was the offspring of a marriage or extramarital liaison with a Jew on or after September 15, 1935." . . .

18. Did all Germans support Hitler's plan for the persecution of the Jews?
    Answer: Although the entire German population was not in agreement with Hitler's persecution of the Jews, there is no evidence of any large-scale protest regarding their treatment. Some Germans defied the April 1, 1933, boycott and purposely bought in Jewish stores, and some helped Jews to escape or to hide, but their number was very small. Even some of those who opposed Hitler were in agreement with his anti-Jewish policies. Among the clergy, Dompropst Bernard Lichtenberg of Berlin publicly prayed for the Jews daily and was, therefore, sent to a concentration camp by the Nazis. Other priests were deported for their failure to cooperate with the Nazis' anti-Semitic policies, but the majority of the clergy complied with the directives against German Jewry and did not openly protest.

Some Neat CDs

- *Mac Globe,* phone (602) 730-9000. Highlights of Mac Globe include a World Map, Country Maps, Country Reports, Comparison Maps, Comparison Charts, and Flags.
- *Mac Timeline,* phone (800) 342-0236. Highlights of Mac Timeline include preprepared timelines of significant events as well as the ability to create one's own timeline.
- *Grolier Encyclopedia,* available from Sherman Turnpike, Danbury, CT 06816. Key lists such as Word Search, Maps, Videos, Pictures, Animations, Timeline, and Knowledge Tree, simplify the process of accessing information.
- *Time Magazine,* available from P.O. Box 40310, Washington, DC 20016. Highlights of Time Magazine CD include weekly issues from 1989, Decades from the 1920s, an Almanac for the States, the United States, and the world. Video clips are included.
- *Maus: A Survivor's Tale* by Art Spiegelman, available from Voyager, Apple Computer Inc. 1994. This CD, which describes the Holocaust in the form of a comic book, is accompanied by a teacher's guide containing excellent activities.
- *Eyewitness History,* available from Aims Media, 9710 DeSoto Avenue, Chatsworth, CA 91311-9734. This CD has recreated a large number of significant historical events.

Some Neat Simulation Games

The following games are available from Broederbond, (800) 521-6263.
- Where in the World Is Carmen San Diego?
- Where in Europe Is Carmen San Diego?
- Where in the U.S.A. Is Carmen San Diego?
- Where in Time Is Carmen San Diego?

The following games are available from MECC, 6160 Summit Drive North, Minneapolis, MN 55430-4003.
- The Oregon Trail
- The Amazon Trail

CHAPTER FOUR

Geography

As a young man, my fondest dream was to become a geographer. However, while working in the customs office, I thought deeply about the matter and concluded that it was far too difficult a subject. With some reluctance I then turned to physics as a substitution.

—Albert Einstein

While Chapter 2 dealt with the National Geography Standards, this chapter will deal with map skills; the five themes of geography as suggested by the National Geographic Society; global education; and some geographical activities for use in the classroom.

WHAT IS GEOGRAPHY AND WHY MUST WE UNDERSTAND IT?

In the global, technologically advanced society in which we all now live, we must understand geography. We have all seen the alarming statistics:

- Forty-five percent of Baltimore's junior and senior high school students could not locate the United States on a map of the world.
- Thirty-nine percent of Boston's high school graduates could not name the six New England states, and on a map of the world some of the youngsters placed Boston in Tibet.
- Twenty-five percent of high school students in Dallas could not name the country directly south of Texas.
- Forty percent of high school seniors in Kansas City, Missouri, could not name even three of South America's dozen countries.
- Sixty-nine percent of 2,200 students in North Carolina could not name a single African country south of the Sahara.

Geography is the science of space and place on the earth's surface. Its subject matter is the physical and human phenomena that make up the world's environments. Geography asks us to look at the world as a whole, to understand the connections between places, to recognize that the local affects the global and vice versa.

Geography combines the physical and human aspects of our world into one field of study. Geography shows the relationship between people and the environment. It is this bridge that makes geography unique among the traditional academic disciplines.

Geography opens the mind to fresh areas of discovery. At first, we are curious about where places are. Then we add more analytical questions, such as what is there and why? Too often, our history students try to explain Hitler's foreign policy, describe the developments in the new African countries, or discuss the Vietnam War without being able to place these events in their appropriate geographical settings. For this reason, every historical event should be studied in its geographical context. Every effort should be made to ensure that students have a mental picture of the historical and geographical setting of an event. Students should be aware not only of the geographical location of the event but also of the influence of geographical factors on people and their environment.

There is a close kinship between geography and history. The historian describes, analyzes, and explains events over time, whereas the geographer describes, analyzes, and explains anything and everything over space. While it is important to stress a sense of time in the teaching of history, it is equally important to try to cultivate a sense of place, a stage on which history is played out. A study of geography and history offers the perspectives of time and place. Unique among subjects taught at school, history and geography are necessarily interdisciplinary, encompassing all other fields of thought. A study of these two disciplines will endow students with a broad knowledge of other times, other places, and other cultures.

GEOGRAPHICAL AND HISTORICAL MAP SKILLS

Geographical Skills

Critical to effective geographic inquiry are four simple cognitive skills:

1. Observation
2. Speculation
3. Analysis
4. Evaluation

Observation, followed by speculation, supported by analysis, and concluding with evaluation of a given geographic scene is a process that not only makes the world more understandable, but trains the student in making sense of the world around her or him. (*Charting a Course: Social Studies for the Twenty-first Century*, p. 44)

Some of the more important geographical skills that need to be mastered are:

1. Identifying the continents, oceans, seas, deserts, and major mountain ranges and rivers
2. Recognizing map symbols
3. Locating absolute and relative positions
4. Reading, interpreting, and making graphs
5. Drawing inferences from a variety of maps

Map lessons need to be teacher-directed: "Teachers can devise map work that enriches involvement and multisensory experiences in a variety of ways in order to increase its learning effectiveness" (Forsyth, 1988) Putting maps in front of students and asking them to study the map is not enough. Students need to be taught how to observe, speculate, compare, analyze, and evaluate maps. What do you look for? What questions can you ask? What do you need to know in addition to what is visible on the map? What kind of conclusions can you draw?

Historical Skills

Integrating map studies into history lessons can develop valuable historical skills:

1. Comparing and contrasting
2. Relating maps to other source material
3. Recognizing relationships
4. Reconstructing historical events
5. Analyzing cartoon maps
6. Identifying historical trends
7. Summarizing basic issues
8. Using sketch maps to illustrate events and activities
9. Noting similarities and differences and drawing conclusions
10. Developing a historical theme
11. Recognizing the influence of geographical factors
12. Writing an essay by referring to a map
13. Identifying and explaining places/events
14. Understanding cause and effect
15. Connecting the present to the past
16. Learning about an area
17. Studying a crisis topic

Criteria for Using Maps in History Teaching

For maps to play a leading role in giving history a sense of place and background, it is necessary that the maps used satisfy two major criteria:

1. The map should be bold and the main features conspicuous. All-purpose historical maps rarely exist. The alternative is for history teachers to produce their own maps and so build up a stock of specific maps that can be used concurrently with a general map.
2. Historical maps should not be overcrowded, as is often the case, with data irrelevant to the history being studied. "Information is more easily remembered if it is first organized in a meaningful way and distinguished from other, irrelevant information. Most maps often present both relevant and unimportant information." (Forsyth, 1988)

The use of maps must be regarded as an integral part of both effective history teaching and evaluation. Once map skills have been taught, learned, and used in the classroom situation, maps should be used as evaluation tools in tests, assignments, and examinations as well.

Suggested Historical Map Activities

What follows are some examples of maps and questions that can be used in teaching and evaluating twentieth-century world history at the high school level. The maps are drawn from a wide variety of sources and in no way are prescriptive in their usage. Any map can be used in a variety of ways. Teachers need to assess their students' needs, aptitudes, and abilities, as well as the lesson plan, and select the maps accordingly. Learning to use maps in a constructive way will add an exciting dimension to history teaching and evaluation.

ACTIVITY   *Recognizing relationships:* Using the maps on this page and page 102 as a guide, show how there is a relationship between the Peace Treaty of Versailles and the foreign policy of Adolf Hitler regarding the following places: (a) the Saar, (b) the Rhineland, (c) Austria, (d) the Sudetenland, (e) Poland.

German Losses after World War I

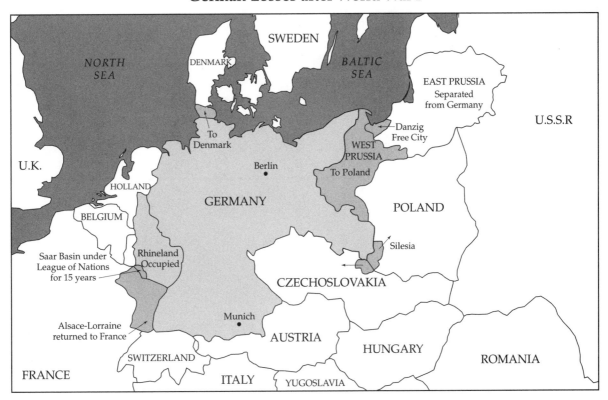

German Expansion 1935–1939

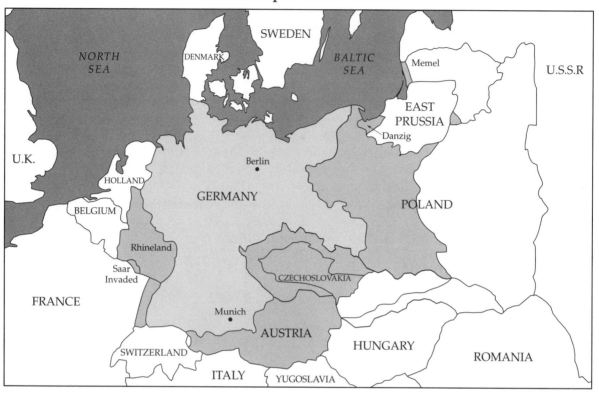

ACTIVITY

Comparing and contrasting maps: Study the three maps on the Arab–Israeli conflict and then answer the following questions:

a. In which year did Israel make the largest territorial gains? Name three major areas which Israel occupied in that year.

b. Why have the Golan Heights been an area of such strategic importance to both the Israeli and Arab nations?

c. Compare the land given to Israel by the United Nations in 1947 to that conquered by Israel in two major wars.

d. Having looked at all three maps, draw a map of the latest developments in the Arab–Israeli territorial conflict.

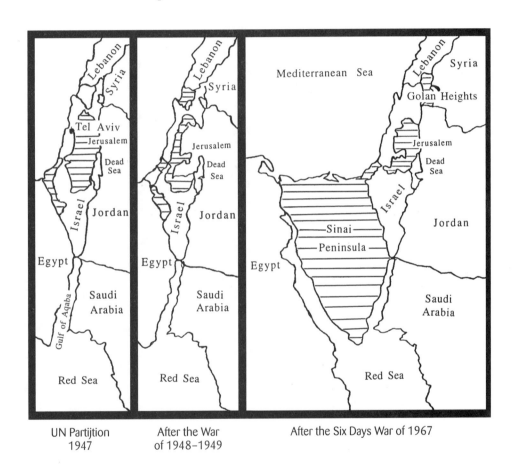

UN Partijtion 1947

After the War of 1948–1949

After the Six Days War of 1967

ACTIVITY *Studying a crisis topic:* Read the explanation of the crisis provided by U.S. President John F. Kennedy and by Soviet Premier Nikita Khrushchev, and study the map of the crisis area.

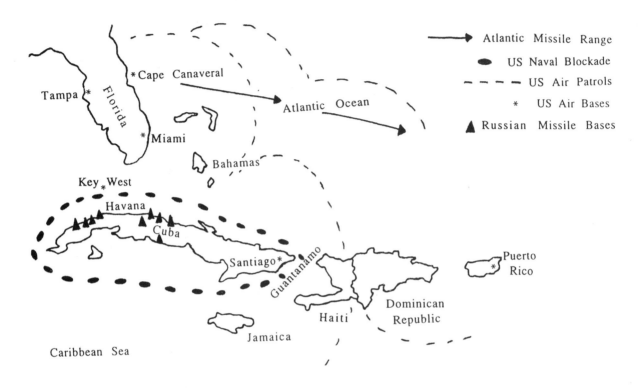

A. Kennedy

This government, as promised, has maintained the closest surveillance of the Soviet military buildup on the island of Cuba. Within the past week, unmistakable evidence has established the fact that a series of offensive missile sites is now in preparation on that imprisoned island. The purpose of these bases can be none other than to provide a nuclear strike capability against the Western Hemisphere. . . . Each of these missiles, in short, is capable of striking Washington, D.C., the Panama Canal, Cape Canaveral, Mexico City, or any other city in the eastern part of the United States, in Central or in the Caribbean.

B. Khrushchev

You want to make your country safe. This is understandable; but Cuba too wants the same thing. All countries want to make themselves safe. But how are we, the Soviet Union, our Government, to assess your actions, which are expressed in the fact that you have surrounded with military bases the Soviet Union, surrounded with military bases our allies: have disposed military bases literally round our country; have stationed your rocket armament there? This is no secret. American officials are demonstratively saying this. Your rockets are situated in Italy and are aimed at us. Your rockets are situated in Turkey. You are worried by Cuba because it is a distance of 90 miles by sea from the coast of America. But Turkey is next to us. Our sentries walk up and down and look at each other.

a. What views are expressed by "A?"

b. How does "B" view the sit

c. What crisis had precipitated this confrontation?

d. Name two places where the U.S.A. had air bases in the Caribbean.

e. Where, exactly, did the USSR have missile bases in the Caribbean?

f. How far is Cuba from the coast of America? How far is Cape Canaveral from Ascension?

g. How was this crisis resolved?

THE FIVE THEMES OF GEOGRAPHY

America 2000 singled out geography and history as core subjects to be taught in the schools. The National Council for Geographic Education has suggested approaching the teaching of geography through five themes:

1. *Location:* To determine absolute location (position on the earth's surface), geographers use a set of imaginary lines that crisscross the surface of the globe—lines of longitude and latitude. They also determine relative location by knowing where something is in relation to things around it.

2. *Place:* The physical and human characteristics of a place give meaning to a site and distinguish it from other places.

3. *Human/environment interactions:* Humans depend on, modify, and adapt to the environment.

4. *Movement:* Geography is movement. All kinds of things move—goods, people, ideas, animals, plants, earth, water, and air. Movement means change—change over distance and change through time. Geography is not static.

5. *Regions:* There are particular unifying features of an area that distinguish the region from surrounding areas. These features may be either natural or cultural, and a place may be part of any number of different regions.

The five themes of geography provide a broad outline for studying any place on earth. What follows is a suggested outline for discovering the geographic diversity of Africa through guided questions using the five themes of geography. A world map, a map of Africa, a map of African tribal lands, and a cultural origins map are included.

Location

- What is the absolute location of the continent of Africa (longitude and latitude)?
- On a blank map of Africa, fill in the Equator, the Tropic of Cancer, the Tropic of Capricorn, and the prime meridian.
- What is the relative location of the continent of Africa (hemispheres, neighboring continents)?

- On a blank map of the world, fill in the Red Sea, the Mediterranean Sea, the Atlantic Ocean, and the Indian Ocean.
- How large is Africa (length and breadth in miles, square mileage)?

Place

- What are the major natural features of the continent (rivers, mountains, deserts, forests)?
- What are the major points of interest (historical, natural, recreational)?
- Find out about the climate of Egypt, Zaire, and South Africa (coldest, hottest, average temperature, and rainfall)? What do you notice?
- Identify some of the native plants and animals throughout Africa.
- Describe the people who live in northern Africa, in central Africa, and in southern Africa (ethnic groups, religion, language, occupations, traditions).

Human/Environment Interactions

- What is the primary land use (agriculture, industry, mining, residential)?
- What are the major industries in the North, in the West, in the East, and in the South?
- What percentage of the population is rural? What percent urban?
- Identify the areas of greatest population density. Discuss what might attract people to these areas.
- How have people and their activities modified the environment (grazing cattle, building dams, clearing forests, etc.)?

Movement

- How do the people travel within Africa? How do they transport goods?
- Who are Africa's main trading partners? List major imports and exports.
- Which diseases are most prevalent and why?
- How do you account for the educational standards in Africa?
- Why do people emigrate from or immigrate to Africa? Provide some immigration and emigration data.

Regions

- On the outline map of Africa, fill in the names of the countries. How have the boundaries of these countries been determined?
- Study the map of original African tribal lands. What do you notice? Are there any major similarities or differences between this map and the map of Africa today (George J. Demko, p. 39)?
- What are the major vegetation regions in Africa (grassland, rain forest, desert, savanna)?

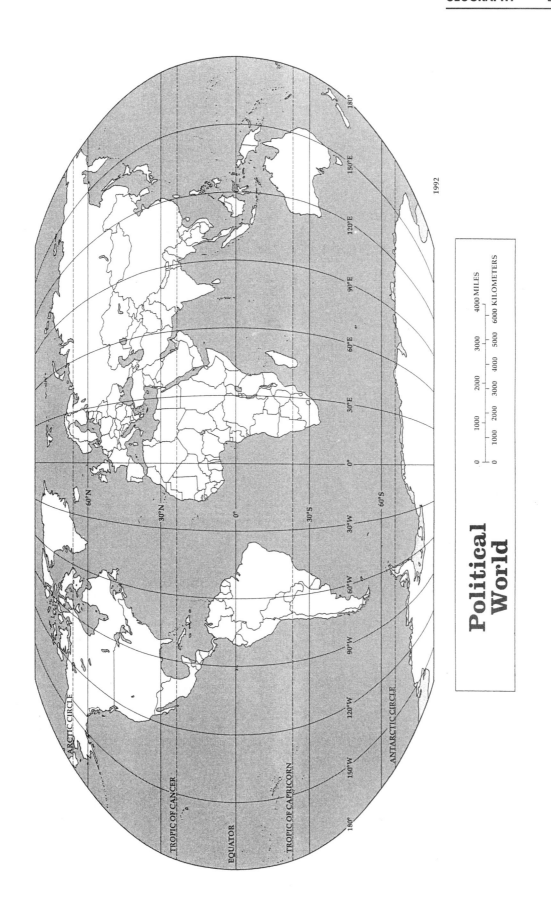

Political World

1992

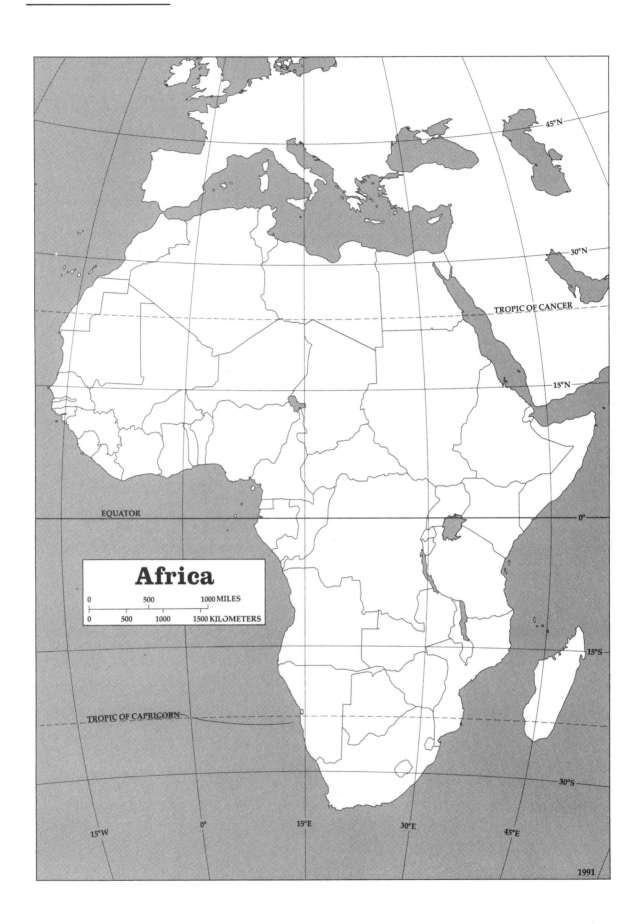

Africa

0   500   1000 MILES
0   500   1000   1500 KILOMETERS

EQUATOR

TROPIC OF CANCER

TROPIC OF CAPRICORN

45°N

30°N

15°N

0°

15°S

30°S

15°W   0°   15°E   30°E   45°E

1991

- How is Northern Africa similar to neighboring countries (language, rainfall, terrain)?
- Find another continent that could be similar to Africa. Give reasons for you selection.

ACTIVITIES: BEYOND THE FACTS

Students should be encouraged to add flesh and blood to the outline that the five themes of geography provide. The *Grolier Encyclopedia* and World Wide Web sites are outstanding reference sources. Activities could in clude:

1. Further research on a particular topic
2. Analyzing literary works such as poems, extracts from novels, and/or videos from Africa
3. Preparing and presenting African personality sketches
4. Reading, editing, and categorizing newspaper articles that deal with Africa
5. Listening to appropriate music from Africa

GLOBAL EDUCATION

Geography asks us to look at the world as a whole, to understand the connections between places, to recognize that the local affects the global and vice versa. The National Commission on Social Studies in the Schools (1989) has stated that although the uniqueness of each culture needs to be understood, "the way to see human history as a whole is to pay special attention to the cultural, economic, and political links that ran across different civilizations and connected them" (p. 14).

Since the mid-1980s there has been a growing awareness of the importance of a global education for American students. In 1985 Downey stressed the importance of preparing students to live in a global society as U.S. citizens found themselves ever more deeply involved in world affairs: ". . . more U.S. citizens are becoming involved in international trade, consuming international products and finding themselves entangled in world wide problems related to pollution, population growth, national security and international political stability. Schools have to prepare tomorrow's citizens to live in a global society" (p. 25).

In 1991 Tye defined *global education* as "learning about those problems and issues that cut across national boundaries, and about the interconnectedness of systems—ecological, economic, cultural, political, and technological. Global education involves perspective taking—seeing things through the eyes and minds of others—and it means the realization that while individuals and groups may view life differently, they also have common needs and wants" (p. 163).

Global education aims at achieving:

1. An awareness that one's world view is not shared universally
2. An understanding of prevailing world conditions and development
3. A cross-cultural awareness that recognizes both similarities and differences between cultures
4. An awareness that there are diverse human choices
5. A broader definition of the term *citizenship* to include not only the nation but the whole world

The 'content' of a global education should include the following parameters.

- *Global issues and problems*—political, social, economic, environmental—that threaten humanity and require joint solutions
- *Human values*—both unique cultural values and universal values that the world shares
- *Global systems*—through which people participate in the world and interact with one another in an organized way
- *Global actors*—including international organizations, national governments, formal and informal groups, and individual citizens

In addition, it is possible to place the vast majority of problems that plague us locally and globally into four categories:

1. *Peace and security:* The arms race, terrorism, national aggression
2. *National/international developments:* Hunger, poverty, overpopulation
3. *Environmental problems:* Pollution, acid rain, nuclear waste disposal, deforestation
4. *Human rights:* Refugees, political prisoners, racism, ethnic cleansing

Creating a Global Awareness at School

If students of the twenty-first century are to learn about the various regions of the world as intimately related and the earth operating as one, then it is imperative that a global awareness be infused in every conceivable way. What follow are some suggestions for creating a global awareness throughout the school building.

1. Every classroom in a school building should have a world map, and every teacher should refer to the map whenever a place, name, or event is discussed.
2. Every school should have a quotation board and a current event board visibly displayed. Global quotations can be collected by faculty and students and changed regularly throughout the school year. The current event board should be changed at least once a week.
3. The librarian can be encouraged to display books on foreign countries and global issues, and the art teacher can display works of art from different cultures.
4. Morning television in the school can be used to mention a major world event, problem, or issue; introduce a foreign student to the school; play music from different countries; or have students share experiences, knowledge, and research about foreign countries.
5. Foreign "hello's" can be displayed around the school, as can flags from many countries.
6. Foreign exchange students can hold a monthly seminar and invite all interested parties to attend. Exchange students should be invited to share information in a variety of classes.
7. Schools can create a global logo, which can, in turn, be transcribed onto T-shirts.
8. ESL (English as a Second Language) students can be integrated into the school system in such a way that their language and culture becomes a basis for global understanding.
9. Pictures of foreign cars, sports, foods, clothing, music, and so on can be displayed in order to focus on our dependency on foreign trade.
10. Special occasions such as International Women's Day (March 8), World Environment Day (June 5), World Food Day (October 16), United Nations Day (October 24), and World Human Rights Day (December 10) can be celebrated.
11. One of the best ways to infuse a global perspective into our schools is to make the newspaper one of the major sources of information in all disciplines. Contact your nearest NIE (Newspapers in Education) office for further guidance.

A second suggestion for infusing a global awareness into our teaching is to require a Global Connection assignment, in which a group of two to four students link people and events across the globe under the topics listed next. Each group is responsible for one decade during this century, and information for each year in that decade must be provided. The students will be responsible for selecting the two most appropriate pieces of information for each year under each topic. Although it is likely that information from Europe and the United States will be easiest to find, it is imperative that Asian, African, and South American information be included. Here is an example:

	History/ Politics	Literature/ Theater	Religion/ Philosophy	Music/ Art	Science/ Technology
1930s					
1940s					
1950s					
1960s					
1970s					
1980s					

Once information has been collected from a variety of resources, which could include *Chase's Annual Events,* world almanacs and *Timetables of History* by Bernard Grun, the information should be summarized, collated, and transcribed onto butcher paper following the example just given. These large sheets of butcher paper will be displayed around the classroom and each group will be responsible for giving a "global report" on its decade. At least one example of appropriate music will be played during the group report. As a conclusion to this assignment, the class as a whole will draw global connections across the decades and across the topics.

GEOGRAPHY ACTIVITIES

A. A General Introduction to Geography

The first two or three days of a geography unit can be spent on introducing (or reintroducing) the whole world to the class, regardless of which country or area might be studied in more depth. It is imperative that large world maps be displayed and that each student be given an outline of a political world map for individual use. One way to approach a general introduction to geography is to use the following song with the accompanying activities.

*Places in the World by Red Grammer**
These are the places in the world.

Some you know and some you don't.
Some you'll visit and some you won't.
Some are near and some are far.
Some sound exotic like Zanzibar,
'Cause these are places in the world.

Bombay, Cape Maine, Mandalay, Baffin Bay,
Baghdad, Leningrad, Ashkabad, Trinidad,
LA, Norway, Paraguay and Monterey,
Singapore, Equador, Bangalore, Baltimore.

---

*Available on *Teaching People, 1986, Children's Group Inc.* By Red and Kathy Grammer. © 1986 Smilin' Atcha Music. Used with permission. From the Red Note Records recording "Teaching Peace" by Red Grammer.

These are places in the world.

Fiji, Sicily, Nagasaki, Tennessee,
Cairo, Quito, Borneo, Idaho,
Taiwan, Dijon, Saigon, Teheran,
Guatemala, Oklahoma, Argentina, North Dakota.

These are the places in the world.

Some are new, some are old.
Some are hot, some are cold.
Some are low, some are high.
Some are wet, some are dry.

'Cause these are places in the world.

Glasgow, Oslo, Fresno, Taingtau,
Falkland, Auckland, Yucatan, Disneyland,
Libya, Namibia, Romania, Pennsylvania,
Bora Bora, Walla Walla, Costa Rica, Bratislava.

These are places in the world.

Krakow, Chongchow, Moscow, Tokelau,
Dominique, Pike's Peak, Mozambique, Bittercreek,
Warsaw, Moosejaw, Saskatoon, Cameroon,
Haifa, Mecca, Bethlehem, Jerusalem.

These are the places in the world.

High on the mountain, down on the plain.
Deep in the jungle in the middle of the rain.
Children laugh and children play,
Everywhere, everyday.
'Cause these are places in the world.

ACTIVITIES

1. Categorize the places mentioned in the song under the following headings: Country, Island, State, City, Bay or Cape, Other.
2. Locate the following places on a world map: Zanzibar, Baffin Bay, Bratislava, Tokelau, Moose Jaw.
3. What is the major similarity in the message of the two songs?

B. World Tour

Starting in E, follow the arrows and you see it is possible to enjoy the "spell" of a world tour by seeing the whole E-A-R-T-H.

There are at least twenty countries (including one overseas territory) you can discover in this way. There are no passport restrictions except that you have to

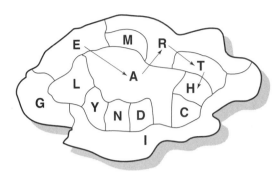

pass directly from one letter to another. But of course you can double back to include a previously used letter.

1. _____ 2. _____ 3. _____
4. _____ 5. _____ 6. _____
7. _____ 8. _____ 9. _____
10. _____ 11. _____ 12. _____
13. _____ 14. _____ 15. _____
16. _____ 17. _____ 18. _____
19. _____ 20. _____

Answers
Italy, Germany, Ireland, India, China, Thailand, Malaya, America, Canada, Chili, Haiti, Tahiti, Trinidad, Nigeria, Niger, Chad, Mali, Algeria, Mariana, Iceland.

C. Continents Drifting

Provide students with the outline map of the earth before the continents drifted. In the space below the map, ask the students to write "what might have happened" if the continents had not drifted.

D. Native Lands

The names by which we know other countries are often quite different from the names the inhabitants of those countries use. For example, the country we call *Greece* is known as *Kypriaki Dimokratia* to the Greeks. The names below may sound like Greek, too, but world travelers should be able to identify at least fifteen of these countries.

1. Al-Mamlaka al-'Arabiya as-Sa'udiya
2. Kalaalit Nunaat
3. Bundesrepublik Deutschland

4. Espana
5. Estados Unidos Mexicanos
6. Hebretasebawit Etyopia
7. Lyoveldio Island
8. Konindrijk der Nederlanden
9. Konungariket Sverige
10. Magyar Nepkoztarasay

11. Nippon
12. Polska Rzeczpospolita Ludowa

13. Republiek van Suid-Afrika
14. Republik Osterreich
15. Republique de Tchad
16. Suomi
17. Eesti Vabariir
18. Eire
19. Turkiye Cumheriyeti
20. Zhonghua Renmin Gonghe Guo

1. (Kingdom of) Saudi Arabia
2. Greenland
3. West Germany (Federal Republic of Germany)
4. Spain
5. Mexico (United Mexican States)
6. (Socialist) Ethiopia
7. (Republic of) Iceland
8. (Kingdom of) the Netherlands
9. (Kingdom of) Sweden
10. Hungary (Hungarian People's Republic)
11. Japan
12. Poland (Polish People's Republic)
13. (Republic of) South Africa
14. (Republic of) Austria
15. (Republic of) Chad
16. Finland
17. Republic of Estonia
18. Ireland
19. (Republic of) Turkey
20. (People's Republic of) China

E. Something to Think About

If we could suddenly shrink the earth's population to a village of precisely 100, but all the existing human ratios remained the same, it would look like this:

- There would be:
    - 57 Asians
    - 21 Europeans
    - 14 Western Hemisphere people (North and South American)
    - 8 Africans
- 70 of the 100 would be nonwhite; 30 would be white.
- 70 of the 100 would be non-Christian, 3 would be Christian.

- 50 percent of the entire world's wealth would be in the hands of only 6 people—and all 6 would be citizens of the United States.
- 70 would be unable to read.
- 50 would suffer malnutrition.
- 80 would live in substandard housing.
- 1 would have a college education.

When one considers our world from such an incredibly compressed perspective, the need for both tolerance and understanding becomes glaringly apparent.

ACTIVITY

1. What surprised you the most about these facts? The least? Give reasons for your answers.

F. Recognizing Individual South American Countries

South American Map Puzzle
The countries of South America are all shown on this page to the same scale, and all are in their north–south positions. Write the names of the countries and their capitals on the blank lines.

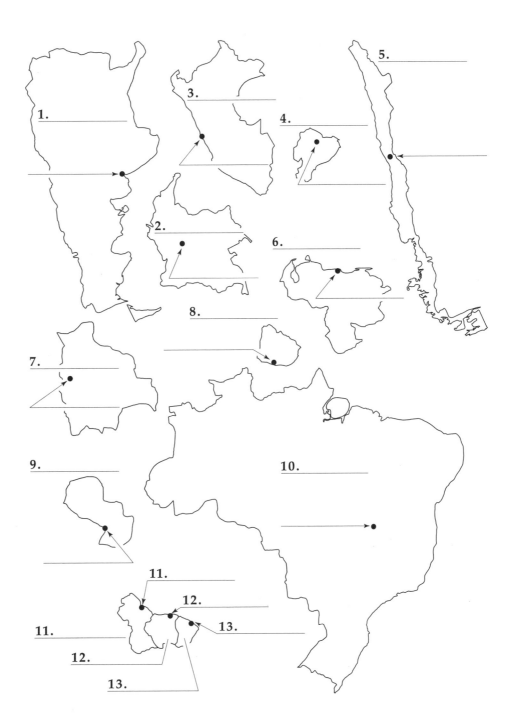

1. _____

2. _____

3. _____

4. _____

5. _____

6. _____

7. _____

8. _____

9. _____

10. _____

11. _____

12. _____

13. _____

11. _____

12. _____

13. _____

G. Comparison Maps

Whenever possible, provide students with land comparison sizes. For example:

- Romania—slightly smaller than Oregon
- Hungary—slightly smaller than Indiana
- Luxembourg—slightly smaller than Rhode Island

- Poland—slightly smaller than New Mexico
- The Great Lakes:
    —Lake Ontario—size of Hawaii and Rhode Island
    —Lake Erie—size of Vermont
    —Lake Michigan—size of Delaware, Vermont, Rhode Island, and New Hampshire
    —Lake Huron—size of Missouri, New Jersey, and Connecticut
    —Lake Superior—size of South Carolina and Rhode Island

ACTIVITY

1. Draw a size comparison map of whatever country or area you are studying and the United States. Be sure to draw the map according to scale.

H. Classifying Country Facts

With so much information available on every country in the world, it is necessary to teach our students how to classify facts. Here is a suggested activity to classify a collection of Canadian facts.

The facts listed here can be classified or placed under main headings. Write the number of each fact under the heading to which it is most closely related. *Note:* Each historical fact has a date. After you have completed the entire activity, read those facts in the order that the events occurred.

1. Canada borders on three oceans: Atlantic, Pacific, Arctic.
2. After more than 150 years of struggle between France and Great Britain, the British won the French and Indian War (1763) and gained control of all of Canada.
3. Canada's population in 1990 was estimated to be about 26,500,000, about 9 or 10 percent of the population of the United States.
4. In Canada's far north, the ground is permanently frozen except for the top two or three feet, which thaw in the summer.
5. The Arctic region has a very small population, mostly made up of about 12,000 Eskimos who earn a living by hunting, fishing, trapping, and working in mines.
6. The first Europeans to sight Canada in about 1000 A.D. were the Vikings.
7. Canada is the second largest country in the world after Russia.
8. Manufacturing occupies more people in Canada than any other economic activity.
9. For at least nine months of the year, most of the Arctic Ocean is frozen over.
10. From east to west, Canada is more than 3,200 miles wide.
11. Quebec, on the St. Lawrence River, was Canada's first settlement (1608).
12. Canada has the longest coastline, almost 60,000 miles including islands, of any country in the world.

13. Canada's leading industry is the manufacturing of food and beverages; second is transportation equipment.
14. In 1931 Canada became a completely self-governing nation within the British Commonwealth of Nations.
15. About three-quarters (75%) of Canada's people live in cities.
16. Some areas on Canada's west coast revive more than 100″ of precipitation in a year, but on the eastern side of the coastal mountains the precipitation is between 14″ and 20″ a year.
17. The people of Canada who are of British descent make up about 40 percent of the inhabitants, whereas people of French origin account for about 27 percent.
18. Toronto, Canada's largest city, has a population of 3,427,000. Ottawa, Canada's capital, has about 819,000 people.
19. About one-third of Canada is covered with forest.
20. Canada imports about 65 percent of its needs form the United States, and sells about 75 percent of its exports to the United States.
21. Some of the islands in Arctic Canada have an average January temperature of − 40°F, but in July an average temperature of about 40° F.
22. The U.S. Rocky Mountains and the Canadian Rocky Mountains are part of the same chain.
23. Mt. Logan in the Yukon Territory, 19,850′ above sea level, is the second highest mountain in North America.

Physical Features	Business and Trade	Climate	Population	History

I. Where in Europe?

It is important to match major historical events and places with their geographical location. In the list that follows, fill in the city or country next to each event or place.

J. Eyewitness Account

Give students the fact sheet on the eruption of Mt. St. Helens. Students can write an eyewitness account of the volcanic eruption as if they were there.

Mount St. Helens Volcano Facts

Mount St. Helens: Named by Captain George Vancouver of the British Royal navy in 1792, in honor of Baron St. Helens, the British Ambassador to Spain. *Catastrophic Eruption in the 20th Century:* May 18, 1980. *Debris Avalanche:* Largest landslide in recorded history—removed more than 1,300 feet of the volcano's summit. *Lateral Blast:* Accelerated to speeds greater than 650 miles per hour and blew down enough timber to build 300,00 two-bedroom homes. *Vertical Ash Eruption:* Rose nearly 16 miles into the atmosphere. *Ash Fall:* Over 500 million tons—enough to bury a football field to a depth of 150 miles. *Pyroclastic Flows:* Were hotter than 800°F. *Mudflows:* Damaged or destroyed 27 bridges, 185 miles of roads, and over 200 homes. *Human Fatalities:* 36 people known dead; 21 peo-

1. Stonehenge _____

2. The Alhambra   _____

3. The Parthenon   _____

4. Eiffel Tower   _____

5. The Colosseum   _____

6. Picadilly Circus   _____

7. Fjords   _____

8. Big Ben   _____

9. Leaning Tower   _____

10. Blarney Stone   _____

11. Bridge of Sighs   _____

12. Vesuvius   _____

13. Black Forest   _____

14. The Kremlin   _____

15. Waterloo   _____

16. Andorra   _____

17. The Louvre   _____

18. Loch Ness   _____

19. Blue Grotto   _____

20. The Tyrol   _____

21. Birthplace of
    Napoleon   _____

22. El Prado   _____

23. Matterhorn   _____

24. Crete   _____

25. Home of Hans
    Christian Anderson   _____

26. Home of Van Gogh   _____

ple missing. *Game Fatalities* (estimated): 5,000 black-tailed deer, 1,500 Roosevelt elk, 200 black bear, 15 mountain goats, and millions of small game, birds, and fish. (Compliments of Foodmasters, Inc.)

K. Guinness Book of Records

Provide numerous copies of the *Guinness Book of Records*. Give each student two or three of the following "records." When they have found the answer and written it on their sheet of paper, each student must pin the piece of paper in the appropriate place on a large world map.

Largest Palace _____

Longest Suspension Bridge_____

Largest Concrete Dam _____

Highest Dam _____

Largest Trash Dump _____Some Interesting Facts

_____

Largest Sundial _____

Largest Employer _____

Oldest Known Flag _____

Largest Mushroom Farm _____Some Interesting

Facts _____

Least Taxed People _____Most Taxed People

_____

Largest Switchboard _____Some Interesting Facts

_____

Largest Temple _____

Largest Ocean _____Square Miles

_____

Average Depth _____

Clearest Sea _____Just Off

_____

Remotest Island _____

Longest and Shortest Rivers _____in

_____

and _____in _____

Highest Waterfall _____ Drop off

_____

Deepest Lake _____ in _____

Measuring _____

Highest Temperature _____ Measured at

_____

Lowest Temperature _____ Measured at

_____

Largest Active Volcano _____

The Greatest Tides Occur In _____

_____ Has Virtually No Tides.

Largest Peninsula _____ Square Miles

_____

Largest Desert _____ Measuring

_____ Square Miles

Largest Industrial Plant _____ Produces

_____

L. Global Deadlines

Provide each student in the class with the following list of global concerns.

1. Depletion of the rain forests
2. Overpopulation
3. Nuclear waste
4. Depletion of the ozone layer
5. Starvation and malnutrition of millions of people.
6. Imbalances in the global economy
7. Pollution
8. Growing numbers of refugees
9. Possible extinction of many species
10. Ethnic cleansing

Each student must rank these concerns according to the priority with which they should receive attention. They do not have to rank the concern according to the seriousness of the problem, but in terms of which problem should be dealt with first. The reasons for their ranking will differ, and these reasons become the basis for a discussion. After each student has completed their ranking, they should be divided into groups based on their first choice. Each group then prepares a proposal as to why their choice is most important and presents this proposal to the class. After the presentations, a variety of discussions can follow. For example, did anyone change his mind after the presentations, or did any group feel they needed more information to make a stronger case for their cause? As a final activity, a discussion regarding priorities is necessary. Does everyone have to have the same priorities? Can any one person or group deal with all the problems in the world? How can differences in opinions help each other rather than hinder each other?

CHAPTER FIVE

National and Global Connections: A Decade-by-Decade Review of the Twentieth Century

Those who do not remember the past are doomed to repeat it.

—George Santayana

Human history is a fascinating story, filled with heroes, villains, myths, reality, fables, foibles, and icons. No one source can ever hope to record in detail all the events and people that make up our history. Can you imagine a history textbook that would chronicle our collective history in exact sequence and chronology? No, nor can I! While it would be a perfectly wonderful resource, it would also be virtually impossible to carry physically and nearly as impossible to store and display. Perhaps the best we can do (as we have done) is to produce a learning resource that either, on the one hand, broadly chronicles the people and events in our history or, on the other, presents a single manuscript focusing on individuals or an event in history. The former are generally called survey textbooks, while the latter are referred to as biographies or single-event chronologies.

These resources have served serious students of history well but have been less successful for those who are less interested in reading or learning history. The problem is that history and geography have been taught mostly from a political point of view. Dates, places, and people are memorized and regurgitated on "chapter tests," which rarely test true knowledge or understanding of history.

An old Senegalese saying states, "What we do not value we choose to forget." So it is with our students, who sit through endless hours of history classes during their school years yet remain functionally illiterate in history and geography. Even worse, teachers, although they may be well versed in the subject matter, have little skill in presenting the material or in motivating and encouraging students to go beyond the text and personalize the information by asking, "How does this affect you?" and "What is its impact on you and your life?" Skillful teachers always draw parallels from history and help their students to see the relevance of history. It is imperative that students who live in a democracy know and understand our past because it points to our collective and personal future. As Santayana reminds us, history isn't "was"—history "is." We must never forget the past, and we must make sure that each generation understands it so that we may avoid repeating the tragic mistakes that pockmark our past and, instead, build a better tomorrow for all of us.

The aim of this chapter, then, is to provide a quick review of our last hundred years—the twentieth century. We will review the people and events that made us what we are today. This is not intended to be a comprehensive list but, rather, a representation, a starting point from which to research, build concepts, and relate the past to the present. It is a resource that clearly illustrates the dramatic changes in our history, identifies patterns in society while opening up some questions and issues about this century. Most of all it is a starting point from which teachers and students can begin to relate the data to their lives and understand the significance of history in them.

Note

It is important to note that much of the information cited in this chapter comes from a variety of resources like almanacs, newspapers, and encyclopedias—all excellent sources for students to be familiar with as they begin developing their own research skills. Some of the data came from the Internet and Encarta, which, I'm sure, will play an even greater role in future research and historiography. The authors would also like to acknowledge some very special resources that proved invaluable in researching the baseline data that was compiled and used in this section of the book. *The Timetables of History: A Horizontal Linkage of People and Events* (Grun, 1975); *The Encyclopedia of American Facts and Dates,* 9th edition (Carruth, 1993); *This Day in American History* (Gross, 1990); and *Our Glorious Century* (Harvey, 1994) not only are rich resources, but we consider them to be the definitive works for historical chroniclers who, like ourselves, seek out and compile both primary and empirical research for historical manuscripts of this nature.

1900–1909: THE TWENTIETH CENTURY BEGINS

Overview

At first glance the initial decade of the twentieth century seems to be one of domestic tranquillity, with few political and social problems facing an American population that was still basking in the glory of the Spanish-American War and was led by an energetic Theodore Roosevelt who was pushing for political, social, economic, and environmental reforms. Indeed, the United States of America came charging into the twentieth century ready to take its place as a world power—one to be reckoned with globally!

In retrospect, however, there were a great many events during this decade that presaged the rest of the century. Certainly the assassination of a U.S. president, the third in less than fifty years, affected Americans directly. So did world events like the Boxer Rebellion, the Sino-Russian war, and Sun Yat-sen's political movement in China. The Boer War and the annexation of Bosnia-Herzegovina by the Austro-Hungarian Empire all would have an impact on U.S. and world history for the next ninety years.

The following pages will chronicle and illustrate some of the most significant facts of the first decade of the twentieth century.

Demographics: 1900–1909

Important Political Leaders

> U.S.—Theodore Roosevelt and William Howard Taft
> Great Britain—James Balfour and H. H. Asquith

Russia—Czar Nicholas II
France—Armand Fallaries
Spain—King Alfonso XIII
Italy—King Victor Emmanuel III
Austro-Hungarian Empire—Emperor Franz Josef
Japan—Emperor Mutshichito
China—Tz'u-hsi (Empress Dowager) and Emperor Pu-yi
Germany—Bernhard von Bülow
Portugal—King Manuel II

Largest Cities

Ten Largest U.S. Cities		*Ten Largest Cities Outside the U.S.*	
1. New York	3,437,202	1. London	4,211,056
2. Chicago	1,698,575	2. Paris	2,536,834
3. Philadelphia	1,293,697	3. Berlin	1,677,304
4. St. Louis	575,238	4. Canton	1,600,000
5. Boston	560,892	5. Vienna	1,364,548
6. Baltimore	508,957	6. Tokio [sic]	1,299,941
7. Cleveland	381,768	7. St. Petersburg	1,267,023
8. Buffalo	352,387	8. Peking	1,000,000
9. San Francisco	342,782	9. Moscow	988,614
10. Cincinnati	325,902	10. Constantinople	980,000

U.S. population: 75,994,575
World population: 1.2 billion

Significant Headlines and News Stories

1900 William McKinley is reelected as U.S. president.
King Umberto of Italy is assassinated.
World Exhibition opens in Paris.

1901 The Boers begin to organize guerrilla warfare in South Africa.
William Howard Taft becomes governor-general of the Philippines.
J. P. Morgan organizes the U.S. Steel Corporation.

1902 National anthracite coal strike.
Casualties of the Boer War: 5,774 British and 4,000 Boers killed.
Aswan Dam opened.

1903 Alaskan frontier settled.
First motor taxis appear in London.
J. P. Morgan founds the International Mercantile Marine Company.

1904 First U.S. Exposition opens in St. Louis.
Steerage rates for immigrants cut to $10.00 by foreign lines.
New York policeman arrests woman for smoking cigarettes in public.

1905 Sinn Fein party founded in Dublin.
The Cullinan Diamond (3,000 carats) is found.
Theodore Roosevelt is awarded the Nobel Peace Prize.

1906 President Roosevelt is the first U.S. president to travel outside the U.S.
U.S. troops occupy Cuba after Liberal revolt.
San Francisco earthquake kills 700; $4 million in property losses.

1907 S.S. *Lusitania* breaks trans-Atlantic record.
Modern zoo opens in Hamburg, Germany.
Universal suffrage instituted in Austria.

1908   Earthquake in Sicily kills 150,000 people.
Ford Motor Company produces the Model T.
Cairo University opens.

1909   Women admitted to German universities.
Anglo-Persian Oil Company founded.
Robert Peary, Matthew Henson, and four Eskimos reach the North Pole.

History and Politics

1900   Boxer Rebellion in China against Europeans.
Commonwealth of Australia created.
William McKinley reelected U.S. president.

1901   President McKinley is assassinated; succeeded by Theodore Roosevelt, who becomes the 26th U.S. president.
Hay-Pauncefort Treaty: U.S. gains control over the Panama Canal.
Queen Victoria dies—succeeded by her son, Edward VII.

1902   Anglo-Japanese Treaty recognizes independence of China and Korea.
Colonial Conference meets in London.
Leon Trotsky escapes from Siberia and settles in London.

1903   Department of Labor and Commerce established by act of Congress.
First cable under the Pacific Ocean is completed.
British complete conquest of northern Nigeria.

1904   Theodore Roosevelt elected U.S. president.
Russo-Japanese War begins.
10-hour work day established in France.

1905   William Haywood founds the Industrial Workers of the World (Wobblies).
Provinces of Alberta and Saskatchewan are formed in Canada.
Norway separates from Sweden.

1906   Pure Food and Drug Act enacted by Congress.
Algeciras Conference gives France and Spain dual control of Morocco.
Alfred Dreyfus rehabilitated.

1907   President Roosevelt bars Japanese immigration.
Oklahoma becomes the 46th U.S. state.
New Zealand becomes a British dominion.

1908   Union of South Africa is established.
William Howard Taft is elected 27th U.S. president.
Tz'u-hsi, Empress Dowager of China, dies.

1909   Dollar Diplomacy initiated in Latin America and Asia.
Civil war breaks out in Honduras.
Turkey and Serbia recognize Austrian annexation of Bosnia and Herzegovina.

Science and Technology

1900   First trial flight of Zeppelin.
First Browning revolvers manufactured.
First transmission of radio waves is achieved by R. A. Fessenden.
F. E. Dorn discovers radon.
Max Planck formulates quantum theory.
Discovery of the Minoan culture results from Arthur Evans's excavations in Crete.

1901   First motor-driven bicycles are made.
        First Mercedes car is constructed by Wilhelm Maybach.
        Max Planck formulates the laws of radiation.
        The hormone adrenaline is isolated.
        W. H. Nernst postulates the third law of thermodynamics.
1902   First arc generator created by Valdemar Poulsen.
        First person to cross the Irish Channel in a balloon is J. M. Bacon.
        H. W. Cushing begins research on the pituitary system of the body.
        Baylis and Starling discover the hormone secretin.
        Charles Richet discovers anaphylaxis (abnormal sensitivity to serum).
1903   First ultramicroscope constructed by R. A. Zsigmondy.
        First electrocardiograph created by Wilhelm Einthoven.
        First successful flight of a powered airplane achieved by the Wright brothers.
        J. J. Thomson discovers the conduction of electricity through gases.
1904   First ultraviolet lamps are invented.
        First telegraphic transmission of photographs done by Arthur Korn.
        First railroad tunnel constructed between Manhattan and New Jersey.
        F. S. Kipping discovers silicones.
        Sir John Fleming discovers the use of thermionic tubes to generate radio waves.
        W. C. Gorgas discovers a way to eradicate yellow fever.
1905   First rayon yarn manufactured commercially.
        First successful blood transfusion is done.
        Albert Einstein formulates the special theory of relativity, the law of mass energy equivalence, the Brownian theory of motion, and the photon theory of light.
        Sigmund Freud develops his three contributions to the theory of sex.
1906   First radio program of voice and music is broadcast in the U.S. by R. A. Fessenden.
        Position of the North Pole discovered by Roald Amundsen.
        Pierre Curie, French Nobelist, dies.
1907   Conditioned reflexes are first studied by Ivan Pavlov.
        First color photography process using a three-color screen is developed by Louis Lumière.
        Ross Harrison develops the first human tissue culture.
        Emil Fischer develops his researches on the chemistry of proteins.
1908   First synthesis of ammonia is done by Fritz Haber.
        Hermann Minkowski formulates a four-dimensional geometry.
        H. Kamerlingh Onnes liquefies helium.
        Bakelite is developed by L. H. Baekeland.
1909   First commercial manufacture of Bakelite marks the beginning of the Plastic Age.
        First research in genetics is begun by T. H. Morgan.
        Paul Ehrlich prepares Salvarsan for cure of syphilis.

Literature and Theater

1900   Colette: *Claudine à l'école* (First Claudine novel).
        Leo Tolstoy: *The Living Corpse*
        Maxim Gorky: *Three People*

1901   Rudyard Kipling: *Kim*
        Thomas Mann: *Buddenbrooks*
        Frank Norris: *The Octopus*
        J. M. Barrie: *Quality Street* (play)
1902   Kipling: *Just-So Stories*
        Beatrix Potter: *Peter Rabbit*
        Nobel Prize for literature: Theodor Mommsen
1903   Jack London: *The Call of the Wild*
        Samuel Butler: *The Way of All Flesh*
        August Strindberg: *The Queen Christina* (historical play)
        Nobel prize for literature: Björnsterne Björnson
1904   James Matthew Barrie: *Peter Pan*
        Henry James: *The Golden Bowl*
        Joseph Conrad: *Nostromo*
        Abbey Theater in Dublin founded.
1905   Nobel Prize for Literature: Henryk Sienkiewicz
        Heinrich Mann: *Professor Unrat* (*The Blue Angel*)
        E. M. Forster: *Where Angels Fear to Tread*
        David Belasco produces *The Girl of the Golden West* in Pittsburgh,
            later made into an opera by Puccini.
1906   George M. Cohan produces *Forty-five Minutes from Broadway* in
            New York.
        Edgar Wallace: *The Four Just Men*
        Upton Sinclair: *The Jungle*
        Arthur Wing Pinero: *His House in Order*
1907   Nobel Prize for Literature: Rudyard Kipling
        Jacinto Benavente: *Los Intereses Credos,* a Spanish comedy
        Maxim Gorky: *Mother*
        Joseph Conrad: *The Secret Agent*
1908   Isadora Duncan becomes popular interpreter of dance.
        The Tiller Girls appear on the London stage for the first time.
        E. M. Forster: *A Room with a View*
        Kenneth Grahame: *The Wind in the Willows*
        Lucy M. Montgomery: *Anne of Green Gables*
        Gertrude Stein: *Three Lives*
1909   Maeterlinck: *L'Oiseau Bleu* (fairytale play)
        H. G. Wells: *Tono-Bungay*
        Jakob Wassermann: *Casper Hauser* (novel)
        Ferenc Molnar: *Liliom* (play)

Music

1900   Puccini: *Tosca* (opera in Rome)
        Edward Elgar: *Dream of Gerontius* (oratorio in Birmingham)
1901   Ragtime jazz develops in the U.S.
        Richard Strauss: *Feuersnot* (opera in Dresden)
        Rachmaninoff: Piano Concerto No. 2
        Stanford: *Much Ado about Nothing* (opera in London)
1902   Enrico Caruso makes his first phonograph recording.
        Leo Blech: *Das War Ich* (comic opera in Dresden)
        Edward German: *Merrie England* (operetta in London)
1903   Oscar Hammerstein builds the Manhattan Opera House in New
            York.

First recordings of an opera: Verdi's *Ernani*
Juan Manen: *Giovanna di Napoli* (opera in Spanish)
1904   London Symphony Orchestra gives its first concert.
First radio transmission of music at Graz, Austria.
Puccini: *Madame Butterfly* (opera in Milan)
1905   Zenobia by L. A. Coerne becomes the first American opera produced in Europe.
Franz Lehar: *The Merry Widow* (operetta in Vienna)
Richard Strauss: *Salome* (opera in Dresden)
1906   Mozart festival held in Salzburg.
Ermanno Wolf-Ferrari: *I Quattro Reseghi* (comic opera)
Ethel Smyth: *The Wreckers* (opera in Leipzig)
1907   The first Ziegfeld Follies staged in New York.
Delius: *A Village Romeo and Juliet* (opera in Berlin)
Leo Fall: *The Dollar Princess* (operetta in Vienna)
1908   11-year-old E. W. Korngold writes his first stage work, the ballet *The Snowman*.
Oskar Strauss: *The Chocolate Soldier* (operetta in Vienna)
Bela Bartók: String Quartet No. 1
1909   Sergei Diaghilev presents his Ballet Russe for the first time in Paris.
Wolf-Ferrari: *Il Segreto di Susanna* (comic opera in Munich)
Ralph Vaughan Williams: *Fantasia on a Theme of Tallis*
Leopold Stokowski named conductor of Philadelphia Orchestra.

Visual Arts

1900   Picasso: *Le Moulin de la Galette* (painting)
Cezanne: *Still Life with Onions*
Renoir: *Nude in the Sun*
Toulouse-Lautrec: *La Modiste*
Film: *Cinderella,* directed by Georges Melies.
1901   Walt Disney is born.
Picasso's Blue Period begins.
Film: *The Little Doctor*
Gauguin: *The Gold in Their Bodies* (painting)
1902   Gauguin: *Raiders by the Sea* (painting)
Monet: *Waterloo Bridge* (painting)
Rodin: *Romeó and Juliet*
Film: *Salome* (Oskar Messter)
1903   Paul Gauguin, the French painter, dies.
Building of the Liverpool Cathedral, designed by G. G. Scott, begins.
Film: *The Great Train Robbery* (longest film to date; 12 minutes)
1904   Picasso: *The Two Sisters* (painting)
Henri Rousseau: *The Wedding*
Films: *Le Barbier de Seville* and *Le Damnation de Faust* (French)
1905   Cezanne: *Les Grandes Baigneuses* (painting)
Henri Rousseau: *Jungle with a Lion*
Picasso arrives in Paris and begins his Pink Period.
Matisse: *Luxe, Calme et Volupte*
Film: First regular cinema established in Pittsburgh, Pennsylvania; first films feature comedian Max Linder.
1906   Aristide Maillol: *Chained Action* (sculpture)

Greta Garbo, film actress, born in Sweden.

Paul Cezanne dies.

1907   First Cubist exhibition held in Paris.

Picasso: *Demoiselles d'Avignon* (painting)

Henri Rousseau: *The Snake Charmer*

Edvard Munch: *Portrait of Walter Rathenau*

Film: Titles replace commentator; slow motion invented by August Musger.

1908   Monet: *The Ducal Palace, Venice*

Maurice Utrillo begins his White Period.

First steel and glass building: A. E. G. Turbine Factory, Berlin, by Peter Behrens

Matisse coins the term *cubism.*

Film: *The Last Days of Pompeii* by Arturo Ambrosio.

1909   Matisse: *The Dance*

Picasso: *Harlequin*

Cinematograph Licensing Act passed in Britain.

Frank Lloyd Wright: Robie House, Chicago

Film: *Carmen;* newsreels; D. W. Griffith features Mary Pickford, the first film star.

Sports

1900   D. F. Davis presents international lawn tennis cup bearing his name.

Ray C. Ewry of the U.S. wins eight gold medals in the Olympic Games.

W. G. Grace ends his cricket career (54,000 runs in his career).

William Muldoon is the first professional wrestling champion.

1901   Boxing recognized as a legal sport in Britain.

First American Bowling Club tournament held in Chicago.

1902   The first Rose Bowl is played; Michigan defeats Stanford, 49-0.

1903   First Tour de France (bicycle race)

In the first postseason baseball series, the Boston Red Sox beat the Pittsburgh Pirates in the first World Series.

1904   World Series between the Giants and Boston canceled as a result of a dispute with Giants manager John McGraw.

U.S. Lawn Tennis Men's Singles won by Holcombe Ward; Women's Singles won by May G. Sutton.

First Vanderbilt Cup auto race won by Mercedes.

Olympic Games held in St. Louis, Missouri.

1905   Ty Cobb begins major league baseball career with the Detroit Tigers.

New York (NL) beats Philadelphia (AL) in the second World Series, 4–1.

World boxing champion James Jeffries retires undefeated.

1906   French Grand Prix motorcar race is first run.

Chicago (AL) beats Chicago (NL) in World Series, 4–2.

Thomas Burns defeats Marvin Hart in 20 rounds in Los Angeles to win world heavyweight boxing championship.

1907   Highest ever break in billiards: Tom Reece plays 449.135 in 85 hours, 49 minutes.

Chicago Cubs defeat Detroit Tigers in World Series, 4–0.

1908   London hosts the Olympic Games; U.S. wins 15 firsts out of 28 events in track and field.

Jack Johnson becomes first black world heavyweight boxing champion.

1909   First six-day bicycle race held in Berlin.

Everyday Life

1900   *Daily Express* appears in London.

The cakewalk is the most fashionable dance.

The Navy purchases its first submarine, equipped with an internal combustion engine and an electric motor, designed by John P. Holland.

Average income: $1,164.

1901   First British submarine is launched.

Mombasa–Lake Victoria railway completed.

Exposition in Buffalo opened, where President McKinley was shot.

Sunday newspaper costs 3 cents, daily newspaper 1 cent.

1902   Metropolitan Water Board established in London.

First automatic vending restaurant opened in Philadelphia.

Anglo-American Pilgrims Association founded.

1903   Motor-car speed limit set at 20 miles per hour in Britain.

First coast-to-coast crossing of the American continent by car takes 65 days.

Richard Steiff designs first teddy bears (named after Theodore Roosevelt).

Wilbur and Orville Wright demonstrate the first motor-driven airplane at Kitty Hawk, North Carolina, with Orville first flying 120 feet in 12 seconds.

Barney Oldfield becomes first man to drive a car at 60 miles per hour.

1904   Helen Keller graduates from Radcliffe College.

Broadway subway opens in New York City.

First American World Exposition in St. Louis.

Paris Conference on white slavery held.

1905   First neon-lighted signs appear.

First motor buses operate in London.

Franklin Delano Roosevelt marries Eleanor Roosevelt in New York City.

Mount Wilson observatory completed in California.

1906   Night-shift work for women is forbidden internationally.

12.5-mile-long Simplon Tunnel between Italy and Switzerland is opened.

Mesa Verde National Park established in Colorado.

Toothbrush: 15 cents

1907   Lord Baden-Powell founds Boy Scout movement.

First daily comic strip, "Mr. Mutt," later "Mutt and Jeff," by Bud Fisher, begins in *San Francisco Chronicle.*

Second Sunday in May is established as Mother's Day.

Man's wristwatch: $2.95

1908   Fountain pens become popular.

The Ford Motor Company introduces the Model T; sells for $850.

General Motors Corporation is formed.

Broadway theater tickets: $2.40.

1909   Girl Guides established in Britain.
        First permanent waves in hair are given by London hairdressers.
        Sigmund Freud lectures on psychoanalysis in the United States.

New Nations, 1900–1909

Australia (1901)
Cuba (1903)
New Zealand (1907)
Norway (1905)
Panama (1903)

Sample Learning Activities

1906   *Pure Food and Drug Act passed by Congress.*
        Students prepare one (or more) paragraph reactions to readings
        from Upton Sinclair's *The Jungle* and photographs or illustra-
        tions from the period.
1909   *Robert E. Peary, Matthew Henson, and four Eskimos first to reach mag-*
        netic North Pole.
        Three groups maintain a one-week journal that represents each of
        the following perspectives: Peary's role, Henson's role as an
        African American explorer, and the Inuit view of their explo-
        ration and survival.

1910–1919: THE WORLD TURNED UPSIDE DOWN

Overview

The second decade of the twentieth century witnessed the first global conflict in
human history, which produced unprecedented human carnage and destruction.
World War I would alter the map of the world, change human attitudes, and,
worse, be the harbinger of an even greater and more destructive global conflict. Yet
the decade was also the time of some of the greatest human accomplishments, including such achievements as the Panama Canal, the Roosevelt Dam, and the
Trans-Siberian Railroad.

Medical and scientific research led to dramatic changes in health care, including immunity tests for diphtheria and the first successful heart transplant done on
a laboratory dog.

American workers gained new rights in the workplace—the eight-hour day
and the five-day work week. This created more leisure time for the average person;
consequently, sports leagues and sporting events began to proliferate. The Professional Golf Association and the National Hockey League were formed, and sports
heroes became national icons.

By the end of the decade, the United States had truly experienced "the best of
times and the worst of times," paving the way for the Roaring Twenties that followed.

Demographics: 1910–1919

Important Political Leaders

> U.S.—Woodrow Wilson
> Great Britain—David Lloyd George and King George V
> France—Georges Clemenceau, Joseph Caillaux, and Raimond Poincaré
> Russia—Czar Nicholas III and Vladimir Lenin
> Greece—Venizelos
> Italy—Benito Mussolini
> Japan—Emperor Yoshihito
> China—Sun Yat-sen and Yuan Shih-kai
> South Africa—Jan Christian Smuts
> Austria—Karl von Stürgkh
> Montenegro—King Nicholas I
> Persia—Tewfik Pasha
> Mexico—Venustiano Carranza
> Poland—Ignace Paderewski

Largest Cities

Ten Largest U.S. Cities		*Ten Largest Cities Outside the U.S.*	
1. New York	4,014,304	1. London	4,536,541
2. Chicago	1,698,275	2. Paris	2,717,068
3. Philadelphia	1,293,697	3. Tokyo	2,088,160
4. Boston	595,083	4. Berlin	2,040,148
5. St. Louis	575,238	5. St. Petersburg	1,678,000
6. Baltimore	508,957	6. Vienna	1,674,457
7. Cleveland	381,768	7. Canton	1,600,000
8. Buffalo	376,618	8. Peking	1,600,000
9. San Francisco	342,782	9. Constantinople	1,400,000
10. Pittsburgh	321,616	10. Osaka	1,300,000

U.S. population: 103.5 million
World population: 1.5 billion

Significant Headlines and News Stories

1910 China abolishes slavery.
       Egyptian Premier Butros Ghali assassinated.
       Union of South Africa becomes a dominion of Great Britain.
1911 Mexican rebels overthrow President Diaz.
       Turkish-Italian war begins.
1912 Woodrow Wilson elected and becomes the 28th U.S. president.
       Titanic sinks; 1,500 persons missing and presumed dead.
       Manchus overthrown in China—China becomes a republic.
1913 Balkan war erupts.
       Mahatma Gandhi arrested in South Africa.
       J. P. Morgan dies.
1914 Panama Canal opens.
       Archduke Franz Ferdinand assassinated in Sarajevo.
       World War I begins in Europe.
1915 Allies retreat from Gallipoli.
       German U-boat sinks the *Lusitania*.

Henry Ford charters the "peace ship" *Oskar II* in an attempt to end World War I in Europe.

1916   General John Pershing and U.S. troops invade Mexico.

Irish Republicans stage Easter uprising in Dublin.

David Lloyd George elected prime minister in Great Britain.

1917   The United States enters World War I.

Bolsheviks seize power in Russia.

U.S. buys Virgin Islands from Denmark.

1918   Armistice signed ending World War I.

President Wilson announces Fourteen Points.

Czar Nicholas and family executed by Bolsheviks.

1919   Peace negotiations begin with Germany, Turkey, and Austro-Hungarian Empire.

Race riots in Chicago.

President Woodrow Wilson wins Nobel Peace Prize.

History and Politics

1910   Montenegro proclaimed a kingdom under Nicholas I.

U.S. Congress passes the Mann Act.

Japan annexes Korea.

1911   Peter Stolypin, Russian Premier, assassinated.

Workmen's compensation passes.

Mexican Civil War ends.

1912   *Pravda* begins publication—Lenin is an editor.

Sun Yat-sen heads Chinese Nationalist Party.

New Mexico (47) and Arizona (48) become U.S. states.

Five thousand women march in Washington, D.C., for suffrage.

1913   16th Amendment passed (federal income tax created).

17th Amendment passed (popular election of senators).

Federal Trade Commission, Department of Labor, and Federal Reserve System established.

1914   Panama Canal opens.

Clayton Anti-Trust Act passed.

Ku Klux Klan numbers 100,000 members in U.S.

1915   First Nobel Prize awarded to father and son (W. H. Bragg and W. L. Bragg).

Chlorine gas used by Germany in World War I.

Aircraft make appearance in World War I.

1916   Louis Brandeis named to Supreme Court.

Eight-hour work day established for railroad workers.

T. H. Lawrence appointed British political and liaison officer of King Faisal's army.

1917   U.S. purchases Dutch West Indies.

U.S. declares war on Germany and its allies.

Mata Hari executed for spying.

1918   Czechoslovakia, Austria, and Iceland become independent nations.

One million U.S. troops in Europe (World War I).

Women over 30 given the vote in Great Britain.

U.S. Congress moves to curtail immigration.

1919   18th Amendment (Prohibition) passed by Congress.

Treaty of Versailles signed, ending World War I.

New German republic established.

Science and Technology

1910 Halley's comet observed.
Marie Curie wins Nobel Prize for "Treatise on Radiology."
Florence Nightingale dies.
Jean Henri Dunant, founder of the Red Cross, dies.

1911 Electric starter for cars invented by Charles Kettering.
First modern air conditioning invented.
Gyro compass patented.
Phenobarbital introduced as a treatment for epilepsy.

1912 Vitamins A, B, and E isolated.
Protons and electrons detected.
Neurological surgery perfected by Dr. Harvey Cushing.

1913 Bahr discovers atom structure.
Diphtheria immunity tests introduced.
First subway opened (Buenos Aires).
X-ray developed by William Coolidge.

1914 Ford Motor Company unveils moving car assembly line.
Wright Brothers get patent on motor-driven airplane.
Robert Goddard experiments with rocket research.

1915 English scientist splits atom.
Einstein's theory of relativity presented.
Vitamin D isolated.

1916 Margaret Sanger opens first birth control clinic.
Submarine ultrasonic detection device invented.
Blood plasma successfully refrigerated.

1917 100-inch reflecting telescope installed on Mount Wilson.

1918 Quantum theory in physics introduced by Max Planck.
Harlow Shapley identifies true dimensions of Milky Way.
Helicopters developed by Hewitt and Crocker.

1919 First experiments with short-wave radio.
F. W. Aston builds mass spectograph and establishes phenomenon of isotopy.
Rutherford demonstrates that the atom is not the final building block of the universe.

Literature and Theater

1910 Little Theater constructed for Hull House players in Chicago.
Mark Twain dies.
E. M. Forster: *Howard's End*

1911 Ezra Pound: *Canzoni*
H. G. Wells: *The New Machiavelli*
D. H. Lawrence: *The White Peacock*

1912 Zane Grey: *Riders of the Purple Sage*
Amy Lowell: *A Dove of Many Coloured Glass*
C. G. Jung: *The Theory of Psychoanalysis*

1913 Sax Rohmer: *Dr. Fu Manchu*
Willa Cather: *O Pioneers!*
Irene and Vernon Castle (dancers) debut on Broadway in *The Sunshine Girl.*

1914 Edgar Rice Burroughs: *Tarzan of the Apes*
Joseph Conrad: *Chance*
Joyce Kilmer: "Trees"

1915 Robert Frost: *A Boy's Will* (poems)
Theodore Dreiser: *The Titan*
Booth Tarkington: *Penrod*

1916 Carl Sandburg: *Chicago Poems*
John Dewey: *Democracy in Education*
Blasco Ibanez: *Four Horsemen of the Apocalypse*

1917 Sigmund Freud publishes *Introduction to Psychoanalysis*.
World Book Encyclopedia introduced.
Sarah Bernhardt (age 72) begins last U.S. tour.

1918 Willa Cather: *My Antonia*
Theater Guild of New York founded by Lawrence Langner.
Pulitzer Prize to Henry Adams for *The Education of Henry Adams*

1919 Hugh Lofting: *Dr. Doolittle*
Carl Sandburg wins the Nobel Prize for "Corn Huskers."
John Reed: *Ten Days That Shook the World*

Music

1910 The tango becomes a popular dance in the U.S.
Puccini: *Girl of the Golden West* (opera)
Stravinsky: *Firebird* (ballet)

1911 Irving Berlin: "Alexander's Ragtime Band" (pop)
Igor Stravinsky: *Petrouchka* (opera)
Richard Strauss: *Der Rosenkavalier*

1912 "Waiting for the Robert E. Lee" (pop)
"When the Midnight Train Leaves Alabama" (pop)
Rudolf Frimi: *The Firefly* (operetta)

1913 Foxtrot (dance) becomes popular.
Debussy: *Jeux* (ballet)
Victor Herbert: *Sweethearts* (operetta)

1914 Irving Berlin: "Watch Your Step, New York"
American Society of Composers and Publishers (ASCAP) founded.
Vaughan Williams: *A London Symphony*

1915 Classic New Orleans jazz is all the rage.
"Pack Up Your Troubles in Your Old Kit Bag" (pop)
"There's a Broken Heart for Every Light in Broadway" (pop)

1916 E. W. Korngold: *Violanta* (opera)
Jazz sweeps America.
Ethel Smythe: *The Boatswain's Mate* (opera)

1917 First jazz recording made by Dixieland Jazz Band.
Chicago becomes jazz center.
Sigmund Romberg: *Maytime* (opera)

1918 Igor Stravinsky: *Histoire du Soldat* (opera)
"Till We Meet Again" (pop)
"K-K-K-Katy" (pop)

1919 "Swanee" (pop)
"How Ya Gonna Keep 'Em Down on the Farm?" (pop)
Los Angeles Symphony Orchestra performs first concert.
Oskar Strauss: *Last Waltz* (operetta)

Visual Arts

1910 American film: *A Child of the Ghetto*
Henri Rousseau: "Le Douanier" (painting)

Frank Lloyd Wright becomes internationally known as an architect.

1911 Matisse: "Red Studio"
Film: *Anna Karenina* (Russian)
Renoir: *Gabrielle with a Rose*

1912 Picasso: *The Violin*
London has 400 cinemas.
Film: *Quo Vadis* (Italian)

1913 Armory Show introduces postimpressionism and cubism.
Film: *The Vampire* (American)
Stanley Spencer: *Self-Portrait*

1914 Henry Bacon designs Lincoln Memorial in Washington, D.C.
Film: *Making a Living* (American)
Braque: *Music*

1915 Film: *Birth of a Nation* (American)
Chagall: *The Birthday*
Film: *The Fire* (Italian)

1916 Dadaist cult develops in Switzerland.
Matisse: *The Three Sisters*
Frank Lloyd Wright designs the Imperial Hotel in Japan.

1917 Picasso designs surrealist sets and costumes for Satie's ballet *Parade*.
Modigliani: *Crouching Female Nude*
J. S. Sargent: *Portrait of John D. Rockefeller*

1918 Film: *A Dog's Life* (American)
Joan Miro first exhibits his works.
Klee: *Gartenplan* (abstract painting)

1919 Ernst Barlach: *Moses* (wooden sculpture)
Monet: *Nympheas*
Film: *J'Accuse* (French)

Sports

1910 Barney Oldfield drives his Benz at a speed of 133 mph at Daytona, Florida.
Jack Johnson, heavyweight champ, defeats Jim Jeffries.
Philadelphia (AL) defeats Chicago (NL), 4–1.

1911 Robert T. Jones wins first golf title at age 9.
Philadelphia (AL) defeats New York (NL), 4–2.

1912 Olympic Games held in Stockholm, Sweden; Jim Thorpe stars for U.S.
Fourth down added to football.
International Lawn Tennis Foundation formed.

1913 First U.S. shuffleboard game instituted (Daytona, Florida).
U.S. team wins Davis Cup.
Philadelphia (AL) defeats New York (NL), 4–1.

1914 Yale Bowl opens—seats 80,000.
Australia wins Davis Cup.
Walter Hagen wins U.S. Golf Association Open.

1915 W. G. Grace, England's greatest cricketer, dies.
Jess Willard wins heavyweight crown from Jack Johnson.
Automobile speed record set—102.6 mph.

1916 Professional Golf Association formed.
Women's International Bowling Congress formed.
Washington State University defeats Brown, 14–0, in first of continuous Rose Bowls.

1917   National Hockey League formed.

First baseball game played in New York Polo Grounds on Sunday. Chicago (AL) defeats New York (NL), 4–2.

1918   Knute Rockne named head football coach at Notre Dame.

Artificial ice first used in Toronto, Canada.

"Exterminator" wins Kentucky Derby.

1919   Black Sox scandal

Jack Dempsey becomes world heavyweight champion.

"Sir Barton" becomes first Triple Crown winner.

Everyday Life

1910   Boy Scouts, Girl Scouts, Camp Fire Girls, National 4-H, and NAACP founded.

Manhattan Bridge (New York) completed.

Father's Day first celebrated in Spokane, Washington.

1911   Gordon-Bennett International Aviation Cup given for the first time.

First flight from Munich to Berlin reaches record height of 12,800 feet.

House paint: $1.60 per gallon.

1912   Process to manufacture cellophane developed.

Macchu-Pichu rediscovered.

First successful parachute jump occurs.

F. W. Woolworth Company founded.

Linoleum: $2.00 per yard

1913   Zippers (in use since 1891) become popular.

Albert Schweitzer establishes hospital in French Congo.

Diagnosis of heart attacks is developed.

Mechanical refrigerators introduced.

New York's Grand Central Station terminal opens.

1914   Almost 10.5 million immigrants enter U.S. during ten-year period.

E. H. Shackleton leads Antarctic expedition.

E. C. Kendall (American) prepares pine thyroxin for treatment of thyroid deficiencies.

Double roll of wallpaper: 15 cents

1915   Henry Ford produces first farm tractor.

First transcontinental phone call made.

Rocky Mountain National Park established.

Motorized taxis appear.

President Wilson marries Mrs. Edith Galt.

Fur coat: $50.00

1916   Coco Chanel introduces women's sportswear.

National Park Service created under U.S. Department of the Interior.

Daylight Savings Time introduced in Great Britain.

Men's tailor-made suit: $15.00

1917   Literacy requirement for U.S. citizenship established.

IQ tests first used.

Bobbed hair styles for women become popular.

U.S. Senate rejects Suffrage Bill.

Converse introduces basketball shoes.

Buffalo Bill Cody dies.

1918   Influenza epidemic kills 548,000 in U.S.

First air mail delivery (Washington, D.C., to New York)

Pop-up toasters introduced.

Daylight Savings Time introduced in U.S.
Electric vacuum cleaner: $40.00
1919 Grand Canyon National Park established.
Zion National Park established.
American Legion formed.
RCA formed.
Shotgun: $10.00
Refrigerator: $900.00

New Nations, 1910–1919

Czechoslovakia (1918)
Finland (1919)
Mongolia (1911)
Poland (1918)
Saudi Arabia (1913)
Yemen (1918)
Yugoslavia (1918)

Sample Learning Activities

1914 Have two groups conduct a debate. One group argues against international involvement in the conflict; the other argues for the inevitability of the Great War.
1917 *The Bolsheviks seize power in Russia.*
Three panel discussions present their views: Bolsheviks, White Russians, and Liberal Democrats (Moderates). Other students judge and select the most convincing panel.

1920–1929: FLIVVERS, FLAPPERS, AND BIG SPENDERS

Overview

The decade of the 1920s was the Jazz Age, the age of the flappers, the era of revolution and reaction to the older generation's lifestyle and values. The era may have been best characterized by the lyrics of "Everybody's Doing It Now," a popular song of the decade. It was a period of escapism, an explosion of colors, sounds, rhythms, and dances. At no other time in our collective history had there been such a dramatic gap between generations of Americans. Socially explicit music and art and the general loosening of social values, reflected in plunging necklines and the shortest skirts in modern history, had worldwide repercussions.

It was a decade of heroes and antiheroes. Red Grange, Babe Ruth, Charles Lindbergh, Jack Dempsey, Rudolph Valentino, Amelia Earhart, and Al Capone became household names throughout the world. The world seemed to become smaller as the concept of internationalism took hold in virtually every field.

While Europe was in a tumult, attempting to cope with the consequences of

World War I, the United States was beginning to thrive. For most of the 1920s, the United States was led by President Calvin Coolidge, a Republican who believed in the importance of business to the nation's economy. Coolidge cut taxes for the wealthy in order to stimulate spending and business growth. This was especially important for Henry Ford, whose Model T, the top-selling car of the decade, made him a billionaire.

Henry Ford came to be a symbol of the prosperity of the 1920s. But just as this "freedom to spend" philosophy promoted economic growth and prosperity, so this same ideal may have led to the stock market crash of 1929, which was felt worldwide. Leading businesses vanished overnight, leading to the Great Depression of the 1930s.

Demographics: 1920–1929

Important Political Leaders

> U.S.—Warren G. Harding, Calvin Coolidge, and Herbert Hoover
> Great Britain—Stanley Baldwin and J. Ramsay MacDonald
> Italy—Benito Mussolini
> China—Chiang Kai-shek
> Japan—Emperor Hirohito
> Vatican City—Pope Pius XI
> USSR—Vladimir Lenin and Joseph Stalin
> France—Aristide Briand and Raymond Poincaré
> Germany—Paul von Hindenburg
> Spain—Primo de Rivera
> Turkey—Mustapha Kemal Ataturk
> Arabia—King Ibn Saud
> Czechoslovakia—Eduard Benes
> Mexico—Emilio Portes Gil
> Iraq—King Faisal I

Largest Cities

Ten Largest U.S. Cities		*Ten Largest Cities Outside the U.S.*	
1. New York	5,620,000	1. London	7,476,000
2. Chicago	2,702,000	2. Berlin	4,000,000
3. Philadelphia	1,824,000	3. Paris	2,863,000
4. Detroit	994,000	4. Tokyo	2,173,000
5. Cleveland	794,000	5. Vienna	1,842,000
6. St. Louis	773,000	6. Buenos Aires	1,637,000
7. Boston	748,000	7. Hankow	1,500,000
8. Baltimore	734,000	8. Osaka	1,500,000
9. Pittsburgh	588,000	9. Moscow	1,500,000
10. Los Angeles	577,000	10. Constantinople	1,400,000

U.S. population: 105.7 million
World population: 1.86 billion

Significant Headlines and News Stories
1920   American Civil Liberties Union founded.
Woodrow Wilson wins Nobel Peace Prize.

Russian–Polish war ends.
Mexico's president, Venustiano Carranza, assassinated.

1921 The Unknown Soldier buried in Arlington National Cemetery.
Vladimir Lenin introduces new economic policy for the USSR.
Japan's Prime Minister Takashi Hara assassinated.

1922 King Tutankhamen's tomb found and opened in Egypt.
Irish Republican Army (IRA) established.
Pope Benedict XV succeeded by Pope Pius XI.
Benito Mussolini seizes power in Italy ("March on Rome").

1923 The Ku Klux Klan begins a reign of terror in the U.S.
Canadian Railways created.
National Women's Party founded.
President Harding dies in office; succeeded by Vice-President Calvin Coolidge, who becomes the 30th U.S. president.

1924 Vladimir Lenin dies at age 54.
Textile Color Card Association of U.S.A. formed in an attempt to standardize system of color.
Ford manufactures its 10 millionth automobile.

1925 Al Capone takes over as underworld boss of Chicago.
Chrysler Motor Company formed.
Teacher John Scopes convicted for teaching Darwin's theory of evolution.
First national spelling bee held.

1926 The Byrd party makes first flight over the North Pole.
Japan plans to increase its military over next 15 years.
Joseph Stalin becomes dictator of the USSR.

1927 Mt. Rushmore completed.
Tokyo Chikatetsu subway opens.
Charles Lindbergh makes first nonstop flight across the Atlantic Ocean.
Holland Tunnel opens—first U.S. underwater vehicle tunnel.

1928 Amelia Earhart becomes first women to fly across Atlantic Ocean.
1,565 Americans die from drinking bad bootleg liquor.
Florida hurricane kills 1,836 people.

1929 The Byrd party flies over magnetic South Pole.
U.S. stock market crashes.
St. Valentine's Day Massacre in Chicago.

History and Politics

1920 19th Amendment (women's suffrage) passed by Congress.
League of Nations holds its first meeting.
British House of Lords divides Ireland into the Protestant North and Catholic South.

1921 Warren G. Harding inaugurated as 29th U.S. president.
U.S. Government Accounting Office (GAO) created by Congress.
Immigration Restriction Act passed.

1922 Benito Mussolini becomes first fascist dictator in Italy.
Lincoln Memorial completed.
Egypt becomes an independent state.
USSR formed.

1923 U.S. withdraws its last troops from Germany.
Adolf Hitler attempts to overthrow German government.
Lenin establishes first Soviet forced labor camps.

1924   Calvin Coolidge elected U.S. president.
        New quota laws further limiting immigration passed.
        J. Edgar Hoover appointed director of FBI.
        Adolf Hitler freed after months of imprisonment.
1925   Syria becomes an independent nation.
        Chiang Kai-shek becomes China's leader.
        President Coolidge runs with the slogan "Keep cool with Coolidge."
        Billy Mitchell trial is held.
1926   Congress establishes the Army Air Corps.
        Hirohito becomes emperor of Japan.
        Saudi Arabia created under King Abdul Ariziba Saud.
        Revenue Act passed (reducing personal income and inheritance
            tax).
1927   President Coolidge states, "I do not choose to run."
        The U.S. Supreme Court rules that illegal income is taxable.
        London breaks relations with Moscow following accusation of es-
            pionage —20 alleged British spies are executed.
1928   Herbert Clark Hoover elected 31st U.S. president.
        Kellogg-Briand Pact (denouncing war) signed by U.S. and 15 other
            nations.
        Stalin launches Five-Year Plan; Trotsky exiled.
        India demands dominion status.
1929   The Great Depression begins.
        Lateran Treaty establishes an independent Vatican City.
        Arab–Jewish riots at the Wailing Wall in Jerusalem.

Science and Technology

1920   Julius Grinkler develops treatment for epilepsy.
        E. V. McCollum finds possible cures for rickets and xerophthalmia.
        U.S. botanist Rudolph Boysen develops boysenberries.
        Trojan condoms invented.
1921   Swiss psychiatrist Herman Rorschach introduces ink blot tests.
        Nobel Prize awarded to Albert Einstein for his discovery of the
            photoelectric effect.
        First birth control clinics founded by Marie Slopes in London.
1922   First commercial insulin to treat diabetes introduced.
        Vitamin D isolated by Elmer McCollum.
        Vitamin E isolated from wheat germ.
1923   Diphtheria immunization introduced.
        Tetanus vaccination developed.
        Sodium amytal first used on humans.
        Schick razors, Maidenform bras, and Sanka coffee introduced.
1924   Willen Einthorea, Dutch scientist, wins Nobel Prize for the inven-
            tion of the electrocardiogram.
        First effective pesticides introduced.
        U.S. physician George Dick and his wife, Gladys, isolate the strep-
            tococcus that incites scarlet fever.
1925   Bell Laboratories is established by AT&T for research.
        Photographs first sent over telephone lines.
        U.S. physiologists Frederica and Holm find that rats do not see well
            when their diets lack vitamin A.
        Niagara Falls is, for the first time, illuminated at night by electric
            lights.

1926   U.S. biochemist James Bachelor Sumner proves that enzymes are proteins.

Thomas Hunt Morgan proves the transmission of heredity through genes.

First trans-Atlantic phone call made.

1927   First iron lung machine installed in New York City hospital.

German physiologists discover a sex hormone that will lead to early tests for pregnancy.

"Peking Man" found.

1928   Paul Dirac devises a theory of the electron.

Scottish bacteriologist Alexander Fleming discovers penicillin.

J. L. Baird demonstrates color television.

1929   First successful use of penicillin for skin infections.

Harvard physician Samuel Levine first notes link between hypertension and fatal heart attacks.

Graf Zeppelin makes an around-the-world flight.

Literature and Theater

1920   Sinclair Lewis: *Main Street*

Edith Wharton: *The Age of Innocence*

New York's Juilliard Foundation founded.

Globe Theater: *Scandals*

1921   Agatha Christie: *Mysterious Affair at Styles*

Globe Theater: *Ziegfeld Follies*

Prokofiev: *The Buffoon* (ballet)

Stravinsky: *The Sleeping Princess* (ballet)

1922   T. S. Eliot: *The Waste Land* (poem)

e. e. cummings: *The Enormous Room*

Willard: *The Cat and the Canary*

James Joyce: *Ulysses*

1923   Schlemmer: *Mechanical Ballet* (ballet)

Kahlil Gibran: *The Prophet*

Robert Frost: "Stopping by Woods on a Snowy Evening"

Edna St. Vincent Millay: *The Harp Weaver and Other Poems*

1924   Michael Arlen: *The Green Hat*

Lowell Thomas: *Lawrence of Arabia*

Sean O'Casey: *Juno and the Paycock*

Noel Coward: *The Vortex*

1925   F. Scott Fitzgerald: *The Great Gatsby*

Adolf Hitler: *Mein Kampf*

Theodore Dreiser: *An American Tragedy*

1926   Ernest Hemingway: *The Sun Also Rises*

A. A. Milne: *Winnie-the-Pooh*

Sinclair Lewis: *Arrowsmith*

Edna Ferber: *Show Boat* (book)

1927   Herman Hesse: *Steppenwolf*

Thornton Wilder: *The Bridge of San Luis Rey*

Oscar Hammerstein and Jerome Kern: *Show Boat* (Broadway musical)

1928   The *Oxford English Dictionary* appears in twelve volumes.

Stephen Vincent Benet: *John Brown's Body*

D. H. Lawrence's *Lady Chatterley's Lover* banned in London.

Sigmund Romberg: *New Moon*

George Gershwin: *An American in Paris*

1929   Erich Maria Remarque: *All Quiet on the Western Front*
        Ernest Hemingway: *A Farewell to Arms*
        William Faulkner: *The Sound and the Fury*

Music

1920   Popular songs: "I'll be with You in Apple Blossom Time,"
            "Whispering"
        Christmas radio concert from Königswusterhausen, Germany.
        Jerome Kern: *Sally*
1921   Rachmaninoff: *Concerto No. 3*
        Prokofiev: *The Love of Three Oranges* (opera)
        Irving Berlin: *Music Box Reviews*
1922   Austria's Salzburg Mozart Festival founded.
        Irving Berlin: "April Showers"
        Louis Armstrong joins "King Oliver's" band.
1923   Sibelius: *Symphony No. 6*
        Bela Bartók: *Dance Suite*
        George Gershwin: *Rhapsody in Blue*
        Pop songs: "Yes We Have No Bananas," "Barney Google"
1924   Rudolf Friml: "Rose Marie"
        Isham Jones: "It Had to Be You"
        Vincent Youmans: "Tea for Two"
        George Gershwin: *Lady Be Good*
1925   *No No Nanette* opens on Broadway
        Louis Armstrong forms the Hot Fives jazz band.
        Harry Akst: "Dinah"
        Jazz, Chicago style, arrives in Europe.
        First Guggenheim Fellowship awarded to Aaron Copland.
1926   Edward "Kid" Ory: "Muskrat Ramble"
        Ray Henderson: "Bye Bye Blackbird"
        Davis and Akst: "Baby Face"
        Sigmund Romberg: "The Desert Song"
1927   Milton Agar: "Ain't She Sweet"
        Walter Donaldson: "My Blue Heaven"
        Sunny Clapp: "Girl of My Dreams"
        George Gershwin: *Funny Face*
1928   Irving Berlin: "Puttin' on the Ritz"
        "Sonny Boy" sells 12 million copies for Al Jolson.
        Lawrence Welk forms his band in Yankton, South Dakota.
        Constant Lambert: "Rio Grande"
1929   Hoagy Carmichael: "Stardust"
        Guy Lombardo and his Royal Canadians play New Year's dance
            music for the next several decades.
        "Singin' in the Rain" and "Tiptoe through the Tulips" become pop-
            ular.
        Aaron Copland: *Symphonic Ode*

Visual Arts

1920   Charlie Chaplin stars in *The Kid.*
        Amedeo Modigliani: "Reclining Nude"
        Douglas Fairbanks and Mary Pickford, silent movie superstars,
            named America's favorites.

1921   Rudolph Valentino: *The Sheik*
Douglas Fairbanks: *The Mark of Zorro*
Eugene O'Neill: *Anna Christie* (theater)

1922   Films: *The Prisoner of Zenda, Blood and Sand, Orphans of the Storm*
Art: *Twittering Machine* (Klee); *Mother and Child* (Picasso)
Frank Lloyd Wright: Tokyo Imperial Hotel

1923   Films: *The Hunchback of Notre Dame, The Ten Commandments, Anna Christie*
Art: *Melancholy* (Picasso); *Freeing of the Peon* (Rivera)
Rin Tin Tin (German shepherd dog) becomes a movie star.

1924   Goldwyn and Mayer film studios emerge.
Films: *The Thief of Baghdad, Life of Abe Lincoln*

1925   Television developed in Europe.
Popular films: *The Freshman, The Gold Rush, The Big Parade*

1926   John Barrymore stars in *Don Juan.*
Fritz Lang: *Metropolis*
Harry Houdini dies.

1927   *The Jazz Singer:* First successful full-length talking movie
Oscars (Academy Awards) are created. First winners: Janet Gaynor, Emil Jannings, and the movie *Wings.*

1928   Walt Disney creates first animated cartoon, *Steamboat Willie.*
CBS founded.
WGY broadcasts first regularly scheduled TV program.

1929   *Broadway* (first film musical)
"Popeye" first appears.
Luis Buñuel and Salvador Dali film: *Un Chien Andalou.*
"Talkies" replace silent movies.

Sports

1920   27-year-old Bill Tilden becomes first American to win Wimbledon.
Eight Chicago White Sox players indicted for "fixing" 1919 World Series.
"Man O'War" retired to stud after winning 20 of 21 races.

1921   Babe Ruth hits 59 home runs.
Jack Dempsey wins world heavyweight boxing championship.
"Behave Yourself" wins the Kentucky Derby.

1922   Negro Baseball League formed.
American Johnny Weissmuller is the first person to swim 100 meters in less than a minute.
Bill Tilden wins third straight Wimbledon title.

1923   Yankee Stadium officially opened.
New York Yankees win their first World Series over the New York Giants, 4–2.
Jack Dempsey retains championship, beating Luis Angel Firpo.

1924   First Winter Olympic Games held in France.
Knute Rockne and the "Four Horsemen" give Notre Dame an undefeated season.
Joe Boyer wins the Indianapolis 500 with an average speed of 98.23 mph.

1925   Bill Tilden wins sixth straight Wimbledon title.
New York Giants professional football team founded.
Walter Hagen wins PGA title.

1926   Gertrude Ederle becomes first woman to swim the English Channel.

Miniature golf invented in Tennessee.

Gene Tunney becomes heavyweight boxing champion.

1927   Babe Ruth hits 60 home runs.

Harry Heilman of the Detroit Tigers bats .398.

New York Yankees beat Pittsburgh Pirates in World Series, 4–0.

1928   Ty Cobb retires from baseball with 4,191 hits and 892 stolen bases.

Johnny Weissmuller wins three gold medals in Olympic Games.

New York Rangers win the Stanley Cup.

Popularity of golf creates demand for nine-hole golf courses to be built.

1929   Notre Dame wins mythical National Championship with 9–0–0 record.

Philadelphia Athletics beat Chicago Cubs in World Series, 4–1.

"Clyde Van Deusen" wins Kentucky Derby.

Everyday Life

1920   Coco Chanel introduces jersey sweaters and pleated skirts.

Life Savers cost 5 cents a roll.

Loaf of bread costs 12 cents.

First air mail flight between New York City and San Francisco.

1921   Pork chops sell for 35 cents per pound.

Mounds chocolate bars, Wise potato chips, and Band-Aids appear.

First Miss America crowned: Margaret Gorman.

Emmett Kelly debuts as the clown Weary Willie in Ringling Brothers, Barnum and Bailey Circus.

1922   Magazines: *Reader's Digest, True Confessions, Better Homes and Gardens*

Kansas City County Club Plaza shopping center is built—the world's first shopping zone outside a town or city center.

Eastern Europe folk embroideries inspire the "peasant" look in Western fashion.

First radio commercial aired.

New York state appellate court rules that the station wagon is a car, not a truck.

1923   Bobbed hair becomes all the rage.

Air mail postage is 8 cents.

A Packard car sells for $2,485, a Rolls Royce for $10,900.

Time magazine first published.

Dance marathons become popular.

1924   Kleenex, electromagnetic incandescent lights, and loudspeakers invented.

Wheaties breakfast cereal introduced.

Average income: $2,196 annually

Only 30 percent of all bread is baked in U.S. homes, down 40 percent from 1910.

New house costs $7,720.

1925   *The New Yorker* is first published.

The Charleston becomes the new dance craze.

First motel opens in San Luis Obispo, California.

Cigarette advertisements feature women smoking for the first time.

Synthetic rubber and Scotch tape introduced.

1926 Safety-glass windshields are installed on Stutz motorcars.

Jean Lanvin opens first boutique for men.

Eton crop haircut replaces bobbed hair.

Italian hairdresser Antonio Buzzacchino invents the permanent wave.

More masculine elements enter feminine clothing.

1927 Average teacher salary: $1,277 annually.

Patent leather shoes introduced.

Cyclone roller coaster introduced at Coney Island.

The foxtrot becomes a popular dance.

First electric jukeboxes introduced.

1928 DeSoto automobile introduced by Chrysler.

Bubble gum, Rice Krispies, and Peter Pan peanut butter introduced.

Hat brims return to fashion.

Hemlines shortest on record.

10 pounds of potatoes sell for 27 cents.

1929 Seven-Up soft drink introduced.

Yo-yo introduced to America.

Average weekly wage: $28.

Hemlines become longer again as fashion leans toward a "more feminine" look.

Business Week begins publication.

New Nations, 1920–1929

Dominican Republic (1924)
Eire (Ireland) (1922)
Lebanon (1920)
Turkey (1923)

Sample Learning Activities

1920 *American women, granted the right to vote by the 19th Amendment, participate in their first national election.*

Four different student groups are formed, with each group presenting speeches as they perceive Carrie Chapman Catt, Susan B. Anthony, Elizabeth Cady Stanton, and Amelia Earhart would have presented them. These speeches must contain references (based on thorough research) to suffrage, temperance, Prohibition, and women's rights.

1927 *Lindbergh's Solo Flight across the Atlantic*

A comparison with modern space travel is made. *The Spirit of St. Louis, Sputnik, Apollo 13,* and *Columbia* missions are charted, with illustrations by four different groups for group presentation to the class.

1930–1939: LEAVING "HOOVERVILLE" ON THE ROOSEVELT ROAD

Overview

In many ways the 1930s were not a pleasant time in which to live. The Great Depression, the rise of fascism, natural disasters like the great midwestern dust storms, and a rise in criminal activities marked the decade. The United States (like much of the world) had enjoyed the prosperity of the 1920s, but the 1930s saw the national economic ship sinking and some 4 million previously productive Americans unemployed, with many standing in free soup lines. The American humorist Will Rogers noted, "we will be the first nation to go to the poor house in an automobile." It was indeed the grimmest of times for many.

Equally troublesome was the rise of fascism in Europe and on this continent. Rumors of German Jews being arrested and deprived of their civil rights led to a rise of anti-Semitic attitudes and actions in this country as well. The Ku Klux Klan was at its zenith, and terrible hate crimes were being perpetrated.

No matter what President Hoover (elected in 1928) did, it seemed to backfire, and the United States sank deeper into an economic depression that was now becoming worldwide in its scope and impact. The ramifications of the Great Depression touched directly or indirectly every human being on the planet, and every nation looked to a Messiah for salvation. In Germany they looked to Adolf Hitler, in Italy to Benito Mussolini, and in the United States to Franklin Delano Roosevelt. It was Roosevelt's plan, his vision, and his actions that provided hope and encouragement for the 13 million who had lost hope. The New Deal, with its "three R's," Relief, Recovery, and Reform, brought about the most sweeping changes ever seen in our history. Agencies and acts like the Civilian Conservation Corps, the Social Security Act, the National Recovery Act, the National Industrial Recovery Act, and the Public Works Administration provided relief and jobs for millions of Americans. Most of all, Roosevelt's "fireside chats," addressed to millions of Americans glued to their radios, gave us confidence in him and his plan. In those dark days, he was a tower of strength and a beacon of light.

Abroad, Hitler, Mussolini, and others used the Depression to rally their people around ideologies of hate and anti-Semitism and to forge the weapons of a second world war that would kill millions and destroy entire nations. World War II, which began in 1939 and lasted until 1945, was one of the great watersheds of history. Because of it, our world would never again be the same.

Demographics: 1930–1939

Important Political Leaders

> U.S.—Franklin D. Roosevelt
> Great Britain—J. Ramsay MacDonald and Neville Chamberlain
> Italy—Benito Mussolini
> China—Chiang Kai-shek
> USSR—Joseph Stalin
> Germany—Adolf Hitler
> Egypt—King Faud I
> France—Edouard Daladier
> Japan—Emperor Hirohito
> Ethiopia—Haile Selassie

Spain—Francisco Franco
Austria—Kurt Schuschnigg
Mexico—Lazaro Cardenas
Iraq—King Faisal

Largest Cities

Ten Largest U.S. Cities		Ten Largest Cities Outside the U.S.	
1. New York	6,930,446	1. London	7,742,000
2. Chicago	3,376,438	2. Berlin	4,013,000
3. Philadelphia	1,951,961	3. Paris	2,880,000
4. Detroit	1,569,662	4. Osaka	2,333,000
5. Los Angeles	1,238,048	5. Tokyo	2,218,000
6. Cleveland	900,429	6. Moscow	2,026,000
7. St. Louis	822,960	7. Buenos Aires	2,022,000
8. Baltimore	804,874	8. Rio de Janeiro	2,004,000
9. Boston	781,888	9. Vienna	2,000,000
10. Pittsburgh	669,817	10. Hankow	1,900,000

U.S. population: 123,188,000
World population: 1.95 billion

Significant Headlines and News Stories

1930   Name of Constantinople changed to Istanbul.
Nazis gain 107 seats in German elections.
Congress creates Veterans' Administration and Federal Bureau of Narcotics.

1931   Nobel Peace Prize: Jane Addams (U.S.) and Nicholas Murray Butler (U.S.)
Al Capone jailed for tax evasion.
Great Britain abandons the gold standard.

1932   German election results: Hindenburg 18 million, Hitler 11 million, Communists 5 million.
13.7 million people unemployed in U.S.
Amelia Earhart becomes first woman to fly solo across the Atlantic.

1933   Nazis erect first concentration camps.
U.S. goes off gold standard.
Francis Perkins, Secretary of Labor, becomes first female cabinet member.
Tennessee Valley Authority (TVA) established.

1934   Hitler and Mussolini meet in Venice.
FBI shoots and kills John Dillinger, "Public Enemy #1."
S.S. Normandie (France) launched: largest ship afloat.

1935   Persia changes name to Iran.
Senator Huey Long assassinated in New Orleans.
Congress of Industrial Organizations (CIO) founded by John L. Lewis.

1936   Bruno Hauptmann convicted of kidnapping Lindbergh baby.
Franklin D. Roosevelt reelected in a landslide.
Floods sweep Johnstown, Pennsylvania.

1937   Amelia Earhart lost in Pacific.
Duke of Windsor gives up British throne and marries a divorcee, Mrs. Wallis Simpson.
Wall Street decline signals serious recession.

1938   Supreme Court rules University of Missouri Law School must admit blacks.

40-hour work week established in the U.S.

20,000 TV sets are in service in New York City.

1939   World War II begins as Germany invades Poland.

Women and children evacuated from London.

Hungary quits League of Nations.

History and Politics

1930   W. H. Taft, former president and Supreme Court Justice, dies.

Charles Evans Hughes appointed Chief Justice of Supreme Court.

White Paper on Palestine halts immigration.

1931   U.S. Senate passes Veterans' Compensation Bill over Hoover's veto.

Hattie T. Caraway (Democrat, Arkansas) is first woman elected to U.S. Senate.

Banguella to Katanga, first trans-African railroad line completed.

1932   Franklin Delano Roosevelt becomes U.S. president.

17,000 World War I veterans arrive in Washington, D.C., demanding cashing of bonus certificates—troops led by General Douglas MacArthur drive them away.

"New Deal" becomes part of the American lexicon.

1933   20th Amendment (change of inauguration date) passed.

Adolf Hitler appointed German chancellor.

21st Amendment (repeal of Prohibition) passed.

Boycott of Jews begins in Germany.

1934   USSR admitted to League of Nations.

Japan renounces Washington Treaties of 1922 and 1930.

Stalin purges Communist party.

1935   Chiang Kai-shek named president of China.

Roosevelt signs Social Security Act.

Wealth Tax Act passed.

1936   Spanish Civil War begins.

Rome–Berlin Axis created.

Chiang Kai-shek declares war on Japan.

Trotsky exiled from the USSR.

1937   U.S. Supreme Court rules in favor of minimum wage law.

Italy withdraws from League of Nations.

Royal Commissioner of Palestine recommends the establishment of both an Arab and a Jewish state in Palestine.

Roosevelt signs Neutrality Act.

1938   Anti-Jewish legislation enacted in Italy.

Roosevelt recalls U.S. ambassador from Germany.

Stanley Reed appointed to U.S. Supreme Court.

1939   Italy invades Albania.

FDR asks Congress for $552 million for defense.

Britain and France recognize Franco's government in Spain.

Science and Technology

1930   U.S. physicist Ernest O. Lawrence develops cyclotron and artificially splits the atom.

Planet Pluto discovered by C. W. Tombaugh.

Max Theiler (South Africa) develops yellow fever vaccine.

Using X-ray, P. J. W. Debye investigates molecular structures.

1931   Thomas Alva Edison dies.

Vitamin A isolated.

Nobelist Otto Warburg (German) for research on enzymes.

George Washington Bridge completed.

1932   Balloon tire produced for farm tractors.

Richard Kuhn investigates riboflavin.

Vitamin D discovered.

1933   Anderson and Millikan discover positrons.

Philo Farnsworth develops electronic TV.

Tadeusz Reichstein synthesizes vitamin C.

Vitamin B is recognized.

Nobel Prize to Thomas Morgan for work on heredity and chromosomes.

1934   Marie Curie dies.

Nobel Prizes to Minot, Murphy, and Whipple for their work on
liver therapy to overcome anemia.

Nobel Prize to Harold Urey (U.S.) for work on heavy hydrogen.

Refrigeration for meat cargoes devised.

1935   Radar equipment built by Robert Watson Watt.

Oil pipelines between Iraq, Haifa, and Tripolis opened.

Prontosic, a sulfa drug to treat streptococcal infections, developed
by German chemist Gerhard Domagk.

1936   Ivan Pavlov, Russian physiologist, dies.

Boulder (Hoover) Dam completed.

Dr. Alexis Carrel develops artificial heart.

Dirigible *Hindenburg* makes trans-Atlantic flight.

1937   Insulin used to control diabetes.

First jet engine built by Frank Whittle.

Bonneville Dam dedicated.

Nylon patented by DuPont.

1938   Barium isotopes first obtained from uranium.

Paul Muller synthesizes DDT.

Sigmund Freud dies.

Igor Sikorsky constructs first helicopter.

Philip Levine and Rufus Stetson (U.S.) discover Rh factor in human
blood.

Isolation of Pyridoxine (Vitamin B_6).

1939   Hans Haas develops underwater photography.

Grand Coulee Dam becomes operational.

Dacron invented by Whinfield and Dickson.

Literature and Theater

1930   W. Somerset Maugham: *Cakes and Ale*

Boston bans all works by Leon Trotsky.

Maxwell Anderson: *Elizabeth the Queen*

Nobel Prize to Sinclair Lewis for *Babbitt*

1931   Pearl Buck: *The Good Earth*

Melvin Dewey creates decimal system for book classification.

Eugene O'Neill: *Mourning Becomes Electra*

1932   Erskine Caldwell: *Tobacco Road*

Dashiell Hammett: *The Thin Man*

Gerhart Hauptmann: *Before Sunset*

1933   Pulitzer Prize to *Men in White* by Sidney Kingsley.
       All books by Jewish and non-Nazi authors burned in Germany.
       Collette: *La Chatte*
1934   Agatha Christie: *Murder in Three Acts*
       Sinclair Lewis: *Work of Art*
       James Hilton: *Good-bye, Mr. Chips*
1935   Pulitzer Prize to *The Old Maid* by Zoe Akins.
       John Steinbeck: *Tortilla Flat*
       T. S. Eliot: *Murder in the Cathedral*
       Walter de la Mare: *Poems 1919*
1936   Dale Carnegie: *How to Win Friends and Influence People*
       Pulitzer Prize to *Gone with the Wind* by Margaret Mitchell.
       Pulitzer Prize to *Idiot's Delight* by Robert Sherwood.
1937   John Dos Passos: *USA*
       Ernest Hemingway: *To Have and Have Not*
       Kenneth Roberts: *Northwest Passage*
1938   Daphne du Maurier: *Rebecca*
       Pulitzer Prize for drama to Robert Sherwood's *Abe Lincoln in Illinois*
       Orson Welles radio broadcast: *War of the Worlds*
       Robinson Jeffers: *Selected Poetry*
1939   Richard Llewellyn: *How Green Was My Valley*
       Jan Struther: *Mrs. Miniver*
       George S. Kaufman and Moss Hart: *The Man Who Came to Dinner*

Music

1930   Bela Bartók: *Cantata Profana*
       Popular songs: "Georgia on My Mind," "I Got Rhythm," "Three
           Little Words," "Body and Soul"
       Igor Stravinsky: *Symphony of the Psalms*
1931   Popular songs: "Minnie the Moocher," "Mood Indigo," " Good Night
           Sweetheart," "When the Moon Comes Over the Mountain"
       Pulitzer Prize to *Of Thee I Sing* by George Gershwin and George S.
           Kaufman.
       Anna Pavlova, Russian ballerina, dies.
1932   John Philip Sousa dies.
       Cole Porter musical *The Gay Divorcee* opens.
       Popular songs: "Brother, Can You Spare a Dime," "Night and Day,"
           "April in Paris," "Let's Have Another Cup of Coffee"
1933   School of American Ballet founded.
       Aaron Copland: *Short Symphony*
       Jerome Kern: *Roberta*
       Popular songs: "Smoke Gets in Your Eyes," "Easter Parade,"
           "Who's Afraid of the Big Bad Wolf?"
1934   Noel Coward operetta: *Conversation Piece*
       Cole Porter: *Anything Goes*
       Popular songs: "Blue Moon," "The Continental"
1935   Electric Hammond organs become popular.
       Jazz becomes "swing."
       George Gershwin's opera: *Porgy and Bess*
       Popular songs: "Begin the Beguine," "I Got Plenty of Nothing,"
           "Just One of Those Things"
1936   Popular songs: "Pennies from Heaven," "Whiffenpoof Song," "I'm
           an Old Cow Hand"

Rodgers and Hart: *On Your Toes*
Richard Strauss opera: *Die Schweigsame Frau*
1937   *I'd Rather Be Right* opens on Broadway.
George Gershwin dies.
Rodgers and Hart: *Babes in Arms*
Popular songs: "The Lady Is a Tramp," "Whistle While You Work,"
    "Harbor Lights," "I've Got My Love to Keep Me Warm"
1938   Benny Goodman Band brings new style to jazz.
Harvard grants honorary doctorate to African American diva Marion Anderson.
Popular songs: "September Song," "A Tisket, a Tasket," "Jeepers
    Creepers," "Falling in Love with Love"
1939   Rodgers and Hart: *The Boys from Syracuse*
Aaron Copland: *Billy the Kid* (ballet)
Cole Porter: *Dubarry was a Lady*
Popular songs: "God Bless America," "Over the Rainbow," "Beer
    Barrel Polka," "I'll Never Smile Again"

Visual Arts
1930   Films: *Blue Angel, All Quiet on the Western Front, Murder, Anna Christie*
Grant Wood: *American Gothic*
George Grosz: *Cold Buffet*
Henri Matisse: *Tiare*
1931   Dali: *Persistence of Memory*
Empire State Building completed.
First color film: Disney's *Flowers and Trees*
Films: *Frankenstein, City Lights, The Front Page*
1932   Burra: *The Cafe* (expressionism)
Edwin Lutyens designs Metropolitan Cathedral in Liverpool.
Academy Award winner: *Grand Hotel*
Shirley Temple appears in her first film.
1933   *Cavalcade* wins Academy Award.
Giacometti: *The Palace at 4 A.M.* (sculpture)
Films: *King Kong, Dr. Jekyll and Mr. Hyde, Dinner at Eight, Little Women*
Matisse: *The Dance*
1934   Dali: *William Tell* (surrealism)
John Piper: *Rye Harbor*
Academy Award winner: *It Happened One Night*
Films: *Lost Patrol, The Thin Man, Of Human Bondage, Design for Living*
1935   Academy Award: *Mutiny on the Bounty*
Stanley Spencer: *Workman in the House*
Films: *Anna Karenina, Becky Sharp, Pasteur*
1936   Laura Knight: *Ballet*
Nazi exhibition of "Degenerate Art" shown.
Academy Award: *The Great Ziegfeld*
Mondrian: "Composition in Red and Blue"
1937   Paul Mellon endows National Gallery in Washington, D.C.
Klee: *Revolution of the Viaducts*
Academy Award: *Life of Emile Zola*
Braque: *Woman with a Mandolin*
1938   Frank Lloyd Wright builds Taliesin West in Phoenix, Arizona.

Gropius and Breuer design Haggarty House in Cohasset, Massachusetts.

Academy Award: *You Can't Take It with You*

The Cloisters added to the Metropolitan Museum.

1939 "Grandma Moses" (Anna M. Roberson) becomes famous U.S. painter.

Kandinsky: *Neighborhood*

Academy Award: *Gone with the Wind*

Jacob Epstein: *Adam* (sculpture)

Sports

1930 "Gallant Fox" wins Triple Crown.

Viktor Barna wins world table tennis championship.

Max Schmeling (German) becomes world heavyweight boxing champion.

1931 Alabama defeats Washington State in Rose Bowl, 24–0.

Mrs. Helen Wills Moody wins U.S. Lawn Tennis championship.

St. Louis (NL) wins World Series, beats Philadelphia (AL) 4–3.

1932 Olympic Games held in Los Angeles, California; winter games in Lake Placid, New York.

Thomas Hampson (England) establishes world record in 800-meter run.

Babe Ruth "calls" his shot in World Series game against Chicago Cubs.

1933 First baseball All-Star game—Comiskey Park, Chicago.

Primo Canera (Italy) wins heavyweight crown.

Fred Perry (England) wins U.S. Lawn Tennis Association championship.

1934 Max Baer wins world heavyweight championship.

Chicago Blackhawks win Stanley Cup.

National Football League established.

1935 "Omaha" wins Triple Crown.

Detroit (AL) beats Chicago (NL) in World Series, 4–2.

James J. Braddock wins world heavyweight title.

1936 Summer Olympic Games held in Berlin—Jesse Owens wins four gold medals.

Baseball Hall of Fame founded in Cooperstown, New York.

Stanford beats Southern Methodist in Rose Bowl, 7–0.

1937 U.S. wins Davis Cup.

Joe Louis wins heavyweight boxing title.

"War Admiral" wins Triple Crown.

1938 Don Budge (U.S.) wins tennis "Grand Slam."

U.S. successfully defends Davis Cup against Great Britain.

Alice Marble wins U.S. Lawn Tennis Association Championship.

1939 Malcolm Campbell establishes water speed record of 368.85 mph.

First baseball game televised.

Everyday Life

1930 Contract bridge is popular card game.

Comic strips grow in popularity.

Photo flash bulb comes into use.

Plexiglas introduced.

1931   Spicer-Dufay process of natural color photography.
Knute Rockne of Notre Dame dies in plane crash.
"Star-Spangled Banner" becomes national anthem.
Growth hormone used clinically for first time.
Milk is 14 cents a quart.

1932   Basic English proposed as international language.
Lindbergh baby is kidnapped.
Imperial Airways serves 22 countries.
Coffee is 39 cents a pound.

1933   First U.S. aircraft carrier *Ranger* is launched.
Approximately 60,000 authors, actors, painters, and musicians emigrate from Germany.
Heywood Broun founds American Newspaper Guild.
Robert Byrd begins second exploration of South Pole.
"Monopoly" game becomes popular.

1934   W. Beebe descends 3,028 feet into the ocean off Bermuda.
Sodium pentothal becomes widely used.
Dionne quintuplets born in Callendar, Québec.
SS Queen Mary launched.
Bread is 1 cent a loaf.

1935   Blood tests will be used in court cases.
SS Normandie crosses Atlantic in 107 hours and 33 minutes.
Alcoholics Anonymous organized in New York City.
Rhumba becomes a fashionable dance.
Beer in cans introduced.

1936   Ford Foundation established.
BBC London inaugurates TV service.
Henry Luce publishes *Life* magazine.
Tampax introduced.

1937   Lincoln Tunnel between New York and New Jersey opened.
Dirigible *Von Hindenburg* crashes at Lakehurst, New Jersey.
Golden Gate Bridge opens.
National Cancer Institute founded.

1938   Teflon coating introduced.
Lambeth walk becomes fashionable dance.
Ballpoint pens come into use.
32,000 people have died in auto accidents during the past five years.
Blood tests required before marriage.
Average salary: $1,368 annually.

1939   Pan-American Airways begins regularly scheduled flights between U.S. and Europe on *Dixie Clipper.*
First baseball game televised.
Nylon stockings first appear.
Swallowing goldfish popular stunt on college campuses.
Round steak 39 cents a pound.

New Nations, 1930–1939

Canada (1931)
Iraq (1932)

Sample Learning Activities

1932   *New Deal begins.*
Students find a New Deal or other Depression era photograph, slogan, or illustration and share it with the class. A short essay or other explanation of the relevance of their choice must also be provided.

1939   *World War II begins in Europe.*
Three groups will be formed, and students must write and direct a play that reflects the "what if's . . ." of World War II. They must select from a teacher-made list such as the following:
. . . Japan attacks the West Coast?
. . . Hitler conquers Europe and Britain capitulates?
. . . The United States decides not to become involved in the European war?
. . . The Germans develop atomic weapons before the United States does?

1940–1949: DECADE OF DESTINY

Overview

The decade of the 1940s dawned on a world in turmoil. Hitler's army had already taken Austria and Poland and was poised to continue its conquest of Europe. In the Pacific, Japan had taken control of Manchuria, Korea, Formosa (now Taiwan), and many ports in eastern China. As European Jews fled the terror of Hitler's "final solution," the United States remained resolutely neutral.

But the decade of the 1940s would end forever the isolationism that had gripped the United States since the end of World War I. Advancing technology would shrink the planet. Many of the world's major cities—Shanghai, London, Warsaw, Berlin, Tokyo—would suffer the devastation of war, only to rise from the ashes. National boundaries around the world would be redrawn, erased, then redrawn again. The world would enter the nuclear age, with all of its promise and peril.

Global events would touch everyday life as well. Scrambling to mobilize military might, Americans would flock to urban areas where factories geared up to produce essential commodities for the war effort. Caught in the wartime housing crunch, war workers would make their homes in anything from a chicken coop to a "hot bed." As military and defense industries depleted the available labor force, new personnel would be needed. Women would enter the workplace in unprecedented numbers. American culture would never be the same.

The world leaders of this decade of destiny read like a "Who's Who" of history. Winston Churchill succeeded Neville Chamberlain as Great Britain's prime minister in 1940. That same year, Franklin Delano Roosevelt was reelected for an unprecedented third—and later for a fourth—term as president of the United States. Joseph Stalin, Communist leader in the USSR, signed secret pacts with the Nazis, then later, under German attack, joined forces with the Allies. Italy, under Benito Mussolini, and Spain, under Francisco Franco, bid for international power. Japan's Emperor Hirohito, at the urging of military opportunist Hedeki Tojo, strove to expand his empire throughout the Pacific. Charles de Gaulle, Dwight D. Eisenhower, Douglas MacArthur, Chiang Kai-shek, Nehru, Gandhi, Mao Tse-tung, and Ho Chi Minh all emerged or departed from the world stage during this era.

During the 1940s, the world witnessed a holocaust of monumental proportions as Hitler systematically ostracized, persecuted, and finally annihilated Europe's Jewish population. Scientists unlocked the key to the atom, producing the most devastating weapon in history. We ended a "hot" war, only to start a Cold War that would continue for another forty years. For the second time in the century, the world would establish a forum to arbitrate world conflicts.

At decade's end, the world map had added the independent nations of India and Israel; divided the nations of Germany, Korea, and China; and witnessed the partitioning of Europe into Western and Communist blocs. Churchill had coined the term *Iron Curtain.* Membership in the United Nations, the North Atlantic Treaty Organization (NATO), and the Organization of American States (OAS) maintained the United States' interest in world affairs. An executive order banned segregation in the military, and a court ruling struck down restrictive real estate covenants designed to discriminate against minority buyers.

During this dramatic decade, the world learned two important lessons. First, it is a very large place that can divide families and isolate neighbors. Second, it is also a very small place, where the actions of any one person or group can have a profound effect on everyone.

Demographics: 1940–1949

Important Political Leaders

> U.S.—Franklin Delano Roosevelt and Harry S. Truman
> China—Chiang Kai-shek and Mao Tse-tung
> Great Britain—Winston Churchill and Clement Atlee
> Germany—Adolf Hitler and Konrad Adenauer
> Egypt—King Farouk
> Italy—Benito Mussolini and Alcidede Gasperi
> Japan—Emperor Hirohito
> France—Charles De Gaulle and Vincent Auriol
> Spain—Francisco Franco
> Israel—Chaim Weizmann
> USSR—Joseph Stalin and Georgi Malenkov
> Argentina—Juan Peron
> Netherlands—Queen Wilhelmina and Queen Juliana
> Czechoslovakia—Klement Gottwald

Largest Cities

Ten Largest U.S. Cities		*Ten Largest Cities Outside the U.S.*	
1. New York	7,454,995	1. London	8,655,000
2. Chicago	3,396,808	2. Bucharest	6,943,293
3. Philadelphia	1,931,334	3. Tokyo	6,457,600
4. Detroit	1,623,452	4. Paris	4,993,855
5. Los Angeles	1,504,277	5. Berlin	4,242,501
6. Cleveland	878,336	6. Moscow	4,137,013
7. Baltimore	859,100	7. Shanghai	3,890,998

8. St. Louis	816,048	8. Osaka	3,221,200
9. Boston	770,816	9. Leningrad	3,191,404
10. Washington, D.C.	663,091	10. Buenos Aires	2,900,000

U.S. population: 131,669,275
World population: 2.1 billion (est.)

Significant Headlines and News Stories

1940   Paris falls to Nazi forces.
Trotsky assassinated in Mexico by Soviet agents.
"Galloping Gertie," suspension bridge over the narrows of Puget Sound, Washington, drops 200 feet into the Sound.

1941   Japanese forces attack U.S. forces in Pearl Harbor, Hawaii.
U.S. citizens of Japanese descent interned on the west coast.
U.S. savings bonds and stamps go on sale.

1942   Japanese forces capture Manila.
Gandhi demands independence for India.
U.S. naval forces defeat Japan in battles of Coral Sea and Midway.

1943   First "Liberty Ships" launched.
Pay-as-you-go tax system instituted.
Shoe and meat rationing begins in the U.S.

1944   The Battle of the Bulge.
Cost of living rises 30% in the U.S.
U.S. forces capture Guam.

1945   Germany surrenders, ending war in the European theater.
Black markets develop throughout Europe.
Atomic bombs are dropped on two Japanese cities (Hiroshima and Nagasaki), forcing Japan to surrender—ends World War II.

1946   New London air terminal opens.
Power in Japan transferred to an elected assembly.
21 nations attend peace conference in Paris.

1947   Peace treaty signed in Paris.
More than one million veterans enroll in U.S. colleges.
Taft-Hartley Act passed.

1948   Soviets blockade Berlin—U.S. airlift begins.
Gandhi assassinated.
First World Health Assembly meets.

1949   Berlin blockade officially lifted.
Dean Acheson appointed U.S. Secretary of State.
U.S. Foreign Assistance Bill grants $5.43 billion to Europe.

History and Politics

1940   Franklin D. Roosevelt elected for a third term.
John L. Lewis, head of the CIO, resigns as its leader.
U.S. gross national product up 10% from 1939.

1941   Germany and Italy declare war on the U.S.
U.S. Office of Price Administration (OPA) established.
U.S. Supreme Court upholds federal wage and hour law restricting 16- to 18-year-olds and setting minimum wage.

1942   Bataan "Death March"
The 26 Allies pledge that none of them will make a separate peace with Axis powers.
U.S. troops land in North Africa.

1943   President Roosevelt meets with Stalin and Churchill at Tehran.
Casablanca Conference takes place.
Italy declares war on Germany.

1944   Franklin D. Roosevelt wins fourth term.
D-Day: Invasion of Europe
Marshal Petain captured and imprisoned in France.

1945   President Roosevelt dies and is succeeded by vice-president Harry S. Truman, who becomes the 33rd U.S. president.
Axis powers surrender, ending World War II.
Allies divide Germany into four zones.

1946   First meeting of United Nations General Assembly in London.
President Truman creates Atomic Energy Commission.
Nuremberg Trials convict Nazi war criminals.
Albania, Hungary, Transjordan, and Bulgaria become independent states.

1947   Jawaharlal Nehru becomes first prime minister of newly independent India.
Marshall Plan for European recovery announced.
India and Burma become independent states.

1948   Harry Truman elected president.
State of Israel created.
Communist coup d'état in Czechoslovakia.

1949   NATO founded.
Bonn named capital of West Germany.
Republic of Eire proclaimed.
Chinese Communists take control of mainland.

Science and Technology

1940   Neptunium discovered by McMillan and Abelson.
Electron microscope developed by RCA.
Penicillin becomes a practical and widely used antibiotic.
Leprosy vaccine developed.
Plutonium discovered by McMillan and Seaborg (U.S.).

1941   Portable military bridges created.
Sulfathiazine used to combat many infections.

1942   Fermi splits the atom.
First automatic computer developed.
First magnetic recording tape.
First turbopropane engine.
Dexedrine produced.

1943   Waksman and Schatz discover streptomycin.
Vitamin K isolated by Henrik Dam and E. A. Doisy.
Polio epidemic strikes U.S.—prompts more research.

1944   DNA isolated.
Uranium reserves built up in U.S.
First cyclotron completed.
Quinine synthesized.
First eye bank established.

1945   Kajos Janossy explores cosmic radiation.
First atomic bombs detonated in New Mexico.
Vitamin A synthesized.
Water fluoridation begins.

1946   Appleton discovers sunspots that emit radio waves.
        Isotope carbon-13 discovered.
        Streptomycin used to fight tuberculosis.
1947   Polio virus isolated.
        First supersonic flight.
        Bell laboratories perfect the transistor.
        Mumps vaccine developed.
1948   Field of chemogenetics established by Charlotte Auerbach.
        Antibiotics aureomycin and chloromycetin developed.
        Mt. Palomar telescope dedicated.
        Long-playing records developed.
1949   Cortisone developed by Hench.
        Neomycin isolated.
        U.S. launches first guided missile.

Music

1940   Stravinsky: *Symphony in C*
        Irving Berlin: *Louisiana Purchase*
        Duke Ellington establishes himself as a jazz pianist and composer.
1941   Roy Harris: *Folk Song Symphony*
        Popular songs: "Chattanooga Choo Choo," "Deep in the Heart of Texas," "I Got It Bad and That Ain't Good"
        Shostakovich: *Symphony No. 7*
1942   Aaron Copland: *Rodeo*
        Richard Strauss: *Capriccio*
        Irving Berlin: *White Christmas*
1943   Aaron Copland: *A Lincoln Portrait* and *Piano Sonata*
        Rodgers and Hammerstein: *Oklahoma*
        Popular songs: "Comin' in on a Wing and a Prayer," "Mairzy Doats"
1944   Aaron Copland: *Appalachian Spring*
        Leonard Bernstein: *On the Town*
        Oxford University establishes a faculty of music.
1945   Benjamin Britten: *Peter Grimes*
        Rodgers and Hammerstein: *Carousel*
1946   Irving Berlin: *Annie Get Your Gun*
        Lerner and Lowe: *Brigadoon*
        Popular songs: "Tenderly," "Zip-a-dee-doo-dah," "Come Rain or Come Shine"
1947   Maria Callas debuts in Verona, Italy.
        John Powell: *Symphony in A*
        Popular songs: "Papa, Won't You Dance with Me," "Almost Like Being in Love"
1948   Cole Porter: *Kiss Me Kate*
        Howard Hanson: *Piano Concerto No. 1*
        Popular songs: "Nature Boy," "Buttons and Bows," "All I Want for Christmas Is My Two Front Teeth"
1949   Arthur Bliss: *The Olympians*
        Leonard Bernstein: *The Age of Anxiety*
        Bela Bartók: *Viola Concerto*
        Popular songs: "So in Love," "Rudolph, the Red Nosed Reindeer," "Riders in the Sky"

Literature and Theater

1940 Ernest Hemingway: *For Whom the Bell Tolls*
Richard Wright: *Native Son*
Rodgers and Hart's *Pal Joey* opens on Broadway.

1941 Noel Coward: "Blithe Spirit"
Winston Churchill: *Blood, Sweat and Tears*
William Shirer: *Berlin Diary*

1942 *Rodeo,* a ballet by Copland and deMille, opens on Broadway.
John Steinbeck: *The Moon Is Down*
Lloyd C. Douglas: *The Robe*

1943 Betty Smith: *A Tree Grows in Brooklyn*
Robert L. Scott: *God Is My Co-Pilot*
Ted Lawson: *Thirty Seconds over Tokyo*
Oklahoma by Rodgers and Hammerstein opens on Broadway.

1944 *I Remember Mama* by John Van Druten opens on Broadway.
W. Somerset Maugham: *The Razor's Edge*
John Hersey: *A Bell for Adano*
Jean Giraudoux: *Madwoman of Chaillot*

1945 Tennessee Williams: *The Glass Menagerie*
Rodgers and Hammerstein: *Carousel*
Richard Wright: *Black Boy*
George Orwell: *Animal Farm*

1946 Robert Penn Warren: *All the King's Men*
John Hersey: *Hiroshima*
Dr. Benjamin Spock: *Baby and Child Care*
Broadway—ballet by Balanchine: *Nightshadow*
Broadway—Eugene O'Neill: *The Iceman Cometh*

1947 Broadway openings: *All My Sons* by Arthur Miller and *A Streetcar Named Desire* by Tennessee Williams
John Gunther: *Inside USA*
James Michener: *Tales of the South Pacific*

1948 *Kiss Me Kate* and *Mr. Roberts* open on Broadway.
W. H. Auden: *Age of Anxiety* (Pulitzer Prize for poetry)
Norman Mailer: *The Naked and the Dead*
Dwight D. Eisenhower: *Crusade in Europe*

1949 George Orwell: *1984*
Nelson Algren: *The Man with the Golden Arm*
John O'Hara: *A Rage to Live*
Broadway: Arthur Miller's *Death of a Salesman* opens.

Visual Arts

1940 Films: Disney's *Fantasia, The Great Dictator* by Chaplin
King's Canyon National Park in California created.
Max Beckman's painting *Circus Caravan* shown.

1941 Films: *Citizen Kane, How Green Was My Valley, Dumbo*
National Gallery of Art opens in Washington, D.C.
Grand Coulee Dam completed.
Art: *Nighthawks* by Hopper shown.
Mount Rushmore completed.

1942 Films: *Bambi, Casablanca, Holiday Inn, Mrs. Miniver*
Art: Braque's *Patience* and Bonnard's *Blue Bird*
Architects develop prefabricated houses.

1943   Art: Henry Moore's sculpture *Madonna and Child*
       Marc Chagall: *The Juggler*
       Films: *Shadow of a Doubt, Watch on the Rhine*
1944   Films: *Going My Way, Laura, Lifeboat*
       Art: Rouault's *Homo, Homini, Lupus*
       Feininger: *Steamboat on the Yukon*
1945   Frank Lloyd Wright previews model for Guggenheim Museum.
       Sculpture: *Lucifer* by Jacob Epstein
       Painting: *Brass Band* by Max Weber
       Films: *The Lost Weekend, They Were Expendable*
1946   Films: *It's a Wonderful Life* (Frank Capra); *Notorious* (Alfred Hitchcock)
       Chagall: *Cow with Blue Umbrella, Head of Thorns*
       Fuller designs Dymaxion House.
1947   Film: *Gentleman's Agreement* directed by Elia Kazan.
       Henry Moore: *Three Standing Figures* (sculpture)
       Art: *Agony* by Gorky; *Das Matterhorn* by Kokoschka
       Howdy Doody appears on television.
       Meet the Press appears on television.
1948   Films: *The Red Shoes, Naked City*
       St. Louis Arch commissioned.
       TV shows: *Toast of the Town, Philco Playhouse, Milton Berle's Texaco
       Theater, Ford Theater*
1949   Film: *The Third Man, Twelve O'Clock High*
       All the King's Men wins Academy Award.
       TV shows: *The Lone Ranger, Hopalong Cassidy, The Perry Como Show,
       Arthur Godfrey and Friends*

Sports

1940   U.S. Lawn Tennis Association men's title won by W. Donald Mc-
       Neill.
       "Bimelch" wins the Belmont and Preakness.
       Cincinnati (NL) beats Detroit (AL) in World Series, 4–3.
1941   "Whirlaway" wins Triple Crown.
       Lou Gehrig dies.
       Baseball helmets tested.
1942   Cornelius Warmerdam sets pole vault record of 3.77 meters.
       First all-star bowling tournament in U.S. held.
       Joe Louis KO's Buddy Baer to retain heavyweight boxing title.
1943   "Count Fleet" wins Triple Crown.
       University of Wyoming wins NCAA basketball crown.
       Detroit wins Stanley Cup in hockey.
1944   "Pensive" wins Kentucky Derby.
       Kenesaw Mountain Landis dies.
       St. Louis (NL) beats St. Louis (AL) in World Series, 4–2.
1945   Rocky Graziano named Boxer of the Year.
       Branch Rickey, Walter O'Malley, and John Smith buy the Brooklyn
       Dodgers.
       Eddie Arcaro rides "Pavot" and "Hoop Jr." to Belmont and Ken-
       tucky Derby wins.
1946   National Basketball Association founded.
       Joe Louis successfully defends his boxing title for the 23rd time.
       "Assault" wins the Triple Crown.

1947   Jackie Robinson becomes first African American to play major
      league baseball.
    Illinois wins Rose Bowl 45–14 over UCLA.
    Jack Kramer wins U.S. singles tennis title.
1948   Olympic Games held in London.
    "Citation" wins Triple Crown.
    Babe Ruth dies.
1949   "Pancho" Gonzales wins U.S. tennis title.
    Ezzard Charles wins heavyweight title from Joe Walcott.
    New York (AL) wins World Series.

Everyday Life
1940   About 40% of U.S. homes have telephones and radios.
    Pennsylvania Turnpike opens.
    U.S. illiteracy rate at all-time low of 4.2%.
    Earl Tupper invents Tupperware.
    Popular dances: jitterbug, conga, Lindy hop
1941   Cheerios cereal goes on sale.
    Regular TV broadcasts begin.
    Rationing begins.
    Lincoln Continental car debuts.
    Slumber parties become popular.
    Coffee is 21 cents a pound.
1942   G.I.s granted free mailing privileges.
    Gasoline rationing begins.
    College enrollments drop dramatically.
    Sugar and coffee rationed.
    Radio show: *Duffy's Tavern*
1943   Cheese, fat, meat, and canned goods rationed.
    "Scrabble" board game becomes popular.
    Postal zones to speed mail delivery adopted.
    Chicago subway opened.
1944   G.I. Bill passed.
    First nightly national newscast aired.
    Newspapers feature G.I. cartoons "Sad Sack" and "Up Front" by
      Bill Mauldin.
    Fashion: Bare midriffs, slim skirts, large hats
1945   FCC designates 13 channels for TV broadcasting.
    Silly Putty developed.
    Fashions emphasize "delicate femininity."
    Sugar rations cut 25%.
    Popular radio shows: *Superman, Inner Sanctum, The Green Hornet,*
      The Red Skelton Show
1946   Bikini swimsuits become popular.
    Fulbright Scholarship program initiated.
    Price controls on meat lifted.
    First prime-time TV schedule published.
1947   First supersonic flight by a U.S. plane.
    1.2 million ex-service people attend college on G.I. Bill.
    Meet the Press first telecast.
    Christian Dior's "New Look" (V-neck, ruffles, flounce skirts)
    "Slinky" toy introduced.

1948   Bernard Baruch coins the term *Cold War*.
        Supreme Court orders equal education for blacks in Oklahoma.
        "New Look" out in fashion—natural lines in.
        Sugar and bread rationing ended.
1949   Antitrust suit seeks to separate AT&T from Western Electric.
        U.S. Air Force XB-47 jet completes transcontinental flight in 3 hours
            46 minutes (607.2 mph).
        Average teacher salary: $3,010 annually
        First prefabricated community completed in Levittown, New York.
        Number of college graduates has doubled since 1940.

New Nations, 1940–1949

    Bhutan (1949)
    Iceland (1941)
    Israel (1948)
    Laos (1949)
    Burma (1948)
    Philippines (1946)
    Syria (1946)

Sample Learning Activities

1941   *Jeannette Rankin, (R) Montana, is the only person to vote "no" on the declaration of war in World Wars I and II.*
        Students research Rankin's decision, discovering the circumstances under which she chose to vote "no." Each student then draws a cartoon that depicts either a pro or con view of Rankin's decisions. Students must explain their cartoons.
1947   *The Marshall Plan is announced, with ramifications for the international economy even in 1997.*
        Students are to use reference sources to prepare a graph that depicts western Europe's growth since 1947 in one of the following: GNP, industrialization, productivity, foreign trade, or education.

1950–1959: AMERICAN PRIDE IS WORLDWIDE

Overview

The 1950s saw the United States emerge as an international superpower that forever ended the traditional isolationist policies it had jealously adhered to since the end of World War I. The decade was one of prosperity for many Americans, but it was also a time of growing social concern and unrest. It was a decade of innocence and ignorance, fear and distrust, hope, faith, and a growing concern for the future. Certainly it was not as confusing a time as the 1960s would become, but in the 1950s many Americans became introspective regarding our social and political institutions, and this laid the groundwork for the more turbulent 1960s.

Big cars, exciting fashions, and new heroes dominated our lives. Elvis, Marilyn Monroe, rock 'n' roll, and the beat generation all became part of our lexicon, while bomb shelters and anti-Communist witch hunts became a national reality. There were also tremendous advances in science and medicine. The polio vaccine was finally introduced after twenty years of experimentation, and humans began to explore outer space. New leaders, new nations, and vibrant political and social movements also emerged during this decade. Some had immediate and dramatic impact, while others took time to ferment and consolidate before they emerged over the next several decades.

Two Olympic Games were held during the decade. One, in Melbourne, Australia, was the first to be held on a continent other than Europe or North America. Sports figures, who would become legends in their own time, emerged and influenced every aspect of our daily lives. Mickey Mantle, Willie Mays, Bill Russell, Carol Heiss, and the Reverend Bob Richards, to mention but a few, had their images on everything from cereal boxes to cigarette advertisements.

Indeed, sports and recreation became more and more important to Americans as we emerged from decades of economic depression and war. People found themselves with more money available for all the new foods and services so long denied and probably nothing had as great an impact on us as did television. The 1950s saw television become an American staple, with news, sports, variety shows, and all kinds of entertainment titillating us and filling our increasing leisure hours.

Everyone who grew up in this decade recalls Howdy Doody; Uncle Miltie; Ed Sullivan; Red Skelton; Arthur Godfrey; Kukla, Fran, and Ollie; Daniel Boone; and Perry Como. They were our entertainment, our link to both the real and the make-believe worlds that took us from the austerity and grimness of the past generations.

For many, it was the best of times as we enjoyed unprecedented prosperity and health. Our influence was recognized around the world. Only a few of us recognized the importance of the struggle for racial equality being waged in this country—or the significance of a far-away place called Vietnam.

Demographics: 1950–1959

Important Political Leaders

> U.S.—Dwight Eisenhower
> China—Mao Zedong and Chou En-lai
> France—Charles De Gaulle
> Great Britain—Anthony Eden, Harold Macmillan, and Queen Elizabeth II
> Egypt—King Farouk and Gamal Abdul Nasser
> USSR—Georgi Malenkov, Nikolai Bulganin, Nikita Khrushchev
> West Germany—Konrad Adenauer
> Japan—Emperor Hirohito
> Italy—Luigi Einaudi
> Israel—Yizhak Ben-Zvi
> Canada—John G. Diefenbaker
> Cuba—Fulgencio Batista
> Ethiopia—Haile Selassie
> India—Pandit Jawaharlal Nehru
> Mexico—Adolfo Mateos

Largest Cities

Ten Largest U.S. Cities		*Ten Largest Cities Outside the U.S.*	
1. New York	7,891,957	1. London	8,930,941
2. Chicago	3,620,962	2. Shanghai	4,630,385
3. Philadelphia	2,071,605	3. Mexico City	4,500,000
4. Los Angeles	1,970,358	4. Tokyo	4,174,505
5. Detroit	1,849,568	5. Moscow	4,137,018
6. Baltimore	949,708	6. Peking	4,100,000
7. Cleveland	914,808	7. Berlin	3,729,300
8. St. Louis	856,796	8. Leningrad	3,191,304
9. Washington, D.C.	802,178	9. Calcutta	3,132,000
10. Boston	801,444	10. Buenos Aires	3,000,371

U.S. population: 150,697,361
World population: 2.3 billion

Significant Headlines and News Stories

1950 Korean War begins.
Puerto Rican nationalists attempt to assassinate President Truman.
Defense Production Act extended.

1951 Juan Peron reelected president in Argentina.
First national telecast aired (Japanese peace conference treaty).
Selective Service System (draft) extended.
General Douglas MacArthur replaced in Korea.

1952 Dag Hammarskjold elected secretary-general of the United Nations.
Coronation of Queen Elizabeth II of England.
Updegraff vs. Board of Regents holds loyalty oath to be unconstitutional.

1953 Korean War ends with armistice.
Department of Health, Education and Welfare established.
Julius and Ethel Rosenberg become the first U.S. civilians to be executed for spying.
Joseph Stalin dies.
Jomo Kenyatta convicted for directing Mau-Mau attacks.

1954 DEW (Distant Early Warning) line installed at the Arctic Circle.
McCarthyism grips U.S.
Brown vs. Board of Education of Topeka (segregated schools ruled unconstitutional).

1955 Blacks boycott Montgomery, Alabama, bus lines.
Suez Canal crisis.
U.S. Air Force Academy created.
Salk polio vaccine introduced.

1956 President Eisenhower reelected.
Hungarian revolt.
Civil Rights Act passes.
Fidel Castro lands in Cuba with a small force.

1957 Vietnam War begins in Asia.
Sputnik I launched from the USSR.
Congress investigates racketeering in the Teamsters' Union.

1958 U.S. launches *Explorer I*.
Antarctica Treaty enacted to preserve the continent.
Democrats gain control of Congress.

1959   John Foster Dulles dies.

New York City forms commission to review possibility of becoming 51st state.

Ban from U.S. mail of D. H. Lawrence's *Lady Chatterley's Lover* is reversed.

History and Politics

1950   Korean War begins.

UN forces land at Inchon.

U.S. recognizes South Vietnamese capital as Saigon.

Great Britain recognizes State of Israel.

1951   22nd Amendment enacted (term limits on U.S. presidents).

North Korea breaks through 38th Parallel and captures Seoul.

Julius and Ethel Rosenberg convicted of espionage and sentenced to death.

1952   Dwight D. Eisenhower elected as the 34th president.

McCarran-Walter Act (immigration quotas) passed.

Israel and Germany agree on restitution for Holocaust.

1953   Earl Warren becomes Chief Justice of U.S. Supreme Court.

Nasser seizes power in Egypt.

Malenkov becomes Soviet premier.

1954   *USS Nautilus,* first U.S. nuclear submarine, launched.

U.S. casualties in Korea: 33,237 dead, 103,376 wounded, 401 missing.

SEATO Pact signed in Manila, Philippine Islands, by 8 nations.

CENTO (Central Treaty Organization) agreement.

1955   AFL-CIO labor unions merge.

Albert Einstein dies.

Bulganin succeeds Malenkov in USSR.

1956   Hungarian revolt against Soviet domination.

Fidel Castro lands in Oriente Province, Cuba.

Pakistan becomes an Islamic Republic.

Japan admitted to United Nations.

1957   Eisenhower Doctrine formulated.

International Atomic Energy Agency statute signed by U.S. and 79 other nations.

Common Market instituted in Europe.

1958   Democrats gain control of the House of Representatives.

United Arab Republic formed.

Khrushchev becomes Soviet chairman.

1959   Alaska and Hawaii are admitted as the 49th and 50th states.

Agricultural Act passed.

Fidel Castro becomes premier of Cuba.

Science and Technology

1950   Plutonium separated from pitchblende concentrates.

Antihistamines become popular remedy for colds and allergies.

Miltown, a meprobamate, becomes a commonly used tranquilizer.

1951   Electric power produced from atomic energy at Arcon, Idaho.

Approximately 400,000 pounds of penicillin and 350,000 pounds of streptomycin produced in United States.

Nobel Prize for chemistry: Edwin McMillan and Glenn Seaborg for their discovery of plutonium.

1952   Contraceptive pills produced.

First hydrogen bomb exploded at Eniwetok Atoll in the Pacific.

Cyram and Becka statistically demonstrate a connection between weather and death frequency.

1953 Cosmic ray observatory erected on Mt. Wrangel, Alaska.

Lung cancer reported attributable to cigarette smoking.

A rocket-powered U.S. plane flies at more than 1,600 mph.

1954 Known chemical elements at the time of the birth of Christ: 9; about 1500 A.D.: 12; around 1900 A.D.: 84; in 1954: 100.

Nobel Prize to Linus Pauling (U.S.) for study of molecular forces.

U.S. submarine *Nautilus* converted to nuclear power.

Dr. Jonas Salk, developer of antipolio serum, starts inoculating school children in Pittsburgh, Pennsylvania.

1955 Ultra-high-frequency (UHF) waves produced at MIT.

Dorothy Hodgkin discovers a liver extract for treating pernicious anemia (Vitamin B_{12}).

Technology to create artificial diamonds reported.

1956 Neutrino produced at Los Alamos, New Mexico.

Dido reactor opened at Harwell, England.

Albert Sabin develops an oral vaccine against polio.

Bell Telephone Company begins to develop a "visual phone."

1957 USSR launches first two earth satellites: Sputnik I and Sputnik II.

Nobelium (element 102) discovered in Stockholm.

Giberellin, a growth hormone, is isolated.

Mackinac Straits Bridge (Michigan), the longest suspension bridge in the world, opens.

1958 U.S. nuclear submarine *Nautilus* passes under polar ice cap.

Van Allen radiation belt around earth is discovered.

U.S. launches *Explorer I.*

1959 First International Congress on Oceanography held in New York.

Nobel Prize to Ochoa and Kornberg (U.S.) for their synthesis of RNA and DNA.

USSR launches satellite with two live monkeys aboard.

First nuclear-powered merchant ship launched: U.S. *Savannah.*

Literature and Theater

1950 Clifford Odets: *The Country Girl*

Ezra Pound: *Seventy Cantos*

Frank Lesser and Abe Burrows: *Guys and Dolls*

Pulitzer Prize: *The Way West* by B. Guthrie, Jr.

1951 Rachel Carson: *The Sea Around Us*

J. D. Salinger: *The Catcher in the Rye*

The King and I by Rodgers and Hammerstein opens on Broadway.

Tennessee Williams: *The Rose Tattoo*

1952 Edna Ferber: *Giant*

Marianne Moore: *Collected Poems* (Pulitzer Prize)

The Shrike by Joseph Krammnius wins Pulitzer Prize for drama.

Agatha Christie's *The Mouse Trap* celebrates 22 years on the stage.

1953 Pulitzer Prize: *The Old Man and the Sea* by Ernest Hemingway

Arthur Miller: *The Crucible*

George Axelrod: *The Seven Year Itch*

Kismet opens on Broadway.

Leon Uris: *Battle Cry*

1954 Bruce Catton: *Stillness at Appomattox* (Pulitzer Prize)

The Pajama Game opens on Broadway.
Terence Rattigan: *Separate Tables*
Tennessee Williams: *Cat on a Hot Tin Roof* (Pulitzer Prize)
1955 Agatha Christie: *Witness for the Prosecution*
Cole Porter's *Silk Stockings* opens on Broadway.
Sloan Wilson: *The Man in the Gray Flannel Suit*
Rudolph Flesch: *Why Johnny Can't Read*
1956 Leonard Bernstein's *Candide* opens on Broadway.
The Diary of Anne Frank by Goodrich and Hacket (Pulitzer Prize).
John F. Kennedy: *Profiles in Courage* (Pulitzer Prize)
Grace Metalious: *Peyton Place*
1957 Dr. Seuss: *The Cat in the Hat*
Ayn Rand: *Atlas Shrugged*
Flower Drum Song opens on Broadway.
Nevil Shute: *On the Beach*
1958 Truman Capote: *Breakfast at Tiffany's*
Boris Pasternak: *Dr. Zhivago*
A Taste of Honey opens in London.
Lorraine Hansberry: *A Raisin in the Sun*
1959 William Gibson: *The Miracle Worker*
Allen Drury: *Advise and Consent* (Pulitzer Prize)
Vance Packard: *The Status Seekers*
The Sound of Music opens on Broadway.

Visual Arts

1950 Chagall: *King David*
Sculpture: *Seven Figures and a Head* by Giacometti
Academy Award: *All About Eve*
Union Building in New York completed.
1951 Frank Lloyd Wright designs Friedman House.
Academy Award: *An American in Paris*
Salvador Dali: *Christ of St. John's on the Cross*
British introduce "X" rating for films.
Picasso: *Massacre in Korea*
1952 Barbara Hepworth: *Statue* (abstract sculpture)
Art Nouveau exhibition in Zurich, Switzerland.
Academy Award: *The Greatest Show on Earth*
Raoul Dufy: *The Pink Violin*
1953 *From Here to Eternity* wins Academy Award.
Cinemascope adopted in U.S. theaters.
Picasso exhibition in Rome.
Henry Moore sculpture *The King and Queen* shown in Athens.
1954 Lynn Chadurck: *Two Dancing Figures*
Graham Sutherland: *Portrait of Churchill*
"Herblock" wins Pulitzer Prize for cartoons.
Henri Matisse dies.
1955 *Marty* wins Academy Award.
"The New Decade" art exhibition opens in New York.
Bernard Buffet: *Circus*
Pietro Annigonis: *Portrait of Queen Elizabeth II*
1956 Popular films: *War and Peace, Lust for Life, Romeo and Juliet, Around the World in Eighty Days*

John Bratby: *A Painter's Credo*
Jackson Pollock dies.

1957 Marc Chagall: *Self-Portrait*
Diego Rivera dies.
H. G. Adam: *Beacon of the Dead*
Academy Award: *The Bridge on the River Kwai*

1958 James Brooks: *Acanda*
Guggenheim Museum in New York opens.
Gigi wins Academy Award.
Oscar Niemeyer designs presidential palace in Brasilia.

1959 Yuchi Inour: *Fish*
Ben Hur wins Academy Award.
Andre Beaudin: *La Lune de Mai*
Cecil B. De Mille dies.

Music

1950 Gian Carlo Menotti opera *The Consul* wins Pulitzer Prize.
"Cool jazz" develops from bebop.
Popular songs: "If I'd Known You Were Coming I'd've Baked a Cake," "Ragg Mopp," "Mona Lisa," "C'est si Bon"

1951 *Billy Budd* opera opens in London.
"Hello, Young Lovers," "Shrimp Boats," and "Cry" are popular songs.

1952 Leonard Bernstein: *Trouble in Tahiti*
Alexi Haieff: *Symphony No. 7*
Popular songs: "I Saw Mommy Kissing Santa Claus," "Jambalaya," "Your Cheatin' Heart"

1953 Bohuslav Martinu: *What Men Live By*
William Schuman: *Mighty Casey*
Popular songs: "Doggie in the Window," "I Believe," "Ebb Tide," "I Love Paris"

1954 First annual jazz festival held in Newport, Rhode Island.
Popular songs: "Hernando's Hideaway," "Hey There," "Mister Sandman"
Aaron Copland: *The Tender Land*

1955 Michael Tippet: *The Midsummer Marriage*
George Antheil: *The Wish*
Popular songs: "Davy Crockett," "Sixteen Tons," "Rock Around the Clock"

1956 Popular songs: "Blue Suede Shoes," "Hound Dog," "Don't Be Cruel"
Elvis Presley becomes the most popular U.S. vocalist.
My Fair Lady opens on Broadway.

1957 The Music Man opens on Broadway.
Stravinsky ballet *Agon* opens.
Bernstein's *West Side Story* opens.

1958 W. C. Handy dies.
Samuel Barber opera *Vanessa* opens.
Popular songs: "Chipmunk Song," "Volare," "Catch a Falling Star," "The Purple People Eaters"

1959 *Fiorello* opens on Broadway and wins Pulitzer Prize.
Gypsy opens on Broadway.

Popular songs: "Tom Dooley," "Mack the Knife," "The Sound of Music," "High Hopes"

Sports

1950 Australia wins Davis Cup.
Ohio State wins Rose Bowl from University of California, 17–14.
U.S. Open in golf won by Ben Hogan.

1951 "Jersey" Joe Walcott wins world heavyweight title.
Frank Sedgman and Maureen Connolly win U.S. Lawn Tennis championship.
"Citation" earns $1 million in horse racing.

1952 Rocky Marciano wins world heavyweight title.
Summer Olympic Games held in Helsinki, U.S. wins 43 gold medals.
Emil Zatopek wins the 5000 meters, 10,000 meters, and marathon races in record time in Helsinki.

1953 Maureen Connolly wins tennis "Grand Slam."
Jim Thorpe dies.
Ben Hogan wins Masters, U.S., and British Opens.
Boston Braves (NL) move to Milwaukee, and St. Louis (AL) moves to Baltimore.

1954 Roger Bannister (Great Britain) breaks four-minute barrier in mile run.
Philadelphia Athletics (AL) move to Kansas City.
Gordon Richards becomes first jockey to be knighted.

1955 "Sugar" Ray Robinson wins world boxing title from "Bobo" Olsen.
Gordon Pirie wins 10,000 meter run in time of 29.19 minutes.
Brooklyn (NL) wins World Series from New York (AL), 4–3.

1956 Olympic Games held in Melbourne, Australia.
"Babe" Didrickson dies.
Connie Mack dies.
"Needles" wins Triple Crown.
Rocky Marciano retires undefeated as heavyweight champion.

1957 New York Giants and Brooklyn Dodgers move to San Francisco and Los Angeles, respectively.
Bobby Fisher (13) emerges as U.S. chess champion.
Iowa wins the Rose Bowl from Oregon State, 35–19.

1958 Eddie Arcaro becomes third jockey to attain 4,000 wins.
"Tim Tam" wins Triple Crown.
"Columbia" defeats "Sceptre" to retain America's Cup.
Pakistani cricket team tours U.S.

1959 Ingemar Johansson (Sweden) wins world heavyweight boxing title.
Los Angeles (NL) beats Chicago (AL) to win World Series, 4–2.
Jack Nicklaus wins amateur golf championship.

Everyday Life

1950 30,000 varieties of roses catalogued.
1.5 million Germans are still missing after World War II.
UN reports that 480 million children worldwide are undernourished.

1951 Color TV introduced in U.S.
William Randolph Hearst dies.

London is largest city in the world with 8.3 million, New York is next with 7.8 million.

1952   Christian Dior fashions are popular.
Biblical city of Jericho excavated.
Germany becomes member of World Bank.

1953   Tornadoes in Texas, Michigan, and Massachusetts kill 350.
Queen Mary of England dies.
All price controls are lifted in the U.S.

1954   1,768 U.S. newspapers publish 59 million copies daily.
Eurovision network established.
U.S. has 6% of world population but 60% of all the automobiles.

1955   82 die in a disaster at LeMans race track.
Commercial TV begins broadcasting in England.
Lufthansa Airlines resumes flights.

1956   Rock 'n' roll dance and music in vogue.
Prince Rainier of Monaco marries U.S. movie star Grace Kelly.
Italian luxury liner *Andrea Doria* sinks off Nantucket Island.

1957   Cities with 1 million population number 71, as against 16 in 1914.
Regular London-to-Moscow flight service resumed.
Desegregation ordered in Little Rock, Arkansas, schools.

1958   The beatnik movement, started in California, goes national.
U.S. unemployment reaches 5.2%.
Brussels World Exhibition held.

1959   World Refugee Year proclaimed.
Total U.S. auto accident deaths total 1.25 million for the decade.
Lady Chatterley's Lover is banned by U.S. Postal Service.

New Nations, 1950–1959

Cambodia (1953)
Guinea (1958)
India (1950)
Indonesia (1950)
Libya (1952)
Malaysia (1957)
Morocco (1956)
Pakistan (1956)
Sudan (1956)
Tunisia (1956)

Sample Learning Activities

1951   *Korean "police action" is undertaken, with ramifications for Asian and U.S. relationships.*
Five groups are formed to represent each of the following nations: Vietnam, Korea, Cambodia, the Philippines, and Indonesia. After researching each nation's history, students share the changes and political concerns after 1951 with the rest of the class.

1957   *The Common Market is established in Europe.*
Students prepare a map that illustrates the major products of western Europe and the conjoint products that are developed.

1960–1969: TROUBLE, TRAUMA, AND TRAVAIL

Overview

The 1960s were more than just a decade in history. They were a state of mind, embodied by America's young people. For the first time, the nation felt the full impact of the baby-boomer generation (those 50 million children born in the post–World War II era) and their attitudes about themselves, their nation, and their place in the world. By 1960, more than one-half of the U.S. population was under 30 years of age, and so it was probably appropriate that the decade began with the election of John F. Kennedy, the youngest person ever elected to that office.

It was an amazing era—a time when we were encouraged (at least at first) to reflect on who we were, question authority, evaluate the meaning of life, scrutinize U.S. society, and test our collective and personal values. When President Kennedy urged us to "Ask . . . what you can do for your country," we did, and a new wave of social consciousness and commitment was born in this nation. In many ways we were naive about the world in which we lived. Although "flower children" talked about love and peace, we were entering one of the most troubled and traumatic decades in our history. Political assassinations, an unpopular war in Asia, escalating Communist threats in Europe and Africa, and race riots at home all led to a growing disillusionment with long-revered American institutions. The 1960s were a watershed in U.S. history, after which we became forever a different nation.

When Richard Nixon was elected in 1968, we were looking into the eye of an economic, social, and political hurricane of awesome proportions. The Kennedy and Johnson eras had seen the Great Society stumble and the Vietnam War—the first televised war—swallow in ever greater numbers not only our economic resources but also thousands of our young men and women. While tens of thousands died in the war to "contain" Communism, thousands also died at home in crime-related activities. Not only were political assassinations shocking Americans, but violent crime was dramatically on the rise. From the assassination of Malcolm X to the Charles Manson murders, the 1960s saw violent crime escalate frighteningly. *The FBI Uniform Crime Report* disclosed that crime in U.S. cities and in rural areas had risen over 30 percent for the decade.

As the decade of the 1960s progressed, many Americans experienced great travail. What started out with hope and great expectations, as cited by our new president, soon gave way to confusion, despair, and civil hostility. Nevertheless, the landing of a person on the moon gave us Americans an opportunity to renew our pride and optimism as we moved into the 1970s.

Demographics: 1960–1969

Important Political Leaders

> U.S.—John F. Kennedy, Lyndon B. Johnson, and Richard Nixon
> Great Britain—Harold Macmillan
> USSR—Nikita Khrushchev and Leonid Brezhnev
> Japan—Emperor Hirohito
> Egypt—Gamal Abdul Nasser
> China—Mao Zedong and Chou En-lai
> Spain—Francisco Franco
> France—Charles De Gaulle

Cuba—Fidel Castro
Italy—Giovanni Gronchi
West Germany—Ludwig Earhardt and Willy Brandt
Vietnam—Ho Chi Minh and Ton Duc Tang
Israel—David Ben Gurion and Golda Meir
Dominican Republic—Rafael Trujillo
Iran—Shah Pahlavi

Largest Cities

Ten Largest U.S. Cities		*Ten Largest Cities Outside the U.S.*	
1. New York	7,781,984	1. Tokyo	9,100,539
2. Chicago	3,550,404	2. London	8,222,340
3. Los Angeles	2,479,015	3. Shanghai	7,100,000
4. Philadelphia	2,002,512	4. Moscow	5,032,000
5. Detroit	1,670,144	5. Mexico City	4,500,000
6. Baltimore	939,624	6. Peking	4,140,000
7. Houston	939,219	7. Buenos Aires	3,703,000
8. Cleveland	876,050	8. Berlin	3,345,000
9. Milwaukee	741,324	9. Sao Paulo	3,147,000
10. San Francisco	740,316	10. Leningrad	3,100,000

U.S. population: 179,323,175
World population: 3.5 billion

Significant Headlines and News Stories

1960   John F. Kennedy elected 35th president.
       U.S. satellite *Discoverer XVII* orbits Earth 29 times.
       Medicare Bill passed by Congress.
1961   23rd Amendment passed, giving citizens of the District of Columbia the right to vote.
       Yuri Gagarin (USSR) becomes the first human in outer space.
       Alliance for Progress Pact provides aid for 10 years to Latin American nations.
1962   Adolf Eichmann (Nazi war criminal) executed in Israel.
       Algeria secures independence from France.
       John Glenn (U.S.) orbits the Earth.
1963   South Vietnamese generals overthrow and kill president Ngo Dinh Diem.
       The U.S., USSR, and U.K. agree to ban atmospheric atomic testing.
       U.S. Supreme Court upholds ban on school prayer.
       President Kennedy assassinated in Dallas, Texas. Lyndon B. Johnson becomes the 36th U.S. president.
1964   Civil Rights Act passed.
       War on Poverty legislation enacted.
       Gulf of Tonkin Resolution (escalation of Vietnam War).
       Anti-U.S. riots erupt in Panama.
       Lyndon Johnson elected to a full term; coins the phrase "Great Society."
1965   Medicare legislation enacted.
       Vatican II Council meets.
       Rebels attempt to overthrow government in the Dominican Republic.

U.S. commits combat troops in Vietnam.

Watts, a section of Los Angeles, erupts in civil riots.

1966 National Organization of Women (NOW) founded.

Robert C. Weaver, first African American to hold a cabinet post, is selected to be Secretary of Housing and Urban Development.

Indira Gandhi elected prime minister of India.

1967 Thurgood Marshall becomes first African American to sit on the Supreme Court.

Six-Day War begins—Egypt, Syria, and Jordan versus Israel.

Civil riots engulf Detroit.

Hanoi attacked by U.S. bombers.

1968 Richard Nixon becomes the 37th U.S. president.

Civil rights legislation enacted.

Warsaw Pact nations (USSR, East Germany, Poland, Hungary, and Bulgaria) invade Czechoslovakia.

1969 Antiwar protests rock U.S.

Neil Armstrong and Buzz Aldrin (U.S.) become first humans to walk on the moon while command pilot Mike Collins orbits the moon.

75,000 U.S. troops withdrawn from Vietnam.

Violent fighting in Northern Ireland between Catholics and Protestants.

History and Politics

1960 Brezhnev becomes president of USSR.

U2 reconnaissance "spy plane" shot down in USSR—pilot Francis Gary Powers captured.

Cyprus becomes independent nation.

First presidential TV debates—Nixon versus Kennedy.

1961 U.S. breaks diplomatic relations with Cuba.

Peace Corps sends first volunteers to Ghana, in Africa.

Bay of Pigs invasion.

Berlin Wall constructed.

1962 Uganda and Tanganyika become independent nations.

Cuban missile crisis.

U Thant elected UN Secretary General.

1963 Winston Churchill becomes honorary U.S. citizen.

200,000 "Freedom Marchers" descend on Washington, D.C.

President John Kennedy assassinated in Dallas, Texas; Lyndon Johnson becomes 36th U.S. president.

Civil rights demonstrations in Birmingham, Alabama.

1964 24th Amendment (abolishing poll tax) ratified.

General Douglas MacArthur dies.

Martin Luther King, Jr., wins Nobel Peace Prize.

Kosygin replaces Khrushchev as Soviet prime minister.

1965 Winston Churchill dies.

750th anniversary of signing of the Magna Carta.

Charles De Gaulle elected French president.

Violence breaks out in Selma, Alabama.

1966 Red Guards demonstrate in China against Western influences.

Nazi ministers Albert Speer and Baldur von Schirach released after serving 20 years imprisonment.

Guyana becomes independent nation.

Israeli and Jordanian forces battle in Hebron.

1967 700,000 marchers support war in Vietnam (New York).

50,000 persons demonstrate against Vietnam War in Washington, D.C.

25th Amendment (presidential succession) ratified.

1968 U.S. Navy intelligence ship *Pueblo* captured by North Koreans.

Reverend Martin Luther King, Jr. assassinated in Memphis, Tennessee.

Senator Robert Kennedy assassinated in Los Angeles.

Pierre Trudeau becomes Canadian prime minister.

Richard Nixon elected 37th U.S. president.

1969 Ho Chi Minh, president of North Vietnam, dies.

Golda Meir becomes Israel's fourth prime minister.

Yasir Arafat elected chairman of PLO.

"Chicago Eight" are indicted for violating antiriot clause.

Lieutenant Calley and Staff Sergeant Mitchell stand trial for My Lai massacre.

Science and Technology

1960 First weather satellite (U.S.) launched.

Optical microwave laser constructed.

Bathyscope *Trieste* descends a record 35,800 feet to ocean floor.

U.S. launches radio-reflector satellite.

1961 Atlas computer installed at Harwell.

Astronaut Alan Shepard (U.S.) makes first suborbital flight.

Lee DeForest, inventor of vacuum tube, dies.

1962 Mariner 2 (U.S.) launched as Venus probe.

U.S. has 200 atomic reactors, USSR 39.

The drug thalidomide, when used by pregnant women, causes children to be born with malformations.

1963 Anti-xi-zeno discovered.

Valentina Tereshkova (USSR), first female cosmonaut orbits Earth for three days.

U.S. astronaut completes 22 orbits.

Dr. Michael DeBakey first uses artificial heart to take over blood circulation during heart surgery.

1964 Hoyle and Marlikar (U.K.) postulate new theory of gravitation.

Rachel Carson dies.

Verrazano-Narrows Bridge opens in New York.

Nobel Prize for chemistry won by Dorothy Hodgkin (U.K.)

1965 Soviet Cosmonaut Leonov "spacewalks" for 10 minutes.

First flight around the world over both poles.

U.S. astronaut Ed White spacewalks for 21 minutes.

1966 USSR sends two male dogs into orbit.

Astronaut "Buzz" Aldrin spacewalks 129 minutes.

U.S. spacecraft "Surveyor One" makes soft landing on the moon.

Nobel Prize for medicine to C. B. Huggins and F. P. Rous for cancer research.

1967 Stanford University biochemists synthesize a version of DNA.

The People's Republic of China explodes its first hydrogen bomb.

Dr. Irving Cooper develops cryosurgery for treatment of Parkinson's disease.

U.S. has 74 nuclear-powered submarines in commission.

1968 First desktop computer introduced.

"Pulsars" discovered by Hewish and Bell (U.K.)

Team of five Harvard chemists announces they have synthesized prostaglandin for treatment of high blood pressure.

1969 Concorde SST makes first test flight.

Mariner spacecraft sends back pictures from Mars.

U.S. takes steps to ban DDT.

Literature and Theater

1960 Robert Bolt: *A Man for All Seasons*

Vance Packard: *The Waste Makers*

Pulitzer Prize to Harper Lee for *To Kill a Mockingbird*

Alberto Moravia: *La Noia*

1961 Ernest Hemingway dies.

James Baldwin: *Nobody Knows My Name*

Joseph Heller: *Catch-22*

Pulitzer Prize in Drama: *All the Way Home*

John Steinbeck: *The Winter of Our Discontent*

1962 Katherine Anne Porter: *Ship of Fools*

Charles Schulz: *Happiness Is a Warm Puppy*

Ken Kesey: *One Flew over the Cuckoo's Nest*

1963 Robert Frost: *In the Clearing*

Barbara Tuchman: *The Guns of August* (Pulitzer Prize winner for nonfiction)

John LeCarré: *The Spy Who Came in from the Cold*

Mary McCarthy: *The Group*

1964 Shakespeare Exhibition at Stratford-on-Avon.

Elizabeth Jennings: *Recoveries* (poems)

Jean-Paul Sartre: *Les Mots*

Peter Weiss: *Marat-Sade*

1965 Norman Mailer: *An American Dream*

Nobel Prize for Literature: M. A. Sholokov

Pulitzer Prize for Poetry: *77 Dream Songs* by John Berryman

T. S. Eliot dies.

W. Somerset Maugham dies.

1966 Truman Capote: *In Cold Blood*

Pulitzer Prize winner: Katherine Anne Porter for *Collected Short Stories*

Sophie Tucker dies.

Jacqueline Susann: *Valley of the Dolls*

1967 Isaac Bashevis Singer: *The Manor*

Leon Uris: *Topaz*

Spencer Tracy dies.

Thornton Wilder: *The Eighth Day*

Langston Hughes dies.

1968 Nobel Prize for literature: Yasunari Rawabatta (Japan)

Gore Vidal: *Myra Breckinridge*

The Great White Hope by Howard Sackler wins Pulitzer Prize for drama.

Edna Ferber dies.

Neil Simon: *Plaza Suite*

1969 Mario Puzo: *The Godfather*

Judy Garland dies.

Michael Crichton: *The Andromeda Strain*
Kurt Vonnegut: *Slaughterhouse Five*

Music

1960   Benjamin Britten: *A Midsummer Night's Dream* (opera)
Oscar Hammerstein dies.
Popular songs: "Itsy Bitsy Teenie Weenie Yellow Polka Dot Bikini,"
"Calcutta," "Let's Do the Twist"

1961   Royal Ballet visits the USSR.
Popular songs: "Moon River," "Exodus," "Where the Boys Are"
Pulitzer Prize winner: *Symphony No. 7* by Walter Piston

1962   Michael Tippet: *King Priam* (opera)
Arthur Miller: *The Crucible*—Pulitzer winner
Popular songs: "Days of Wine and Roses," "Go Away Little Girl,"
"Blowin' in the Wind"

1963   Popular songs: "Danke Schoen," "Those Lazy Hazy Days of Sum-
mer," "Call Me Irresponsible"
Joan Baez and Bob Dylan are most popular U.S. singers.
Edith Piaf dies.

1964   Cole Porter dies.
Jerry Bock: *Fiddler on the Roof*
Popular songs: "Hello Dolly," "From Russia with Love," "Chim
Chim Cheree," "I Want to Hold Your Hand"

1965   Leonard Bernstein: *Chichester Psalms*
Nat "King" Cole dies.
Popular songs: "King of the Road," "Downtown," "Hard Day's
Night"

1966   *Man of La Mancha* opens on Broadway.
40th World Music Festival held in Stockholm.
New Metropolitan Opera House opens in New York.
On a Clear Day You Can See Forever opens on Broadway.
Popular songs: "Born Free," "Ballad of the Green Berets"

1967   Opera: *Mourning Becomes Electra*
Woody Guthrie dies.
Cabaret opens on Broadway.

1968   Pascal: *George M* opens on Broadway.
Aretha Franklin and Jimi Hendrix are popular musicians.
Popular songs: "Hey Jude," "Stoned Soul Picnic," "Mrs. Robinson"

1969   Duke Ellington is presented with Medal of Freedom.
Woodstock
1776 opens on Broadway.
Coco opens on Broadway.
Popular songs: "A Boy Named Sue," "Aquarius," "In the Year
2525"

Visual Arts

1960   Picasso Exhibition held at Tate Gallery, London.
John Bratby: *Gloria with Sunflower*
Academy Award: *The Apartment*
Clark Gable dies.

1961   Grandma Moses dies.
Academy Award: *West Side Story*

Gary Cooper dies.

Sir Edward Maufe completes Guildford Cathedral, England.

1962 Academy Award: *Lawrence of Arabia*

Marilyn Monroe dies.

Oskar Kokoschka: *Ringed with Vision*

1963 *Mona Lisa* exhibited in New York.

Popular art displayed at Guggenheim Museum.

Academy Award: *Tom Jones*

Goya exhibit held at Royal Academy, London.

1964 Picasso: *The Painter and His Model*

Academy Award: *My Fair Lady*

Allen Jones: *Green Girl*

1965 "Op" art becomes the rage.

Academy Award: *The Sound of Music*

Picasso: *Self-Portrait*

1966 Academy Award: *Who's Afraid of Virginia Woolf?*

Kumi Sugai: *Mer Soleil* (abstract painting)

Temples and statuary of Abu Simbel in Egypt are moved to save them from the rising waters of the Aswan Dam.

1967 Academy Award: *Guess Who's Coming to Dinner*

Marc Chagall: *The Blue Village*

Charmion von Wiegand: *The Secret Mondella*

1968 Buckminster Fuller awarded gold medal by Royal Institute of British Architects.

Mickey Mouse celebrates 40th birthday.

Oliver wins Academy Award.

1969 Academy Award: *Midnight Cowboy*

Museum of Modern Art in New York pays $6 million for Gertrude Stein art collection.

Rembrandt self-portrait sold for $1.26 million.

Sports

1960 Olympic Games held in Rome, Italy; Wilma Rudolph (U.S.) wins three gold medals.

Bobby Fischer (16) successfully gains U.S. chess title.

Floyd Patterson (U.S.) regains world heavyweight boxing championship.

1961 Roger Maris breaks Babe Ruth's home run record with 61.

Australia defeats Italy (5–0) to win Davis Cup.

"Carry Back" wins Triple Crown.

1962 Arnold Palmer wins second consecutive British Open.

Rod Laver (Australian) wins Tennis Grand Slam.

"Weatherly" (U.S.) defeats "Gretel" (Australia) 4–1 to win America's Cup.

1963 Stanley Cup won by Toronto Maple Leafs.

Sonny Liston retains heavyweight boxing title by KOing Floyd Patterson.

Los Angeles (NL) defeats New York (AL) to win World Series, 4–0.

Arthur Ashe becomes first African American on U.S. Davis Cup team.

1964 Summer Olympic Games in Tokyo—USSR wins 41 gold medals, U.S. 37.

Cassius Clay wins world heavyweight boxing title.

"Northern Dancer" wins Triple Crown.

Jack Nicklaus is top money winner in golf—$113,284.50.

1965 Ten British professional soccer players are found guilty of "fixing" matches.

Amos Alonzo Stagg, football coach, dies.

Michigan University defeats Oregon State University in Rose Bowl, 34–7.

1966 Italian Bridge team wins seven consecutive titles.

Jim Ryun (U.S.) sets record for mile run, 3:51.3.

England defeats West Germany to win soccer's World Cup.

1967 Mickey Mantle hits 500th career home run.

Mrs. Billie Jean King wins almost every American and international tennis title available to women.

Green Bay Packers, coached by Vince Lombardi, win third consecutive NFL championship.

1968 Mexico City hosts Olympic Games and hosts more than 6,000 athletes (U.S. wins 41 gold medals).

Bob Beamon sets long-jump record with leap of 29'-2.5".

U.S. wins Davis Cup from Australia (4–1).

1969 18th Chess Olympiad won by USSR.

George Archer wins U.S. Open golf championship.

"Majestic Prince" wins horse racing's Triple Crown.

Everyday Life

1960 85.5 million TV sets in U.S.

Etiquette expert Emily Post dies.

Charles Van Doren is among 21 contestants on TV show *21* arrested for perjury.

1961 Tanganyika Conference moves to protect wildlife.

Last journey of Orient Express (Paris–Bucharest) train.

UN condemns apartheid.

1962 James Meredith, African American student, denied admission to University of Mississippi.

The Sunday Times issues first color supplement.

Eleanor Roosevelt dies.

44% of world's adult population is illiterate.

1963 U.S. unemployment rate reaches 6.1%.

Great Train Robbery in Great Britain nets £2.5 million.

Earthquake in Skopje, Yugoslavia kills 1,100.

1964 Race riots erupt in several U.S. cities as reaction to enforcement of civil rights laws.

The Beatles arrive in the U.S.

New York World's Fair opens.

The Watusi, Frog, Monkey, and Funky Chicken are dance crazes.

1965 Major tornadoes strike midwestern U.S.

Edward R. Murrow dies.

U.S. spends more than $26.2 billion for public school education.

1966 Miniskirts come into fashion.

The Salvation Army celebrates its centenary.

U.S. spends $17.4 million on alcoholic beverages.

1967 Expo '67 opens in Montreal.

Albert H. de Salvo ("Boston Strangler") sentenced to life in prison.

Lake Point Tower (Chicago) at 645 feet becomes the world's tallest reinforced concrete apartment building.

British model "Twiggy" takes U.S. by storm.

1968   U.S. gross national product is at $861 billion.

Aswan Dam in Egypt completed.

U.S. figure skater Peggy Fleming wins the only U.S. gold medal in the Winter Olympic Games.

1969   *Saturday Evening Post,* founded in 1821, suspends operations.

Camille, the strongest hurricane since 1935, devastates Gulf Coast area.

Charles Manson murders rock the nation.

World population growing by 2% annually.

Woodstock

70% of Americans polled by Gallup feel U.S. influence in the world is declining.

New Nations, 1960–1969

Barbados (1966)	Malawi (1964)
Benin (1960)	Singapore (1965)
Botswana (1966)	Maldives (1965)
Burkina Faso (1960)	Mali (1960)
Burma (1962)	Malta (1964)
Cameroon (1960)	Mauritania (1960)
Central African Republic (1960)	Nauru (1968)
Chad (1960)	Niger (1960)
Congo (1960)	Nigeria (1963)
Cote d'Ivoire (1960)	Rwanda (1962)
Cyprus (1960)	Senegal (1960)
Dominica (1967)	Sierra Leone (1961)
Equatorial Guinea (1968)	Singapore (1965)
Gabon (1960)	Somalia (1960)
The Gambia (1965)	Republic of South Africa (1961)
Guyana (1966)	Swaziland (1968)
Jamaica (1962)	Tanzania (1964)
Jordan (1946)	Togo (1960)
Kenya (1963)	Uganda (1962)
Kuwait (1961)	Western Samoa (1962)
Lesotho (1966)	Zambia (1964)
Madagascar (1960)	

Sample Learning Activities

1962   *The Cuban Missile Crisis occurs; has the possibility of escalating into World War III.*

Students role-play the important decisions facing Kennedy, Khrushchev, Castro, and others during the hours of crisis. Students also document the reactions and responses to actions taken by each side—for example, troop movements, deployment of bombers, speeches made, and rhetoric published by the media.

1969   *The first man walks on the moon; international politics and science are affected.*

Students create collages with the themes of science, technology, and government investment in research. In small groups, students use various research materials to determine what the "real" industrial/technological capabilities of the leading nations of the world were.

1970–1979: THE SHRINKING OF AMERICA

Overview

The United States, once the "world's policeman" commanding respect around the globe, saw its power and prestige wane during the 1970s. The war in Vietnam was going badly, and Americans were becoming increasingly disillusioned with a conflict that seemed to have no end. Indeed, when the conflict ended, many Americans felt disgraced not only by our involvement but also by our failure to beat a "third-rate" power.

An imposed Arab oil boycott brought Americans to their collective knees as they suddenly became aware that two-thirds of their oil supply was controlled by OPEC nations who could dictate to us how much oil we would get and how much it would cost. Other international incidents also made the United States appear to be an inept, bungling nation, a mere shadow of what it had been! When Iranian extremists captured the U.S. embassy in Teheran and took a number Americans hostage, the Carter administration seemed paralyzed and unable to resolve the issue. This further frustrated the American people. Suddenly, it seemed, we had become a second-rate nation—a "Paper Dragon," as the Chinese had put it.

At home, things were not much better. Race riots, anti-war protests (some ending in violence, as happened at Kent State University where student protesters were shot) and a sagging economy seemed to spell doom on the domestic front. Watergate and the disgrace surrounding the Nixon presidency led to growing cynicism about politics, leadership, and America's role in a rapidly changing world. More than at any other time in our history, the United States of America seemed directionless. Politically, this was a dark time for many Americans. Even the end of the Vietnam War brought little joy. After all, we had lost the war and were being called war-mongers. All around the world, our credibility was sadly damaged.

Even the space program, once the jewel in our crown, was essentially dismantled by lack of money (siphoned off for the Vietnam War) and, worse, lack of interest. The accident at the Three Mile Island nuclear power plant sounded the death knell for America's desire to create and develop nuclear power stations that would supposedly eliminate our need for foreign fuel sources.

Aside from Vietnam and Watergate, perhaps the two greatest traumas of the decade, the most significant human interest stories that seemed to profoundly affect our lives, were the mass murders/suicides of the Jonestown cult followers and the *Roe v. Wade* decision in 1973, which sparked the Right-to-Life movement. Yes, the Soviet invasion of Afghanistan and the U.S. boycott of the 1980 Olympics were newsworthy—but Jonestown and *Roe v. Wade* touched the very core of America—religion and family values.

Demographics: 1970–1979

Important Political Leaders

    U.S.—Richard Nixon, Gerald Ford, Jimmy Carter
    Japan—Emperor Hirohito
    China—Mao Zedong, Deng Xiaoping
    USSR—Leonid Brezhnev
    Great Britain—Edward Heath
    France—Giscard d'Estaing and Charles De Gaulle
    Egypt—Anwar Sadat
    Italy—Francesco Cossiga
    Israel—Menachem Begin, Yitzhak Rabin
    Spain—Francisco Franco, King Juan Carlos
    Yugoslavia—Josip Broz (Tito)
    India—Chandburg Singh, Indira Gandhi
    West Germany—Helmut Schmidt, Konrad Adenauer
    Canada—Pierre Trudeau
    Chile—Salvador Allende
    Uganda—Idi Amin

Largest Cities

Ten Largest U.S. Cities		*Ten Largest Cities Outside the U.S.*	
1. New York	7,771,730	1. Tokyo	11,350,000
2. Chicago	3,325,263	2. London	7,763,000
3. Los Angeles	2,782,400	3. Paris	7,196,000
4. Philadelphia	1,926,529	4. Moscow	7,061,000
5. Detroit	1,492,914	5. Shanghai	6,900,000
6. Houston	1,213,064	6. Sao Paulo	5,684,706
7. Baltimore	895,222	7. Bombay	5,574,261
8. Dallas	836,121	8. Calcutta	5,071,161
9. Washington, D.C.	764,000	9. Rio de Janeiro	4,207,322
10. Indianapolis	742,612	10. Peking	4,010,000

        U.S. population: 203,302,031
        World population: 3.78 billion

Significant Headlines and News Stories

    1970   Anti–Vietnam War protests intensify in U.S.
           Four students killed, nine wounded at Kent State University.
           Arab commandos hijack three jets bound for Europe and U.S.
    1971   U.S. planes bomb Vietcong supply routes in Cambodia.
           China joins the United Nations.
           Women granted right to vote in Switzerland.
           Civil war in Pakistan.
    1972   Watergate affair begins.
           President Nixon visits China.
           President Nixon signs SALT I agreement with Soviet leader Leonid
              Brezhnev.
           Ceylon changes name to Sri Lanka.
           Arab guerrillas storm Israeli Olympic compound in Munich—kill
              11 Israeli athletes.

1973 Military coup in Chile.
Vice-president Spiro Agnew resigns.
Fourth Arab–Israeli war begins (Yom Kippur War).
Israeli Prime Minister Golda Meir dies.
Arab oil embargo—quadruples price of oil in U.S.
1974 Terrorism continues in Northern Ireland and England.
Nelson Rockefeller nominated to serve as vice-president.
President Ford pardons Richard Nixon and extends limited amnesty to Vietnam War draft evaders.
1975 Vietnam War ends.
Ethiopian Emperor Haile Selassie deposed after a 44-year reign.
Portugal's rule over all African colonies ends.
Juan Carlos I becomes King of Spain.
Apollo–Soyuz test project in outer space.
1976 Mao Zedong of China dies.
Women admitted to U.S. military academies.
Québec seeks independence from Canada.
Jimmy Carter elected 39th U.S. president.
1977 *Roots* by Alex Haley attracts huge TV audiences.
U.S. and Panama agree to return control of canal to Panama.
President Carter pardons Vietnam War draft "dodgers."
1978 Unmanned space ship *Pioneer* reaches Venus.
World's first test-tube baby born in Great Britain.
Karol Wojtyla becomes first non-Italian Pope in 450 years—renamed Pope John II.
1979 Nuclear accident at Three Mile Island power plant in Pennsylvania.
Israel and Egypt sign peace treaty.
100 U.S. embassy staff taken hostage in Teheran, Iran.
USSR invades Afghanistan.

History and Politics
1970 Gambia becomes a republic within the British Commonwealth.
French president de Gaulle dies.
Paris Peace Talks end second year without progress toward peace in Vietnam.
1971 Idi Amin seizes power in Uganda.
26th Amendment enacted, changing voting age to 18.
"Pentagon Papers" appear in *New York Times.*
1972 SALT I Treaty signed with the Soviets.
U.S. returns Okinawa to Japan.
J. Edgar Hoover dies.
Richard M. Nixon reelected for second term.
1973 *Roe v. Wade* decision.
Kissinger signs Vietnam Peace Agreement, ending Vietnam War.
Lyndon Johnson dies.
Militant Native Americans occupy South Dakota hamlet of Wounded Knee.
1974 Impeachment charges brought against President Nixon.
Richard Nixon becomes first person to resign U.S. presidency.
Gerald Ford becomes 38th president.
1975 King Faisal of Saudi Arabia assassinated.
Franco, Spanish dictator, dies; monarchy restored.

1976 U.S. and USSR sign an agreement banning underground nuclear testing.

U.S. celebrates its bicentennial.

Isabel Peron is deposed in Argentina.

1977 Begin becomes prime minister of Israel.

Bhutto overthrown in Pakistan.

Space shuttle *Enterprise* tested on back of a 747.

U.S. and Canada sign pact for Alaskan oil pipeline.

1978 California voters approve Proposition Thirteen.

The Bakke decision is handed down declaring racial quotas illegal.

Camp David Accords signed by Sadat, Carter, and Begin.

Begin and Sadat share Nobel Peace Prize.

1979 Iran deposes Shah Reza Pahlavi.

Ayatollah Khomeini returns to Iran from his exile in Paris.

U.S. embassy in Teheran taken by Iranians, 100 U.S. hostages held.

Sandinistas take power in Nicaragua.

Soviets invade Afghanistan.

Science and Technology

1970 *Apollo 13* launched from Cape Kennedy.

150-inch reflecting telescope at Kitt Peak Observatory completed.

Luna 16, unmanned Soviet spacecraft, returns from moon with rock samples.

1971 U.S. satellite *Mariner 9* orbits Mars.

U.S. *Apollo 14* and *Apollo 15* crews explore moon's surface.

U.S. astronomers discover two "new" galaxies.

1972 Richard Leakey and Glynn Isaac discover 2.5-million-year-old skull in Africa.

Soviet spacecraft *Venus 8* soft-lands on Venus.

The Tasadays, a Stone Age tribe, are found living in caves in the Philippine Islands.

1973 Nobel Prize in Medicine: Konrad Lorenz (Austria)

U.S. space probe *Pioneer 10* translates TV pictures from 81,000 miles from the surface of Mars.

Dr. Paul Dudley White, American heart specialist, dies.

1974 India becomes sixth nation to explode nuclear device.

Freon said to endanger ozone layer.

High-energy neutrons produced in cyclotrons are used to treat cancer.

1975 Paleontologists discover the oldest American fossil, a 620-million-year-old marine worm.

Astronomers discover a new galaxy ten times larger than the Milky Way.

Godfrey Hounsfield (England) designs an X-ray scanner giving clear cross-section of a patient's body.

1976 "Lyme" arthritis first isolated near Lyme, Connecticut.

Indonesia launches a commercial satellite.

Pioneer 10 travels through Saturn's rings and heads toward Pluto.

1977 Fluorocarbons are banned.

FDA claims saccharin may cause cancer.

Scientists discover DNA contains more information than previously thought.

1978 Controversy over cloning of human beings.
Interferon used as treatment in "hopeless" cancer cases.
AMA concludes 14-year study showing cigarette smoking causes heart disease and cancer.

1979 A "black hole" is discovered in the Milky Way.
Viking I discovers Jupiter has a ring and fourteenth moon.
Chinese dentists claim 90% success rate for replanting teeth.

Literature and Theater

1970 Nobel Prize for Literature: Alexander Solzhenitsyn (USSR).
Neil Simon: *Last of the Red Hot Lovers*
William Meredith: "Earth Work" (poems)

1971 Nobel Prize for Literature: Pablo Neruda (Chile)
Bernard Malamud: *The Tenant*
Edward Albee: *All Over*

1972 *Fiddler on the Roof,* longest running musical, closes.
Ezra Pound dies.
Nobel Prize for Literature: Heinrich Boll (Germany)

1973 J. R. R. Tolkien (Britain) dies.
David Storey: *The Changing Room*—best play of the season
Pearl Buck dies.

1974 Patrick White: *The Eye of the Storm*
No Pulitzer Prize for literature or drama awarded this year.
Isaac Singer: *A Crown of Feathers and Other Stories*

1975 Soprano Beverly Sills debuts at the Metropolitan Opera in New York.
A Chorus Line opens on Broadway.
Ciro Algra: *El Paso de los Garos*
Vincent Bugliosi: *Helter Skelter*

1976 Leon Uris: *Trinity*
Alex Haley: *Roots*
California Suite, a play by Neil Simon, opens.

1977 David Mamet: *American Buffalo*
Annie opens on Broadway.
Colleen McCollough: *The Thornbirds*

1978 Nobel Prize in Literature to Isaac Bashevis Singer.
John Irving: *The World According to Garp*
James Michener: *Chesapeake*
Liza Minnelli wins Tony for *The Act.*

1979 Pulitzer Prize to Norman Mailer for *The Executioner's Song*
Tom Wolfe: *The Right Stuff*
Jerzy Kosinski: *Passion Play*

Music

1970 New York City Ballet presents 500th performance of *The Nutcracker.*
Broadway: *Company, Applause*
London Contemporary Dance Theater is first modern dance company in England.

1971 Broadway: *Godspell, Jesus Christ Superstar*
Carole King: *Tapestry*
Elton John: *Tumbleweed Connection*

1972 Broadway: *Pippin, Grease*

Helen Reddy: "I Am Woman" becomes a popular song expressing a theme of the women's movement.

Robert Moog patents the Moog synthesizer.

1973   Billy Joel: "The Piano Man"

Stevie Wonder: "You Are the Sunshine of My Life"

Opera: *Death in Venice* (Benjamin Britten)

1974   Duke Ellington dies.

Popular music groups: Chicago, Steely Dan, Jefferson Starship, Santana, The Eagles

1975   Bruce Springsteen: "Born to Run"

Nureyev performs *Sleeping Beauty* ballet in London.

Bee Gees, "Jive Talkin'" introduces disco music.

1976   Peter Frampton (Britain) chosen Artist of the Year.

Stevie Wonder: *Songs in the Key of Life*

Bob Marley popularized reggae music.

1977   Disco dance music is all the rage.

"Punk rock" or "new wave" music gains popularity.

Brel performed by Jaques Brel is biggest musical hit in France.

1978   Dolly Parton named Country Music Association's Entertainer of the Year.

Irish flutist James Galway has best selling hit in the U.K.: "Annie's Song"

ABBA becomes the most popular group since the Beatles.

1979   Elton John is first rock star to tour USSR.

Paris Opera presents *Lulu.*

Visual Arts

1970   Academy Award: *Patton*

Japanese department store Ichi-Ban-Kan opens in Tokyo.

Rowan and Martin *Laugh-In* is top TV show.

1971   Kennedy Performing Arts Center opens in Washington, D.C.

Academy Award: *The French Connection*

"Conceptual" art becomes new U.S. craze.

1972   Academy Award: *The Godfather*

Raphael painting *Madonna and Child* sells for $3 million.

Max Fleischer, creator of "Popeye," dies.

1973   Academy Award: *The Sting*

World Trade Center opens in New York City.

Jack Lemmon wins Oscar for *Save the Tiger*

1974   110-story Sears Tower in Chicago becomes world's tallest building.

Samuel Goldwyn dies.

Upstairs, Downstairs is popular TV series.

Academy Award: *The Godfather, Part II*

1975   *All in the Family* is top TV show for fifth straight year.

Academy Award: *One Flew Over the Cuckoo's Nest*

Mary Hartman, Mary Hartman is popular "off-color" TV show.

Gary Trudeau wins Pulitzer Prize for editorial cartooning.

1976   Academy Award: *Rocky*

15.1% of all U.S. households have color TV sets.

Stanley Forman of the Boston *Herald-American* wins Pulitzer Prize for photography.

Cristo designs *Running Fence,* a 24-mile curtain along the Pacific coast.

1977   *Annie Hall* wins Academy Award.

TV series *Roots* breaks all audience records.

In Paris, Georges Pompidou National Centre for the Arts and Culture opens.

1978   Vietnam is subject of two movies, Academy Award winner *The Deer Hunter* and *Coming Home.*

Ralph Bakshi: *Lord of the Rings*

Walter Kerr (*New York Times*) and William Safire (*New York Times*) won Pulitzer Prizes for criticism and commentary, respectively.

1979   Academy Award: *Kramer vs. Kramer*

ESPN starts broadcasting.

The Icebergs, a painting, sells for $2.5 million.

Sports

1970   Brazil wins World Cup in soccer.

Joe Frazier becomes world heavyweight boxing champion.

Tony Jacklin becomes first Briton to win U.S. Open in fifty years.

1971   Hank Aaron hits 600th home run, only the third player ever to do so.

Chichester crosses Atlantic Ocean alone in *Gypsy Moth II* (22 days).

Mrs. Billie Jean King becomes first woman athlete to earn $100,000 in a single season.

1972   11th Winter Olympic Games held in Sapporo, Japan.

Summer Olympics held in Munich—U.S. takes 50 gold medals.

Bobby Fischer (U.S.) wins chess title from Boris Spassky (USSR).

Jackie Robinson, first African American major league baseball player, dies.

1973   Designated hitter introduced in the American League.

George Foreman wins world heavyweight boxing title.

"Secretariat" wins Triple Crown.

Cambridge crew defeats Oxford in their 148th race.

1974   Muhammad Ali regains world heavyweight championship.

Frank Robinson becomes first African American baseball manager.

Little League bars foreign teams and allows girls to participate.

Hank Aaron sets new major league home run record.

1975   Jackie Tonawanda, a woman, is denied a boxing license in the state of New York.

Chris Evert wins $40,000, highest prize ever won on women's tennis tour.

European baseball finishes first season; Israel Sabres take first place.

1976   Winter Olympics held at Innsbruck, Austria, where 1,054 athletes from 37 nations participates.

1977   Steve Cauthen (17) is first jockey to earn $6 million.

St. Louis outfielder Lou Brock sets base-stealing record with 893.

Pete Maravich of New Orleans leads NBA scorers with 31.7 average.

1978   Nancy Lopez wins 5 consecutive golf tournaments.

Argentina wins World Soccer Cup.

Tracy Caulkins (15) sets 14 U.S. records in swimming.

1979 Tracy Austin (16) becomes youngest women's champion in U.S. Tennis Open history.

Lou Brock gets 3,000 hits.

Carl Yastrzemski hits 400th home run.

Pete Rose hits 2,427th single.

Everyday Life

1970 Hundreds of U.S. universities and colleges are either closed or on strike to protest the Vietnam War.

A report shows *Sesame Street* is improving young children's reading skills.

An estimated 231 million TV sets are in use around the world.

1971 U.S. Supreme Court rules hiring policies must be the same for both sexes.

Justice Department reports that nearly half of the nation's major crimes are committed by juveniles.

Cigarette advertisements banned from TV.

Mass murderer Charles Manson convicted and sent to prison for life.

1972 Six cigarette manufacturers agree to include health warnings on their package.

Life magazine ceases publication.

U.S. military draft phased out.

1973 14 states restore death penalty.

Ford Motor Company fined $7 million for violating Clean Air Act.

American Hospital Association publishes 12-point patient Bill of Rights.

1974 "Streaking" spreads across America.

More than $1.9 billion is spent by moviegoers to see *The Sting* and *The Exorcist*.

Federal Trade Commission requires advertisers to support nutritional claims about food values.

1975 Elizabeth Seton becomes first U.S.-born saint in Catholic Church.

World population passes 4 billion.

Insurance companies drop malpractice insurance for medical doctors.

1976 Women, participating for the first time, win 13 of 32 Rhodes scholarships.

National survey of high school seniors finds 53% have tried marijuana.

Department of Health finds Americans' health generally good. Life expectancy:

White women: 79.2 years	Nonwhite women: 72 years
White men: 67.4 years	Nonwhite men: 62 years

1977 John Neumann becomes first American male to become a saint in the Catholic Church.

U.S. Supreme Court rules spanking in school by officials is not a violation of pupils' constitutional rights.

Trans-American oil pipeline begins operation.

1978 Mass murders/suicides at People's Temple, Jonestown, Guyana, claims 911 victims.

Federal judge in Ohio rules that high school girls should not be prevented from participating with boys on same teams.

Irene Miller and Vera Komarkova become first Americans and first women to climb Annapurna in Nepal (26,545 feet).

1979   Mother Teresa of India awarded Nobel Peace Prize.

Three Mile Island nuclear accident forces thousands to evacuate from their homes.

Pope John II tours U.S.

New Nations, 1970–1979

Afghanistan (1973)	Papua New Guinea (1975)
Angola (1975)	Qatar (1971)
The Bahamas (1973)	St. Lucia (1979)
Bahrain (1971)	St. Vincent and the Grenadines (1979)
Bangladesh (1971)	Saõ Tome and Principe (1975)
Cape Verde (1975)	Seychelles (1976)
Comoros (1975)	Solomon Islands (1978)
Djibouti (1977)	Sri Lanka (1972)
Fiji (1970)	Suriname (1975)
Grenada (1974)	Tonga (1970)
Guinea-Bissau (1978)	Trinidad and Tobago (1976)
Kiribati (1979)	Tuvalu (1978)
North Korea (1973)	United Arab Emirates (1971)
Mozambique (1975)	Vietnam reunited (1976)
Namibia (1978)	Republic of Zaire (1971)

Sample Learning Activities

1975   *Vietnam War ends; repercussions are felt by the U.S., as well as ramifications for the world at large.*

Students interpret video excerpts from the period, such as the films *All the President's Men* and *Woodstock,* as well as performances by groups like Crosby, Stills, Nash, and Young; Ohio; The Doors; and Sly and the Family Stone.

Group examination of the U.S. role in international affairs following Vietnam is predicated on the idea that the U.S. was "beaten" for the first time in over a century. Students should ask: "How will the U.S. respond to other foreign crises?" "How does the rest of the world now regard the U.S.?" They should find examples to support their answers.

1979   *Three Mile Island accident.*

Students prepare a report on toxic waste sites, pollution, and cleanup efforts in their local area. Comparisons to the Chernobyl nuclear meltdown in the USSR can be made.

Later, students can further examine human interaction with the environment around the globe. Individually or in groups, students can research such places as Alaska (pipeline and mining), Kuwait (after the Gulf War), Russia (mining and weapon plants), Brazil (the rain forest), Argentina (mining), the Great

Lakes states (industrial manufacturing), and central Europe (industrial manufacturing, mining, etc.).

The class can role-play a session of Congress and debate the benefits and dangers of nuclear power. The debate should conclude with the passing of a bill that the students have developed regarding the future of nuclear power in this country.

Students also can examine the "health" of the nation in areas that have nuclear power, fossil fuel power, and chemical plants. They can discuss cancer rates and birth defects, also.

1980–1989: RESOLUTION, RESTORATION, AND CONSERVATION

Overview

Not since the conclusion of World War II had the national political climate changed as much as it would in the 1980s. This decade would see the end of the Cold War that had dominated world attention for more than 40 years, including the democratization of the Soviet Union, the destruction of the Berlin Wall, and the reemergence of the United States as a peacekeeper and a world power exerting its influence all over the globe.

As the 1970s ended, the United States found itself desperately trying to rebuild its image and reestablish economic stability. A hopeful nation elected Ronald Reagan to the presidency, and the former film star began to promote the idea of a new and more dynamic America to friends and foes alike. Although the economy seemed healthy throughout the 1980s, it was actually in bad shape; we, along with many other nations, would suffer from a worldwide recession. That, however, was not known in 1980, and the business of rebuilding the American image began by focusing on the defeat of the so-called Evil Empire (Communism) wherever it existed. Exercising U.S. political, economic, and military muscle became a guiding principle of U.S. foreign policies. The so-called Brush Fire wars (Grenada, 1983; Panama, 1989) were initiated and completed to illustrate our resolve to be the protector of democracy around the world.

The 1980s were a time when the United States reaffirmed itself globally, but at a cost of domestic programs that served millions of people who relied on government aid for their very existence. Both the Reagan and Bush administrations were politically conservative, which, in this context, meant that individual states, rather than the federal government, would be responsible for identifying and serving their own needy populations. Long-established programs were systematically disposed of, creating hardship for millions. Subsequently, with the general downturn of the economy, the poor became more numerous, and homelessness became part of the American lexicon, and the American reality, in virtually every community.

Another issue that plagued the 1980s was the alarming increase in international terrorism. It seemed that no one was safe if targeted by an extremist group for destruction. But that was still an issue foreign to most Americans; it concerned only those traveling abroad or reporting the news elsewhere. Terrorism would strike the United States in earnest in the 1990s, but for now the concern was still remote.

The decade ended with a dramatic series of "impossible" events. The Berlin Wall came tumbling down, the Cold War ended, and the Soviet Union began to break up. Certainly the 1989 Tienanmen Square massacre in China reminded us that Communism was still alive and well, but it seemed less of a threat to our national security than formerly. Indeed, as the 1990s approached, it appeared that the United States had righted itself and would again become the Great Power in the world, filling the void left by the breakup of the USSR and, more important, serving notice to all the United States was back.

Demographics: 1980–1989

Important Political Leaders

U.S.—Ronald Reagan and George Bush
Great Britain—Margaret Thatcher
France—François Mitterand
Egypt—Hosni Mubarak
Israel—Yitzak Shamir
West Germany—Helmut Kohl
USSR—Alexei Kosygin, Konstantin Chernenko, and Mikhail Gorbachev
Japan—Emperor Hirohito
Jordan—King Hussein
Canada—Brian Mulroney
Cuba—Fidel Castro
Vatican City—Pope John II
East Germany—Erich Honecker
Iran—Ayatollah Khomeini
Iraq—Saddam Hussein
India—Indira Gandhi, Rajir Gandhi
Mexico—Miguel Aleman Valdes

Largest Cities

Ten Largest U.S. Cities		*Ten Largest Cities Outside the U.S.*	
1. New York	7,262,700	1. Tokyo-Yokohama	25,434,000
2. Los Angeles	3,254,340	2. Mexico City	16,901,000
3. Chicago	3,009,530	3. Sao Paulo	14,911,000
4. Houston	1,728,910	4. Seoul	13,665,000
5. Philadelphia	1,642,900	5. Osaka-Kobe-Kyoto	13,562,000
6. Detroit	1,086,220	6. Buenos Aires	10,750,000
7. San Diego	1,015,190	7. Calcutta	10,462,000
8. Dallas	1,003,520	8. Bombay	10,137,000
9. San Antonio	914,350	9. Rio de Janeiro	10,116,000
10. Phoenix	894,070	10. Cairo	9,500,000

U.S. population: 226,545,805
World population 5.19 billion

Significant Headlines and News Stories
1980 "O! Canada" becomes the Canadian national anthem.
U.S. boycotts Summer Olympic Games because of Soviet invasion of Afghanistan.
Mount St. Helen's in Washington State erupts.
1981 Sandra Day O'Connor becomes first woman appointed to Supreme Court.

U.S. hostages released by Iranians.

Attempted assassination of President Reagan fails.

1982   Israel invades Lebanon to root out Palestinian terrorists.

U.S. Marines land in Beirut, Lebanon.

Soviets occupy Kabul and most of Afghanistan.

1983   James Watt resigns as Secretary of the Interior.

Large amounts of dioxin found in soil around Times Beach, Missouri.

Famine strikes Africa and other parts of the world.

1984   The U.S. restores full diplomatic relations with the Vatican after 117 years.

U.S. Embassy in Beirut bombed—200 Marines killed.

1985   TWA jet hijacked in Athens, Greece.

Union Carbide Corporation sued by the government of India for the plant disaster in Bhopal that killed 1,700 people.

Cyclone kills 10,000 in Bangladesh.

1986   Spacecraft *Challenger* is lost in accident.

Number of AIDS deaths increases tenfold in five years.

Debt crisis in South Africa threatens worldwide economic crisis.

1987   Kurt Waldheim of Austria becomes first head of state to be put on "excluded" list barring him entry into the U.S.

Lech Walesa becomes a leader in Polish politics.

Lieutenant Colonel Oliver North testifies about the Iran-Contra affair.

1988   The Cold War ends!

General Manuel Noriega of Panama convicted.

George Bush elected 41st president of the United States.

1989   The Berlin Wall comes down!

Thousands killed in Tienanmen Square massacre in China.

UNESCO reports that over one-third of the world's population is illiterate.

History and Politics

1980   Ronald Reagan elected 40th president of the U.S.

U.S. boycotts Summer Olympic Games.

U.S. breaks diplomatic relations with Iran.

Cyrus Vance resigns as Secretary of State over Iran-Contra hostage situation.

1981   Nationwide air traffic controllers strike.

Two Libyan jets shot down by U.S. forces.

Sandra Day O'Connor becomes first woman appointed to Supreme Court.

1982   Alexander Haig resigns as Secretary of State.

ERA fails to achieve ratification.

Pope John II escaped an assassination attempt in Portugal.

1983   Spaceship *Challenger* launched.

Harold Washington becomes first African American mayor elected in a major U.S. city.

U.S. troops invade the island of Grenada.

1984   School prayer amendment defeated in Senate.

Walter Mondale versus Ronald Reagan in national election.

Brunei becomes an independent nation.

1985 President Ronald Reagan visits China.

President Ronald Reagan meets with Gorbachev of the USSR.

IRA terrorists continue to challenge British rule in northern Ireland.

1986 *Roe v. Wade,* providing constitutional protection in abortion cases, upheld.

Swedish Premier Olaf Palme killed by gunmen in Stockholm.

U.S. corporations withdraw from South Africa.

1987 Worst stock market crash in history—Dow falls 508 points.

President Reagan vetoes Clean Water Act.

U.S. hostage in Lebanon slain by terrorists holding him captive.

1988 USSR withdraws from Afghanistan.

Ferdinand and Imelda Marcos of the Philippine Islands are convicted by federal grand jury.

Cities of Philadelphia (Republican) and Atlanta (Democrat) host national political conventions.

1989 Burning of the U.S. flag is protected by the First Amendment.

The U.S. invades Panama in an effort to arrest General Manuel Noriega.

Czechoslovakian parliament ends Communist rule and promises free elections.

Science and Technology

1980 First successful synthesis of interferon—effective against viral diseases.

Of the 68 nuclear plants operating, 38 failed to meet safety regulations.

U.S. declares state of emergency at the Love Canal, New York, area contaminated with toxic waste.

1981 Herpes simplex virus successfully suppressed with acyclovir.

Space shuttle *Columbia* launched.

Risk of coronary death linked to high levels of cholesterol.

1982 *Time* magazine names the computer "man of the year."

Halley's comet sighted.

Barney Clark gets first artificial heart.

1983 First California condor chick hatched in San Diego Zoo.

Barney Clark dies after 117 days with artificial heart.

Sally Ride becomes the first woman and Lieutenant Colonel Guion Bluford becomes the first African American to fly in the space shuttle *Challenger.*

1984 First successful surrogate mother conception announced.

Identification of virus thought to cause AIDS found.

First successful baboon heart transplant performed on a human infant ("Baby Fae").

Effective chicken pox vaccine developed.

1985 Wreck of the luxury liner *Titanic* found.

1986 First test tube baby in America born in Cleveland, Ohio.

First nonstop flight around the world without refueling completed by *Voyager.*

1987 Azidothymide (AZT) patented to assist AIDS victims.

Gene splicing introduced.

1988 Ban on smoking on passenger planes is implemented.

The B-2 "Stealth" bomber is shown publicly.

1989 Nuclear fission at room temperature is claimed by two University of Utah chemists.

Space shuttle launches *Galileo* spacecraft on its trip to Jupiter.

Literature and Theater

1980 U.S. Ballet Theater celebrates 40th anniversary.
The Clan of the Cave Bear by Jean Auel
Children of a Lesser God by Mark Medoff opens in New York.
Agnes of God by John Pielmeir opens.
Executioner's Song by Norman Mailer wins Pulitzer Prize.

1981 *Crimes of the Heart* by Beth Henley wins Pulitzer Prize.
A Soldier's Play by Chris Fuller opens.
Transit of Venus by Shirley Hazzard wins National Book Critics Award.

1982 *Cats* opens.
Little Shop of Horrors opens.
John Updike's *Rabbit Is Rich* wins Pulitzer Prize.

1983 100th anniversary of New York City Metropolitan Opera.
Ironweed by William Kennedy wins National Book Critics Award.
Pulitzer Prizes awarded to Alice Walker for *The Color Purple* and Russell Baker for *Growing Up.*
Brighton Beach Memoirs by Neil Simon opens.
A Chorus Line becomes longest running Broadway musical.

1984 *La Cage aux Folles* by Jerry Herman wins Tony Award.
Pulitzer Prize awarded to David Mamet for *Glengarry Glen Ross.*
Donald Duck celebrates 50th birthday.

1985 *Biloxi Blues* by Neil Simon wins Tony Award.
Pulitzer Prize to Alison Lurie for *Foreign Affairs.*
Big River, a musical by Roger Miller and William Hauptman, opens.

1986 *Me and My Girl* opens.
Robert Penn Warren becomes the first official U.S. poet laureate.
Lonesome Dove by Larry McMurtry wins Pulitzer Prize.
Accidental Tourist by Anne Tyler and *Common Ground* by J. Anthony Lukas win Critics Award.

1987 *Les Miserables* opens.
Richard Wilbur becomes second U.S. poet laureate.
A Summons to Memphis wins Pulitzer Prize.
Fences by August Wilson wins Tony Award.
Sleeping Beauty ballet opens.

1988 *Phantom of the Opera* opens.
Beloved by Toni Morrison and *Driving Miss Daisy* by Alfred Urey win Pulitzer Prizes.
Irving Berlin celebrates 100th birthday.
Howard Nemerov named third U.S. poet laureate.

1989 *Heidi Chronicles* and *Grand Hotel* open on Broadway.
Saul Bellow wins Critics Award for his two books, *A Theft* and *The Bellarossa Connection.*
Anne Tyler wins Pulitzer Prize for *Breathing Lessons; 42nd Street* becomes second longest running musical on Broadway.

Music

1980 John Williams succeeds Arthur Fiedler as director of Boston "Pops."

Christopher Cross wins Grammy Award for "Sailing."
Video cassettes and MTV are introduced.

1981   Kim Carnes: "Bette Davis Eyes"
John Lennon and Yoko Ono: *Double Fantasy*

1982   Toto: "Rosanna"
Manhattan Transfer: "Boy from New York City"

1983   Michael Jackson: "Beat It"
"Thriller" by Michael Jackson becomes the all time best-selling album.

1984   *Flashdance* wins Grammy Award.
Tina Turner: "What's Love Got to Do with It?"

1985   "We Are the World"—USA for Africa
Phil Collins: "Against All Odds"

1986   Steve Winwood: "Higher Love"
Paul Simon: "Graceland"

1987   U2: "The Joshua Tree"

1988   George Michael: "Faith"
Bobby McFerrin: "Don't Worry, Be Happy"

1989   Bonnie Raitt: "Nick of Time"
Bette Midler: "Wind Beneath My Wings"

Visual Arts

1980   *Kramer vs. Kramer* wins Academy Award.
Notebook Sketches by Leonardo da Vinci sold at auction for $5,280,000.

1981   Picasso *Self-Portrait* sold for $5,300,000.
Ordinary People wins Academy Award.
Raiders of the Lost Ark opens in theaters.

1982   *ET the Extraterrestrial*

1983   *The Day After* TV show attracts 100 million viewers.
Final episode of *MASH* draws 125 million viewers.
Gandhi wins Academy Award.

1984   *Indiana Jones and the Temple of Doom* is most popular movie.
Thriller video on MTV.
Sculpture *Big Crinkly* by Alexander Calder sold at auction for $852,000.
Cagney and Lacey wins Emmy Award.

1985   *Rambo, First Blood, Part II*
Back to the Future becomes a popular movie.
Rubens Peale with a Geranium by Rembrandt sold at auction for $4.02 million.
Amadeus wins Academy Award.
"Art of India: 3000 B.C. to A.D. 1300" exhibit opens.

1986   *Ferris Bueller's Day Off* and *The Color of Money* are popular movies.
Out of Africa wins Academy Award.
Cagney and Lacey wins Emmy Award.

1987   *Platoon* wins Academy Award.
Irises by Vincent Van Gogh sold for $5.3 million.
Emmy Award to *LA Law*.
Georgia O'Keeffe works sell for $1.9 million.

1988   Bill Cosby's TV show rated #1.

"Art Treasures of the Hermitage" opens in Metropolitan Museum
of Art in New York.
The Last Emperor wins Academy Award.
Art Institute of Chicago expands.
Jackson Pollock painting *Search* sold for $4.8 million.
Andy Warhol collection sold for $25.3 million.
1989   Picasso's *Pierrette's Wedding* sold for $51.3 million.
Rain Man wins Academy Award.
Indiana Jones and the Last Crusade most popular movie of the year.
Do the Right Thing (film by Spike Lee)

Sports

1980   Winter Olympic Games, Lake Placid, New York
U.S. hockey team upsets highly favored USSR.
U.S. defends "America's Cup" against Australia.
1981   First major league baseball strike loses one-third of season.
Indiana University wins NCAA basketball crown.
1982   National League wins its 11th straight All-Star game.
"Gato del Sol" wins the Kentucky Derby.
1983   Pan American Games held in Caracas, Venezuela. U.S. wins 137
medals.
Bowie Kuhn not rehired as Major League Baseball commissioner.
1984   Winter Olympic Games held in Sarajevo—U.S. wins four gold
medals.
USSR boycotts Summer Olympics in Los Angeles, California, and
U.S. wins 83 gold medals.
1985   Jockey Willie Shoemaker becomes first rider to win $100,000,000 in
purse money.
Tom Seaver of the Chicago White Sox becomes 17th pitcher to win
300 games.
Pete Rose breaks Ty Cobb's record with his 4192nd base hit.
1986   Greg LeMond becomes first American to win the "Tour de France."
Three-point goal instituted in men's basketball.
1987   Martina Navratilova wins her sixth Wimbledon Tennis Crown.
40th anniversary of Little League baseball.
Pan American Games held in Indianapolis, Indiana.
1988   Fifteenth Winter Olympic Games held in Calgary, Canada. U.S.
wins six medals—Bonnie Blair (speed skating) and Brian Boi-
tano (figure skating) win gold.
Jackie Joyner-Kersee sets heptathlon record win of 7215 points in
Summer Olympics.
"Little 500" bicycle race in Indiana admits an all-woman team for
first time in 37 years.
1989   Greg LeMond of U.S. wins his second "Tour de France."
Pete Rose banned from baseball for gambling.

Everyday Life

1980   John Lennon of the Beatles murdered.
First female candidates graduate from U.S. service academies: 61
from West Point; 55 from Annapolis; and 97 from the Air Force
Academy.
Mount St. Helens erupts.
Sexual harassment of women prohibited by act of Congress.

1981   Wage discrimination struck down.

Title IX enacted.

First Mexican American mayor, Henry Cisneros, elected in San Antonio, Texas.

John Hinckley attempts to kill President Reagan.

Iranian hostage crisis ends.

U.S. employs grain embargo against USSR.

1982   Hard winter freeze kills 261 people in the Midwest, the South, and the Plains.

Dow Jones average hits all-time high of 1070.25.

Cyanide poison found in Tylenol pills—7 die.

Air Florida jet crashes into Potomac River Bridge—several die.

U.S. Marines land in Beirut, Lebanon.

1983   Cost of living index rose 3.2%.

"Yuppie" look becomes popular in fashion.

Home video games become popular.

Computer-based technology becoming significant.

First U.S. woman astronaut goes into space.

1984   Richard Miller, first FBI agent charged with espionage, is arrested.

Bill protecting student meetings for religious or political purposes outside of normal school days is signed by President Reagan.

Margie Velma Barfield becomes the first woman to be executed in the U.S. in 22 years.

Dr. Kathryn Sullivan becomes the first woman to walk in space.

Discovery of 7000-year-old human skulls with brains found in Florida peat bog.

1985   U.S. passes economic sanctions against South Africa.

Luxury liner *Achille Lauro* is hijacked in the Mediterranean by Arab terrorists.

Christa McAuliffe, teacher and mother of three, is selected to go on space shuttle.

1986   U.S. imposes economic sanctions against Libya.

New gun control laws passed.

Rev. Donald Pelotte becomes first Native American to be ordained a Catholic priest.

Third worst mass murderer in U.S. history, Patrick Henry, is executed in Oklahoma.

1987   Reverend Jim Bakker resigns his TV ministry in disgrace.

Hospital orderly Donald Harvey is convicted of killing 24 people in Ohio.

President Reagan lifts sanctions against Poland.

1988   U.S. troops sent to Honduras.

Governor Evan Mecham of Arizona convicted for misconduct.

Senate passes bill to protect ozone shield.

Eugene Antonio Marino becomes first African American Catholic archbishop in the U.S.

First nightly TV news anchorman, Douglas Edwards, retires.

Samuel Leroy Mandel (104), the oldest living U.S. veteran, dies.

Lauro Cavaros becomes first Hispanic to be elevated to a cabinet post—Secretary of Education.

1989   The Exxon Valdez runs aground in Alaska, causing the worst oil spill in U.S. history.

USS Iowa gun turret explodes, killing 47 sailors.

13-year-old U.S. students rank last in math and science exams and knowledge—Korea, Great Britain, Ireland, Spain, and four Canadian provinces rank higher.

106,000 new cases of AIDS reported.

Douglas Wilder of Virginia becomes first African American governor.

Sam Moore Walton is listed as the richest American—worth $8,700,000,000.

New Nations, 1980–1989

Antigua and Barbuda (1981)
Belize (1981)
Brunei (1984)
Republic of Cape Verde (1980)
Myanmar (1989)
St. Kitts and Nevis (1983)
Vanuatu (1980)

Sample Learning Activities

1981   *Sandra Day O'Connor named to the Supreme Court.*

Five classroom groups compare the accomplishments of Sandra Day O'Connor with those of other modern women, including the following: Dixie Lee Ray, Coretta Scott King, Geraldine Ferraro, and Barbara Jordan.

1989   *Tienanmen Square in Beijing erupts in violence.*

A panel discussion held in class includes U.S. "delegates," student "protesters," neutral observers, and Chinese government "officials." Each individual role plays his or her opinion of the crisis.

1990–2000: MARCHING INTO THE TWENTY-FIRST CENTURY— AMERICA AT THE CROSSROADS

Overview

1990 began not only the final decade of the twentieth century but also the final decade of the millennium. The significance of this boggles the mind when one thinks of what a hundred, let alone a thousand, years means in the total history of humankind. Consider this: in the year 1000 A.D., Leif Erickson was exploring North America and Christianity had already been introduced to both Iceland and Greenland. Judaism had moved its spiritual center from Mesopotamia to Spain. Arabs and Jews had become court physicians in Germany. Sridhan, an Indian mathematician, had recognized the importance of the concept of zero. There were several references to aborted attempts to fly or float on air. The Chinese were perfecting gunpowder. In literature, *Beowulf* was written in England, Foochow in China wrote *Bridge of Ten Thousand Ages,* and in Japan Sei Shonogan wrote *The Pillow Book,* a diary of a woman's thoughts and experiences at the Imperial Japanese Court. The Mayan civilization was disappearing from the Yucatan peninsula, while the Tiahuanco civilization was spreading throughout Peru with the planting and cultivating of corn and potatoes.

All too frequently we forget that the present and the future are forever securely anchored in the past. To ignore that concept is foolish at best. Even a thousand years ago, there were men and women who were intensely interested in history, literature, and science and who used accomplishments of previous generations to make their lives better for themselves and their posterity. So it has been throughout the collective and individual history of humankind, and so it will be with us as we move into the twenty-first century. We, too, will build not only on previous decades of the twentieth century but also on every previous century in this millennium.

Although this decade is far from over, there is plenty of evidence to indicate that the 1990s may be one of the most interesting, exciting, and perilous decades yet recorded. Already there have been dramatic changes in the political world map as well as advances in science and technology that were previously the stuff of science fiction. Yet although we are advancing swiftly in many areas, we are still plagued by those ancient enemies—plague, famine, and war. To realize our potential as human beings and make this a great world in which to live, we must resolve these enduring human problems as we move into the twenty-first century. Threats to the environment, the population explosion, and genocide—to name only a few of our most serious problems—must be addressed if we are to survive on this small planet. To paraphrase Santayana, if we do not learn from our past mistakes, we are doomed to repeat them.

Demographics: 1990–2000

Important Political Leaders

U.S.—Bill Clinton
Russia—Boris Yeltsin
France—Jacques Chirac
United Kingdom—John Major
Italy—Silvio Berlusconi
China—Li Peng
Japan—Emperor Ahito
Spain—King Juan Carlos I
Israel—Yitzhak Rabin and Benjamin Netanyahu
Egypt—Hosni Mubarak
Australia—William Hayden
Canada—Jean Chretien
Germany—Helmut Kohl
South Africa—Nelson Mandela
India—Dayai Sharma
Argentina—Carlos Menen
Peru—Alberto Fujimori
Cuba—Fidel Castro
Czech Republic—Vaclav Klaus
El Salvador—Armando Calderon Sol
Mexico—Ernesto Zedillo Ponce de Leon
Jordan—King Hussein I
Syria—Hafez Assad

Largest Cities

Ten Largest U.S. Cities		Ten Largest Cities Outside the U.S.	
1. Greater New York	18.1 million	1. Tokyo	26.5 million
2. Greater Los Angeles	14.5 million	2. Mexico City	20.8 million
3. Greater Chicago	8.1 million	3. Sao Paulo	18.7 million
4. Greater San Francisco	6.2 million	4. Seoul	16.8 million
5. Greater Philadelphia	5.9 million	5. Beijing	12.3 million
6. Greater Detroit	4.4 million	6. Bombay	12.1 million
7. Greater Boston	4.1 million	7. Calcutta	11.5 million
8. Greater Washington, DC	3.9 million	8. Rio de Janeiro	11.4 million
9. Greater Dallas-Ft. Worth	3.8 million	9. Buenos Aires	10.9 million
10. Greater Houston	3.7 million	10. Moscow	10.4 million

U.S. population: 263,814,000
World population: 5.5 billion

Significant Headlines and News Stories

1990   U.S. Air Force bombs Baghdad—Gulf War begins.

Thousands die as civil war tears at Somalia.

Millions of gallons of crude oil spilled off the coast of Galveston, Texas.

Nelson Mandela released from prison in South Africa after 17 years.

1991   USSR and U.S. begin massive arms reduction.

Millions of Kurds flee repression in Iraq.

Saddam Hussein sets Kuwait oil fields afire, causing massive environmental damage.

General Norman Schwarzkopf becomes a national hero.

Edwin Austin Tracy, an American hostage in Beirut, is released in Syria.

1992   "Ethnic cleansing" causes thousands of deaths in Bosnia.

Clinton, Rabin, and Arafat are named "The Big Three" by *Time* magazine.

World Trade Center in New York is bombed by terrorists.

1993   China carries out underground nuclear testing—U.S. follows soon after.

U.S. troops begin to leave Somalia.

President Clinton pushes for sweeping health care reforms.

U.S. conducts air drops over Bosnia.

1994   UN approves troop withdrawal from Somalia.

Former President Reagan stricken with Alzheimer's disease.

Whitewater affair embroils the White House.

Former President Richard Nixon dies.

1995   O. J. Simpson acquitted of murder.

Oklahoma City Federal Building bombed.

Jobless rate continues to decline—stands at 5.6%.

U.S. pilot Scott O'Grady downed and rescued in Bosnia.

1996   Unabomber suspect arrested in Lincoln, Montana.

TWA Flight 800 crashes—230 killed.

Swiss banks found holding Nazi gold from World War II.

1997   _____

           _____

           _____

           _____

1998   _____

           _____

           _____

           _____

1999   _____

           _____

           _____

           _____

2000   _____

           _____

           _____

           _____

History and Politics

1990   The Gulf War begins when Saddam Hussein fails to withdraw from Kuwait.

L. Douglas Wilder becomes first African American governor of Virginia.

Boris Yeltsin elected president of Russia.

Romanian uprising overthrows Communist government (President Ceausescu and wife executed on December 25, 1989).

1991   Slovenia and Croatia become independent nations as Yugoslavia dissolves.

Boris Yeltsin becomes head of USSR as Gorbachev resigns.

USSR breaks up into several independent states and calls itself the Commonwealth of Independent States (CIS).

Bosnia-Herzegovina conflict begins.

1992   William Clinton elected 42nd president of the United States.

Serbia and Montenegro claim sovereignty as independent nations.

The United Nations gains nine new members, all former Soviet Union members.

Hanna Suchocka becomes first woman to become prime minister of Poland.

1993   U.S. discovers North Korea is testing nuclear weapons.

Hindus and Moslems clash in Bombay; 550 die.

Israel and the PLO reach agreements for peace.

Warlords in Mogadishu, Somalia support insurgents.

1994 Congress approves General Agreement on Tariffs and Trade (GATT).

Republicans capture both Houses of Congress in general election.

CIA official Al Drichames arrested for selling secrets to the Russians.

Civil war in Rwanda kills thousands of civilians.

1995 Newton Gingrich sworn in as Speaker of the House—first Republican speaker in 40 years.

United Nations celebrates its 50th anniversary.

Palestine currently has 3.1 million refugees residing there.

The U.S. has 385,000 refugees.

1996 Russian troops invade Chechnya

U.S. Congress passes new and more restrictive immigration laws.

William Clinton reelected for second term as U.S. president.

The Republican party retains control of both houses of Congress.

_____

1997 _____

_____

_____

_____

1998 _____

_____

_____

_____

1999 _____

_____

_____

_____

2000 _____

_____

_____

_____

Literature and Theater

1990 Pulitzer Prize drama: *The Piano Lesson* by August Wilson

Sebastian de Grazia: *Machiavelli in Hell*

Kennedy Center Honors to Katharine Hepburn (actress) and Billy Wilder (director).

John Guare: *Six Degrees of Separation*

Oscar Hijuelos: *The Mambo Kings Play Songs of Love*

1991   Neil Simon: *Lost in Yonkers*
       Kennedy Center Honors to Fayard and Harold Nicholas (dancers)
           and Gregory Peck (actor).
       John Updike: *Rabbit at Rest*
       Laurel Thatcher Ulrich: *Diary 1785–1812*
       Brain Friel: *Dancing at Lughnasa*
1992   Robert Schenkkan: *The Kentucky Cycle*
       Kennedy Center Honors to Paul Newman (actor), Joanne Wood-
           ward (actress), Ginger Rogers (dancer/actress), and Paul Tay-
           lor (dancer).
       Frank McGuinness: *Kiss of the Spider Woman*
       James Tate: *Selected Poems*
       Jane Smiley: *A Thousand Acres*
1993   *London Suite, Having Our Say,* and *After-Play* all open on Broadway.
       David Levering Lewis: *W. E. B. DuBois: Biography of a Race*
       Sunset Boulevard by Andrew Lloyd Webber opens in Los Angeles.
       Richard Reeves: *President Kennedy*
       Three Hotels, a drama by Jon Robin Baitz, opens.
1994   *NRTA/AARP Bulletin* is the best-selling magazine in 1994.
       John Grisham: *The Chamber*
       Rosie Daly: *In the Kitchen with Rosie*
       Pope John Paul II: *Crossing the Threshold of Hope*
       Henry Kissinger: *Diplomacy*
1995   Julia Alvarez: *In the Time of the Butterfly*
       Newbury Book Award to *Walk Two Moons* by Sharon Creech.
       Tony Award winner: *Love! Valour, Compassion* by Terrence McNally
       John Hope Franklin wins Spingarn Medal.

1996   _____

       _____

       _____

       _____

1997   _____

       _____

       _____

       _____

1998   _____

       _____

       _____

       _____

1999   _____

       _____

       _____

       _____

2000 _____

_____

_____

_____

Science and Technology

1990 Congress, the National Institute of Health, the U.S. Department of Energy, and many foreign countries are cooperating to map out every gene on the 23 human chromosomes (*genomes*, or "all genetic material that composes a living person"). Doing this may lead to cures for life-threatening diseases, and other important scientific discoveries are being made through gene splicing.

Ulysses, an international project to study the poles of the Sun and interstellar space, was launched on October 6. It will make its "first solar encounter" in 1994.

The Hubble Space Telescope, an observatory, was launched in April. It is considered the first of four "Great Observatories."

The SR-71 A/B "Blackbird" set a transcontinental speed record by flying 2404 miles in 1 hour, 7 minutes, 53.69 seconds at a speed of 2124.51 mph. Afterwards it was donated to the Smithsonian Institution.

Eight men and women entered Biosphere II.

1991 Global warming is considered "the hottest topic in environmental conservation" by the World Almanac.

The potential health effects on humans of electromagnetic radiation from computer screens raise concerns. The most common type has been associated with certain cancers, miscarriages, and birth defects.

The space probe *Magellan* begins radar probing the surface of Venus in order to map it.

The Gamma Ray Observatory is launched in April from the space shuttle *Atlantis*—it is the second "Great Observatory."

The F-117-A "Stealth" bomber is used in the Gulf War.

1992 The federal government proposes $4.1 billion for biotechnology research into altering the genetic constitution of living organisms.

NASA resubmits plans for a space station that could be built more efficiently than the former plans stated. It will be cheaper, smaller, and easier to assemble while in orbit.

NASA schedules a mission to study conditions on Mars for a Martian year, called the "Mars Observer."

1993 Nobelists in Physics: Bertram N. Brockhouse (Canadian) and Clifford Shulk (U.S.).

Superconducting supercollider is developed with the hope of giving high-energy physics. It is located in Ellis County, Texas, and its laboratory "will comprise a 54 mile circular tunnel in which superconducting magnets will accelerate counter-rotating proton beams." The operation of the lab should increase the collision energy to 20 times the current capability. The experiments conducted in the lab should contribute to magnetically leviated, high-speed trains, energy storage systems used to conserve fuel, and more efficient electrical power. *Time* magazine states that it became doomed when its cost went from $5 billion to $11 billion.

Scientific fraud: Robert Galio hid the fact that a French scientist, Luc Montagnier, had sent him a virtual genetic twin of an AIDS virus that he was studying in 1983. Gallo took credit for isolating the virus. In 1989, the *Chicago Tribune* published an article that motivated the federal government to investigate the case. The time wasted in this conflict could have been used more profitably to study the AIDS epidemic further.

Biotechnology: The federal government will increase its funding in this field to about $4 billion. Because of the recent emphasis on genetic engineering, scientists are working to improve agriculture, medicine, and the environment through the fusion of cells of two different species.

Princeton Plasma Physics Laboratory: After twenty years of work, scientists created a nuclear reaction with tritium and deuterium gas, heated with radio beams. The reaction, which produced temperatures hotter than the sun, will be used in the future as a safe, clean source of power using fuels taken from ordinary water.

Eight men and women emerge from Biosphere II.

Mark Norell discovers a fossil embryo of a baby dinosaur in the Gobi Desert.

1994   Nobel Prize to Dr. George Hammond, who created the field of photochemistry.

Spaceship *Columbia* orbits for 14 days, 17 hours, 54 minutes, and 50 seconds.

Scientists make new assumptions about the evolution of humans. They now wonder if humankind started in various places around the world, rather than in Africa, or if humans left Africa eons earlier than was thought.

Scientists discovered bones of an *afarensis*, a forerunner of modern humans, which supports a theory that humans sprang from a single, long-lived species.

Fermi National Accelerator Laboratory (Chicago): Scientists finally sighted a "top" quark, which will lead to a search through a fascinating microcosmos. Quarks make up different types of matter and rays.

A comet disintegrates and hits Jupiter, causing tremendous explosions on the planet.

Hubble: Discovered rings lit up around a supernova that are light-years in diameter.

Hubble scientists believe that they have found a black hole.

Archaeologists discover evidence that *Tyrannosaurus rex* was warm-blooded.

1995   Nobel Prize in Chemistry to Paul Crutlen (Germany) and two Americans, Mario Molina and F. Sherwood Zawling, for their work on ozone layer depletion.

Russian spaceship *Mir* docks with U.S. craft *Atlantis.*

1996   Last full lunar eclipse of the millennium.

Radioactive mouse trapped at Hanford nuclear site in Washington State.

Manuel Patarroyo submits SPF660 vaccine as a cure for malaria.

_____

1997   _____

_____

_____

1998   _____

_____

_____

_____

1999   _____

_____

_____

_____

2000   _____

_____

_____

_____

Music

1990   Phil Collins named Artist of the Year.

Pulitzer Prize to Mel Powell for _Duplicates: A Concerto for Two Pianos and Orchestra._

Grammy Award to Quincy Jones for "Back on the Block."

Soundtrack of the Year: _Pretty Woman_

Top country recording: "Nobody's Home" by Clint Black

Classical Artist of the Year: Vladimir Horowitz

1991   Kennedy Center Award winners: Roy Acuff, Betty Comden, Adolph Greene, and Robert Shaw

Top R&B recording: "Written All Over Your Face" by the Rude Boys.

Pulitzer Prize to Shulamat Ran: _Symphony_

Grammy Award: Natalie Cole with Nat King Cole for "Unforgettable"

Jazz Artist of the Year: Wynton Marsalis

1992   Kennedy Center Award recipients: Lionel Hampton and Mstislav Rostropovich

Top pop album: _Ropin' the Wind_ by Garth Brooks

Top R&B single recording: "Come and Talk to Me"

Top classical album: _Baroque Duet_

Top pop single: "End of the Road" from Boyz 2 Men

1993   Grateful Dead concert is top money grosser.

Rod Stewart named Artist of the Year.

Pulitzer Prize to Christopher Rouse for _Trombone Concerto._

Whitney Houston wins Grammy Award for *The Body Guard.*
Academy Award song: "Can You Feel the Love Tonight?" (*The Lion King*)

1994 Barbra Streisand had top-grossing North American concert tour appearances (7).
The Rolling Stones are top grossing band.
All 4 One's "I Swear" goes platinum.
Top musical: *Sunset Boulevard*

1995 Rock is still the top-selling genre in music.
Lifetime Achievement Awards: Carol Channing and Harvey Sabinson

_____

_____

1996 _____

_____

_____

1997 _____

_____

1998 _____

_____

_____

1999 _____

_____

_____

2000 _____

_____

_____

_____

Visual Arts

1990 *Cheers* is most popular TV program.
Dances with Wolves is best picture of the year.
An average of 95.4 million people watch prime-time TV—6 hours, 35 minutes average daily viewing time.

1991 *60 Minutes, Roseanne,* and *Murphy Brown* are top TV programs.
Silence of the Lambs is best picture of the year.
Drawings of Henry Fuseli, a forerunner of surrealism, are displayed at the National Academy of Design in New York.

"Art in Germany 1909–1936" on display at Milwaukee Art Museum.

1992 *60 Minutes* is most popular TV program.
Schindler's List is best picture.
98% of all U.S. homes have television.
30% of all U.S. homes have two televisions.

1993 *60 Minutes* is most popular TV program.
Forrest Gump is best picture.
The Sistine Chapel: Michelangelo's masterpiece gets a facelift.
65% of all U.S. homes receive basic cable service.

1994 Outstanding films: *Apollo 13, Pulp Fiction,* and *Pocohontas*
Mrs. Doubtfire is most popular video.
Super Nintendo Donkey Kong Country is top-selling video game.
Seinfeld is a popular TV comedy.
Terra cotta figures (2000 years old) are found in the grave of Chinese Emperor Jing.

1995 *Braveheart* is best picture.
Emmy Award: *NYPD Blue*
ER is a popular TV series.
Pritzker Architecture Award: Tadeo Ando

1996 *Wheel of Fortune* and *Jeopardy* remain favorite syndicated TV programs.
Friends becomes a popular TV series.

_____

_____

1996 _____

_____

_____

1997 _____

_____

_____

1998 _____

_____

_____

_____

1999 _____

_____

_____

_____

2000 _____

_____

_____

_____

Sports

1990   Baseball owners lock players out of spring training.

Pirmin Zurbriggen of Switzerland wins World Cup Alpine Skiing Championship.

Betsy King wins U.S. Women's Open Golf Championship.

James "Buster" Douglas wins world heavyweight boxing title.

1991   World League of American Football debuted with 10 teams.

National Hockey League players went on strike.

Rick Mears wins Indianapolis "500."

Rod Carew named to Baseball Hall of Fame.

1992   Winter Olympics staged in Albertville, France.

Freestyle ballet, skiing, and curling added to the Olympic Games.

Stefan Edberg wins U.S. Open tennis title.

Tom Seaver, pitcher, named to Baseball Hall of Fame.

1993   Fencing World Championships held in Essen, Germany.

Syracuse wins NCAA lacrosse championship.

Steffi Graf wins Wimbledon title.

American League wins baseball's All-Star Game, 9–3.

1994   George Foreman, at 45, is the oldest person to win heavyweight boxing crown.

Winter Olympics staged in Lillehammer, Norway.

World Cup Soccer competition held for the first time in the U.S.

Baseball teams go on strike, halting the season.

Brazil wins World Cup soccer title.

1995   Cal Ripken breaks Lou Gehrig's consecutive game streak (2,131).

Steffi Graf (Germany) and Pete Sampras (U.S.) win Wimbledon crowns.

Houston Rockets repeat as NBA champions.

1996   University of Kentucky wins NCAA basketball championship.

University of Michigan wins NCAA hockey championship.

University of Tennessee wins NCAA women's basketball championship.

Nick Faldo wins Masters golf title.

1997   _____

_____

_____

_____

1998   _____

_____

_____

_____

1999   _____

_____

2000   _____

Everyday Life

1990   *Cheers, 60 Minutes,* and *Murder, She Wrote* are top TV programs.
College enrollment (all schools): 12,935,000.
Median home value: $79,100 (high: Hawaii, $245,300; low: Mississippi, $45,000).
22,844,000 U.S. households touched by crime.

1991   144 law enforcement officers killed in the line of duty.
21,505 Americans murdered.
The Three Tenors in Concert is top music video.
Mount Pinatubo erupts in the Philippines—U.S. forces evacuate Clark Field.

1992   36.9 million Americans are living below the poverty level.
Fewer people around the world are smoking cigarettes.
The Ventura River in California overflows—U.S. Army rescues home owners and campers.
Haitian refugees deported from U.S. back to Haiti.

1993   5.7 million women eligible for child support.
Brady Bill (gun control) passes in Congress.
Wall Street Journal has a circulation of 1.8 million.
NAFTA passes.

1994   50th anniversary of D-Day is celebrated.
ESPN has 16.2 million subscribers.
CNN has 11.6 million subscribers.
Jacqueline Kennedy Onassis dies.
Alaska jury orders Exxon to pay Alaska $5 billion.
"Gangster" style clothing is in fashion.

1995   O. J. Simpson murder trial.
10% of U.S. households with computers have CD-ROM installed.
Oklahoma City Federal Building destroyed by terrorists; many killed.
Seinfeld a popular TV program.

1996   Tenth anniversary of Chernobyl nuclear accident.
Ford Motor Company recalls thousands of its automobiles and vans.
Bankruptcies in U.S. reach all-time high—1 million.
New York Times is most widely read U.S. newspaper.

1997   _____

1998 _____

_____

_____

_____

1999 _____

_____

_____

_____

2000 _____

_____

_____

_____

New Nations, 1990–1999

Andorra (1993)	Latvia (1991)
Armenia (1991)	Lithuania (1990)
Azerbaijan (1992)	Macedonia (1991)
Belarus (1991)	Marshall Islands (1990)
Bosnia and Herzegovina (1991)	Mauritius (1992)
Burkina Faso (1990)	Micronesia (1991)
Cape Verde (1993)	Moldova (1991)
Croatia (1991)	Namibia (1990)
Czech Republic (1993)	Palau (1994)
Eritrea (1993)	Slovakia (1993)
Estonia (1991)	Slovenia (1992)
Georgia (1991)	Tajikstan (1991)
United Germany (1990)	Turkmenistan (1991)
Kazakhstan (1991)	Ukraine (1991)
Kyrgyzstan (1991)	Uzbekistan (1991)

Sample Learning Activities

1991 *Soviet Union dissolves.*

Five groups and leaders are chosen to represent the following republics: Latvia, Lithuania, the Ukraine, Georgia, and Kazakhstan. A map of the republic is drawn; the group researches each republic and then shares the unique challenges of their republic with the rest of the class.

1995 In follow-up to the above, a debate can be held on the state of the Commonwealth today. Should the republics rejoin to form a unified "soviet"? Students can also debate the distribution of resources (natural, monetary, and military), making a strong argument for their republic to receive its fair share.

CHAPTER SIX

Teaching History Is a Daily Event

*"When I want to understand what is happening today
or try to decide what will happen tomorrow, I look
back."*

—Oliver Wendell Holmes, Jr.

THE CALENDAR

An ordinary daily calendar just might be the most complete, cheapest, and most accessible teaching resource in social studies education. Most teachers highlight a special day here and there, but rarely do they use the calendar as a teaching tool to help enrich social studies content.

In the hands of a skillful teacher, the calendar can become an exciting instructional tool. Besides serving as a means to mark significant historical dates or as a reminder of someone's birthday, the calendar may also be used to initiate creative writing sessions, art projects, and panel groups, or to initiate research projects. In short, the calendar can supplement traditional social studies materials and help breathe life into the daily curriculum. It can be used as a tool to help students learn basic research skills and can also serve as the starting point in inquiry-oriented lessons, providing some answers while students resolve the "why" from the history content. Finally, the calendar may well serve as a bridge from the past to the present and the future.

The following pages outline some significant dates and offer some enjoyable learning and teaching activities. Teachers are encouraged to refer daily to a calendar and to help their students develop a concept of time and history. Classroom calendars (recording daily school and community events) or class timelines are enjoyable and informative by-products enjoyed by students in this process.

General Information about Calendars

1. *Calend* was the name the ancient Romans gave to the first day of each new month. After the fall of Rome, this was adopted and changed to *calendar* by the new Christian nations in Europe.
2. The concept of a calendar (the measuring of days) has been around since ancient times. Many ancient cultures, such as the Babylonians, Mayans, Egyptians, and Romans, developed a "calendar" to measure time. Some were lunar (based on the moon), while others were solar (based on the sun). But all were vital in everyday life for the people in these societies.
3. The Jewish calendar also has twelve months called Tishri, Heshvan, Kislev, Tebet, Shevat, Adar, Nisan, Iyar, Sivan, Tammuz, Ab, and Elul.

The Jewish calendar year is calculated by adding 3760 to the date of the Christian calendar. For example, in 2000 the Jewish calendar would be 5760. The number 3760 represents the years the Jewish culture existed before the birth of Jesus Christ, hence the difference in years.

4. The Islamic calendar marks its beginning with Muhammad's flight from Mecca to Medina in A.D. 632 (Christian calendar). Consequently, the year 2000 in the Islamic calendar would be 1368. This, too, is a twelve-month calendar. The months are Muharran, Safar, Rabi I, Rabi II, Jumada I, Jumada II, Rajab, Shabau, Ramadan, Shawwal, Zulkadah, and Zulhijjah. There are 354 days in the Islamic calendar.

5. The Chinese calendar began in 2367 B.C., which makes the year 2000 in the Christian calendar "4367." This calendar is based on cycles of 60. For example, the year 2000 will be the 17th year in the 78th cycle. The Chinese New Year comes no earlier than January 20th and no later than February 20th.

6. The current Christian calendar (Gregorian calendar) was adopted by Pope Gregory XIII in 1582. This calendar has a cycle of 12 months, with 10 or 11 of those months having at least 30 or 31 days. The exception is February, which has 28 days except in a leap year, when it has 29. The calendar is based on the life of Jesus Christ, the Christian savior. The abbreviation A.D. refers to the years following Christ's birth; B.C. refers to the years prior to the birth. Non-Christians sometimes use B.C.E. to refer to "Before Christian Era" and C.E. for "Christian Era."

7. The days of the week are probably derived and named from ancient calendars:
   Sunday—for Helios (Greek god of the sun)
   Monday—for Selene (Greek goddess of the moon)
   Tuesday—for Tyr (Norse god of war)
   Wednesday—for Woden (Norse ruler of the gods)
   Thursday—for Thor (Norse god of thunder)
   Friday—for Frigga (Norse goddess of marriage)
   Saturday—for Saturn (Roman god of time)

Sample Learning Activities for the Calendar

Activity 1: Time
Each student finds one quote pertaining to time and brings it to class. The teacher prepares a large clock, and the quotes can be arranged so that the face of the clock is made up of quotes. (Examples of quotes are: "Time waits for no man"; "For those who love, time is eternity"; "Till the end of time"; "It's always the right time to do right").

Activity 2: Basic Research Skills

1. Students can research Galileo Galilei, with particular reference to his "pendulum" discovery. A pendulum can then be constructed in class and Galileo's theory demonstrated.
2. Students can research the life and times of Louis XVI of France, with particular reference to his interest in fixing clocks. Parts of a clock can be reassembled in class.

Activity 3: Art
Given the derivation of the days of the week, students can choose one god or goddess and draw their interpretation of that deity.

Activity 4: Music and Time
Find a selection of songs that contain the word time, the days of the week, or the months of the year. Edit snippets of these songs onto a tape. Students listen to each song and write down all the references to time, days, or months. Examples of songs are: "Calendar Girl," "Come September," "Time and the River," "Eight Days a Week," "Never on Sunday," and "Autumn in New York."

Activity 5: Now and Then
On any special day or holiday, students can role-play a "now and then" situation. For example, on Lincoln's birthday, one student can role-play Lincoln for the 1860s while another can role-play the same scenario from a present-day perspective.

JANUARY

The month of January was named for Janus, a Roman god with two faces looking in opposite directions, one face to the future and the other to the past.

Some Interesting Facts about January

1. January is the first month of the year according to the Gregorian calendar.
2. The Anglo-Saxons called January "wolf month" because wolves came into the village in the winter (January) in search of food.
3. The snowdrop is the special flower of the month because it often blooms in the snow.
4. The garnet is the gem for January.

Activity 1

Date: January 10

Event: Sherlock Holmes's birthday.

Lesson plan: Students will have a better understanding of mystery, detection literature, and the nuts and bolts of writing mystery fiction stories.

Activity: Students will read a variety of mystery or detective stories and write one mystery of their own about some aspect of our school. These mysteries will then be drawn at random for the class to solve together over the period of three days.

Questions:

1. Who was Sherlock Holmes?
2. What impression did the character of Sherlock Holmes make on you?

January

1	2	3	4	5	6	7
Paul Revere (American patriot, b. 1735) Betsy Ross (American patriot, b. 1752) Emancipation Proclamation anniversary (1863)	First commemorative stamp issued, 1893, depicted Christopher Columbus's voyage Georgia Admission Day, 4th state, 1788	Lucretia Mott (abolitionist, b. 1793) Alaska Admission Day, 49th state, 1959	Louis Braille (invented Braille system, b. 1809) Trivia Day Utah Admission Day, 45th state, 1896	George Washington Carver (inventor and scientist, b. 1864) Nellie Ross Taylor of Wyoming (first woman governor, 1925)	Carl Sandburg (poet and biographer, b. 1878) New Mexico Admission Day, 47th state, 1912	Millard Filmore (13th president, b. 1800) First U.S. presidential election held, 1789
8 Elvis Presley (musician, b. 1935) Battle of New Orleans, 1815 11th amendment to U.S. Constitution passes (1798)	**9** Richard Milhous Nixon (37th President, b. 1913) Connecticut Admission Day, 5th State, 1788	**10** Ethan Allen (American revolutionary, b. 1738) Oil discovered in Texas, 1901 French-Indian War ended, 1763	**11** Alexander Hamilton (American statesman, b. 1755) Nepal National Unity Day	**12** Jack London (American author, b. 1876) Ira Hayes' birthday (raised flag at Iwo Jima) Tanzania, Zanzibar Revolution Day	**13** Stephen Foster (composer, d. 1864)	**14** Henry Ford inaugurated assembly line, 1914 Benedict Arnold (American traitor, b. 1741) Ratification Day of U.S. Constitution, 1787
15 Martin Luther King, Jr. (civil rights leader, b. 1929) Humanitarian Day (Chicago area)	**16** Ethel Merman (Broadway musical star, b. 1909) Religious Freedom Day	**17** Benjamin Franklin (American statesman, scientist, author, b. 1706) U.S. Air Force bombed Iraq, Gulf War begins 1991	**18** A. A. Milne (*Winnie the Pooh*, b. 1882) Daniel Webster (American orator and statesman, b. 1789)	**19** James Watt (invented steam engine, b. 1736)	**20** U.S. Presidential Inauguration Day Anniversary of first basketball game, Springfield, MA, 1892	**21** Thomas "Stonewall" Jackson (Confederate General, b. 1824) John Fitch (American inventor, b. 1743)
22 First F. W. Woolworth store opened in New York, 1879	**23** National Handwriting Day John Hancock (American statesman, first signer of Declaration of Independence, b. 1737)	**24** 20th amendment passed (presidential term limits, 1961) Eskimo Pie patented by Christian Nelson, 1922 Gold discovered in California, 1848	**25** Robert Burns (Scottish poet, b. 1759) Alexander Graham Bell with Thomas A. Watson made another historic phone call between New York and San Francisco	**26** Australia Day Republic Day in India Michigan Admission Day, 26th state, 1837	**27** Thomas A. Edison granted patent for incandescent light, 1880 Lewis Carroll (Alice in Wonderland, b. 1832) Wolfgang Amadeus Mozart (composer, b. 1756)	**28** Great Seal of the U.S. anniversary, 1782 First ski tour in 1934 at Woodstock, VT First community telephone exchange opened, New Haven, CT 1878
29 William McKinley (25th president, b. 1843) Kansas Admission Day, 34th state, 1861 Thomas Paine (author of *Common Sense*, b. 1837)	**30** Franklin Delano Roosevelt (32nd President, b. 1882) Adolf Hitler appointed chancellor, 1933 Mohandas Gandhi assassinated, 1948	**31** Jackie Robinson (baseball player, b. 1919) Franz Schubert (composer, b. 1797) Explorer I launched, 1st U.S. satellite, 1958				

3. What techniques did the author, Sir Arthur Conan Doyle, use to create suspense in his books?
4. What techniques did you use to create your own mystery, and why did you choose to use these methods or techniques?

Skills taught: Writing skills and cognitive thinking skills involved with writing and solving mysteries

Resources: Plenty of Sherlock Holmes books and any other high-quality mysteries like the works of Agatha Christie

Activity 2

Date: January 15

Event: Martin Luther King, Jr.'s birthday

Lesson plan: Students will have a better understanding of the feelings for the dreams of Martin Luther King, Jr. They will also have a better insight into their own dreams for the future.

Activity: Read or listen to King's speech. As a class, discuss Martin Luther King, Jr.'s, dreams. Have students write about a dream of their own.

Questions:

1. Why was Martin Luther King a major historical figure in our country?
2. What does King's speech mean to you?
3. If you were alive in King's time, what would you have contributed to the cause of equality for all people?
4. What is a problem in our society today, and what can you do to improve or solve that problem?

Skills taught: Reading and comprehension

Resources: A video or written copy of the famous speech, "I Have a Dream" given by Martin Luther King, Jr., on August 28, 1963, at the Lincoln Memorial in Washington, D.C.

FEBRUARY

The month of February comes from the Latin word *februarie,* which means to purify.

Some Interesting Facts about February

1. February is the shortest month of the year (28 days; 29 in leap year).
2. According to tradition, the Roman Emperor Augustus took one day from February and added it to August, which is the month named after him, leaving February as the month with 28 days.

3. The primrose is the flower of February.
4. The amethyst is the gem for February.

Activity

Date: February 21, 1858

Event: Edwin Holmes invented the burglar alarm.

Lesson plan: Students will have a better understanding of why and how the burglar alarm was invented.

Activity: Each student will have the opportunity to do some research from trade books and encyclopedias on how burglar alarms were invented. After learning about the burglar alarm, students will create their own alarms, either drawing them on paper or building them in a variety of media.

Questions:

1. Who was Edwin Holmes?
2. Why did he see a need to create a burglar alarm?
3. If you were to build an alarm, what would you be protecting, and how would you build this special alarm to protect it?
4. If you were a burglar, what would you do if you found out that there was an alarm created to catch you?

Skills taught: Critical thinking, analytical, and evaluation skills

Resources: Trade books and encyclopedias about Edwin Holmes and burglar alarms

Activity 2

Date: February 22

Event: George Washington's birthday

Lesson plan: Students will have a better understanding of George Washington's life and some of his character traits that led to his being the first president of the United States.

Activity: Cut out a picture of the American flag. For each star or stripe, students will write facts about George Washington, the era in which he lived, or reasons that he is so respected and honored today.

Questions:

1. Who was George Washington?
2. What do you think it was like growing up during the time of George Washington and his presidency?

FEBRUARY

1	2	3	4	5	6	7
American History Month Black History Month Langston Hughes (poet, b. 1902)	Groundhog Day William Ross Bennett (American poet, b. 1886) Treaty of Guadalupe Hidalgo, 1848	Norman Rockwell (b. 1894) First paper money issued in America, 1690 Elizabeth Blackwell (first female American physician, b. 1821)	Charles Lindbergh (b. 1902) USO's birthday since 1941 George Washington chosen president, 1789 Rosa Parks (b. 1913)	Hank Aaron (baseball player, b. 1934) John Jefferson (1st U.S. weatherman, b. 1744)	Babe Ruth (baseball player, b. 1895) Ronald Reagan (40th president, b. 1911) Massachusetts Admission Day, 6th state, 1788	Charles Dickens (b. 1812) Grenada Independence Day Laura Ingalls Wilder (author, *Little House* series, b. 1867)
8	9	10	11	12	13	14
Confederate States of America formed, 1861 Boy Scouts of America founded, 1910	William H. Harrison (9th president, b. 1733) Alice Walker (author of *The Color Purple*, b. 1944)	Postal telegraph introduces singing telegram, 1933 25th amendment (presidential succession, 1967)	Thomas Edison (inventor, b. 1847) Inventor's Day	Harry Lidfield becomes first automobile fatality, 1898 Abraham Lincoln (16th president, b. 1809)	Grant Wood (American artist, b. 1892) First U.S. public school established, Boston, 1635	St. Valentine's Day Arizona Admission Day, 48th state, 1912 Oregon Admission Day, 33rd state, 1859
15	16	17	18	19	20	21
Susan B. Anthony (b. 1820) Galileo (scientist, b. 1564)	Lithuania Independence Day	Geronimo died, 1909 Michael Jordan (basketball player, b. 1963) Maria Anderson (opera singer, b. 1902)	Clyde Tombaugh discovered the planet Pluto, 1930 Cyprus: Green Monday Gambia: Independence Day President's Day	Nicolaus Copernicus (astronomer, b. 1473) Franklin D. Roosevelt signs Executive Order 9066 interning Japanese on West Coast, 1942	John Glenn, Jr. (first American in space, 1962) Frederick Douglass (Abolitionist, b. 1817)	Richard Trevitchick invents first steam locomotive, 1804
22	23	24	25	26	27	28
George Washington (first president, b. 1732) French-Fry Friday, Tri-Cities, WA Frederick Chopin (b. 1810)	W. E. B. DuBois (Black American educator, b. 1868) Santa Ana attacked the Alamo	Winslow Homer (painter, b. 1836) Wilhelm Grimm (author of Hansel and Gretel, b. 1873)	Pierre Augustine Renoir (b. 1841) Buffalo Bill Cody (b. 1846) Samuel Colt (Colt handgun, b. 1836) 16th amendment (1913)	Grand Canyon became National Park, 1919 Levi Strauss (blue jeans, b. 1829)	Dominican Republic Independence Day Henry Wadsworth Longfellow (American poet, b. 1829) Cesar Chavez b. 1927 (immigrant rights)	Republican Party formed in Ripon, WI, 1854
29						
Leap Year Day						

3. If you could be any president in the history of our country, which one would you be and why?
4. Using what you know about our nation's history, what do you suppose were some of the major problems facing our country during Washington's presidency?

Skills taught: Reading, comprehension, and writing

Resources: Resources include books on George Washington and the history of that era as well as books researching the changes in the American flag throughout our history.

MARCH

The month of March is named to honor Mars, the Roman god of war.

Some Interesting Facts about March

1. March is the month that ends winter and begins spring.
2. March comes in like a lion and goes out like a lamb.
3. The violet is the official flower for March.
4. The bloodstone and aquamarine are the gems for March.

Activity 1

Date: March 3, 1814

Event: National Anthem Day

Lesson plan: Students will have a better understanding of why and how we acquired "The Star-Spangled Banner" as our national anthem.

Activity: Students will create their own words to the musical background of "The Star-Spangled Banner" dealing with current events around the world. This can be achieved as a class or in small groups. Ideas can be collected and these can be sung at the next assembly or open house.

Questions:

1. Who wrote "The Star-Spangled Banner" and when?
2. What were the circumstances surrounding the creation of this song?
3. Why do you think this song was chosen as our national anthem?
4. What effect will your song have on the history of our class, school, state, or country?

Skills taught: Research, outlining, and music appreciation

Resources: "The Star-Spangled Banner" by Francis Scott Key

MARCH

1
Congress passed Civil Rights Act, 1875
Nebraska Admission Day, 17th state, 1803
President JFK created Peace Corps, 1961
22nd amendment (1951)

2
Dr. Seuss (b. 1904)
Sam Houston (politician, b. 1793)
Texas Independence Day

3
Florida Admission Day, 27th state, 1845
National Anthem Day, 1931
A. G. Bell (telephone, b. 1847)
Jackie Joyner-Kersee (athlete, b. 1962)

4
Vermont Admission Day, 14th state, 1791
Thomas Jefferson inaugurated at new capital, Washington, D.C., 1801
Jane Goodall (zoologist, b. 1934)

5
Australia's Labour Day
Crispus Attucks Day (first African American killed in Boston Massacre, 1770)
Iditarod Day, Alaska

6
Michelangelo (b. 1475)
Elizabeth Barrett Browning (poet, b. 1806)
Dred Scot decision, 1857

7
Luther Burbank (horticulturist, b. 1849)
Bell granted patent for telephone, 1876

8
International Women's Day

9
Charles Graham receives first patent for false teeth, 1822
Yuri Gagarin (Russian cosmonaut, b. 1934)
Amerigo Vespucci (explorer, b. 1491)

10
Anniversary of Salvation Army in the U.S., 1880
Harriet Tubman Day (Abolitionist)

11
Johnny Appleseed Day
Canadian Commonwealth Day

12
U.S. Post Office established, 1789
American Girl Scouts founded, 1913
Virginia Hamilton (author, b. 1936)

13
First earmuffs patented, 1877
Grenada National Holiday
Good Samaritan Involvement Day

14
Lucy Hobbs Taylor (first American female dentist, b. 1833)
Albert Einstein (b. 1879)
Casey Jones (railroad legend, b. 1849)

15
Maine Admission Day, 23rd state, 1820
Andrew Jackson (7th president, b. 1767)

16
James Madison (4th president, b. 1751)
Robert Goddard Day (first rocket built and launched)
Freedom of Information Day

17
St. Patrick's Day
Camp Fire Boys and Girls birthday

18
Rudolph Diesel (inventor, b. 1858)
Steven Grover Cleveland (22nd and 24th president, b. 1837)
Alexei Leonov (floats in space, 1965)

19
Australia: Canberra Day
Swallows return to San Juan Capistrano, CA

20
Earth Day
Mitsumasa Anno (author, b. 1926)
Lois Lowry (*Number the Stars*, b. 1937)
Fred Rogers ("Mr. Rogers," b. 1928)

21
Benito Juarez (Mexican statesman, b. 1806)
Persia becomes Iran, 1935
Vernal Equinox
Johann Sebastian Bach (composer, b. 1685)

22
Marcel Marceau (pantomimist, b. 1923)
Johann Wolfgang Von Goethe dies, 1832

23
"Give me liberty or give me death" speech, Patrick Henry, 1775
Elisha Otis installed the first passenger elevator, 1857
23rd amendment

24
First American gasoline powered car sold, 1898
Art Week
Harry Houdini (magician, b. 1874)

25
Béla Bartók (composer, b.1881)
Greek Independence Day
Gloria Steinem (feminist, b. 1934)

26
Robert Frost (poet, b. 1874)
Bangladesh Independence Day
Sandra Day O'Connor (Supreme Court Justice, b. 1930)

27
Dr. Abraham Gesner discovered process to refine oil into kerosene, 1856
First color TV broadcast (1955)

28
Teacher's Day in Czech Republic
Three Mile Island Nuclear Accident, 1979

29
John Tyler (10th president, 1790)
Coca-Cola invented, 1886
Pearl Bailey (singer, b. 1918)

30
Treaty of Paris ended Crimean War, 1856
Anna Sewell (*Black Beauty*, b. 1820)
Vincent Van Gogh (painter, b. 1853)
15th amendment, 1870

31
Eiffel Tower opened in Paris, 1889
Treaty of Karogawa opened Japan to the West, 1854

Activity 2

Date: March 29, 1886

Event: Invention of Coca-Cola

Lesson plan: Students will have a better understanding of the invention of cola and the production of cola drinks today.

Activity: Students will take a tour of the Coca-Cola processing plant and write a letter to the president of Coca-Cola, presenting an invention for a new drink, its ingredients, and a reason that people will buy it.

Questions:

1. Why do you think Coca-Cola is so popular today?
2. What did you learn at the Coca-Cola factory?
3. What were your reasons for creating the drink that you did?
4. How will you get people to try your newly invented drink?

Skills taught: Interviewing, recording, and writing

Resources: Students will tour a Coca-Cola processing plant.

APRIL

The name April comes from two possible sources. One source may be the Latin word *Aprilis*, meaning "to open," because in the temperate zones of the Northern Hemisphere growth starts in flowers and trees and the hibernating animals are coming out of their dens. The other source may be the word for the Greek goddess of love, *Aphrodite*.

Some Interesting Facts about April

1. It is the fourth month of the Gregorian calendar.
2. April has 30 days.
3. It is considered the first month of spring in the Northern Hemisphere and the first month of fall in the Southern Hemisphere.
4. Many religious holidays all over the world are celebrated in April, such as the Christian Easter (usually in April), the Jewish Passover, the Chinese Pure and Bright Festival, and the Canadian and British St. George's Day (patron saint of England).
5. The daisy is the official flower for April.
6. The diamond is the gem for April.

Activity 1

Date: April 18

Event: "Paul Revere's Ride" in 1775

Lesson plan: Students will research the mythology of the ride of Paul Revere (he, along with Dr. Prescott and Billy Dawes, actually made the ride) and discuss why only he receives credit.

Activity: Read Longfellow's poem "Paul Revere's Ride." Also read excerpts from *Johnny Tremain* by Esther Forbes. Display a map of the Boston-Concord-Lexington (Massachusetts) area.

Questions:

1. Why did the three patriots ride that night?
2. What impact did their ride have on the American Revolution?
3. Trace the route on a blank map of the area.
4. Calculate the distance they rode.
5. Write a newspaper article as if the event were actually happening.

Skills taught: Reading, listening, map skills, computation, and analysis

Resources: Johnny Tremain by E. Forbes (Houghton Mifflin, 1946); *Paul Revere's Ride* by H. W. Longfellow (Greenwillow, 1985); and *The World Almanac and Book of Facts* (World Almanac, 1990).

Activity 2

Date: April 22

Event: Earth Day

Lesson plan: Students will be able to name local environmental pollutants and describe what can be done to eliminate them.

Activity: Obtain posters and other information about Earth Day and other environmental information. Discuss and display the posters around the room.

Questions:

1. What would a home be like if no one took out the garbage?
2. What would happen to our world if no one ever cleaned up the garbage and trash?
3. Name some things we have on our campus that are environmental pollutants (paper scraps, plastic, etc.).
4. List some serious environmental pollutants (nuclear waste, acid rain, etc.). Do some artwork or get pictures from magazines to make a bulletin board depicting some pollutants found in the local area.

Skills taught: Listening, observing, writing, drawing, and critical thinking

Resources: Various posters and handouts on Earth Day; *Where the Sidewalk Ends* by Shel Silverstein (Harper & Row, 1974).

April

1	2	3	4	5	6	7
April Fool's Day	Hans Christian Andersen (author, b. 1805) Ponce de Leon arrives in America, 1513 International Children's Book Day	Washington Irving (American author, b. 1783) Pony Express opens, 1860 First American circus opens in Philadelphia, 1793	Martin Luther King, Jr., assassinated in Memphis, 1968 Flag Act of 1818 Maya Angelou (author and poet, b. 1928)	Booker T. Washington (education advocate, b. 1856) Buddha Day, Japan	First modern Olympic games, 1896 First theater in colonies, Williamsburg, VA, 1716 U.S. declares war on Central Powers, 1917	World Health Day
8 Buddha's birthday Holocaust Remembrance Day Hank Aaron breaks Babe Ruth's home run record, 1974	**9** American Civil War ends, 1865	**10** Walter Hunt patents safety pin, 1898 SPCA created, 1866 Francis Perkins (first female Secretary of Labor, b. 1882)	**11** Jackie Robinson becomes first African American to play major league baseball, 1947	**12** Russian Yuri Gargarin becomes first human in space, 1961 American Civil War begins, 1861	**13** Thomas Jefferson (3rd president, b. 1743) First elephant arrives in U.S., 1796	**14** Titanic sinks, 1912 Thomas Edison invents kinescope motion pictures, 1894 President Abraham Lincoln assassinated, 1865
15 First organized automobile race in U.S., 1900 Boston Marathon Income Tax Day Thomas Hart Benson (painter, b. 1889)	**16** Wilburt Wright (aviator, b. 1867) Slavery abolished in Washington, DC, 1862 Charlie Chaplin (actor, b. 1889)	**17** Verrazano Day (discovery of New York Harbor, 1524) Sirimavo Bandavanaiko (world's first female prime minister, Sri-Lanka)	**18** San Francisco earthquake and fire, 1906 Anniversary of Paul Revere's ride (made by Paul Revere, Dr. Samuel Prescott, and Billy Dawes)	**19** Lord Byron, died in Greece, 1824 First Boston Marathon, 1897	**20** Apollo 16 astronauts explore the moon, 1972 Adolf Hitler (dictator, b. 1889)	**21** Friedrich Froebel (German educator, b. 1872, founded first kindergarten, 1837) John Muir (explorer, b. 1838) Charlotte Brontë (English novelist, b. 1816)
22 Earth Day, 1970 First National League Baseball game (Philadelphia vs. Boston)	**23** James Buchanan (15th president, b. 1791) Shakespeare (playwright, b. 1664) Book Day in Spain Granville Woods (telegraph, b. 1856)	**24** First soda introduced, 1874 Library of Congress Day First American League game (Cleveland vs. Chicago)	**25** Automobile license plates required, 1901 Iceland: First day of Summer	**26** James Audubon (b. 1785) Charles Francis Richter (Richter scale, b. 1900)	**27** Ulysses S. Grant (18th president, b. 1822) Edward Gibbon (historian, b. 1737) Samuel F. B. Morse (b. 1791)	**28** Maryland Admission Day, 7th state, 1788 James Monroe (5th president, b. 1758) Great Poetry Reading Day
29 Confederate Army Memorial Day	**30** Louisiana Admission Day, 18th state, 1812 Vietnam War ends, 1975 Hamburgers first introduced at St. Louis World's Fair, 1904					

MAY

The month of May is probably named for Maia, the Roman goddess of spring and growth. The name seems to be related to the Latin word for growth and warmth.

Some Interesting Facts about May

1. It is the fifth month of the year.
2. May has 31 days.
3. May Day (May 1) has been celebrated since ancient Roman times with parades, flowers, dancing, and other festivities.
4. The famous horse race, the Kentucky Derby, has been run in May since 1875.
5. The lily of the valley is the official flower for May.
6. The emerald is the gem for May.

Activity 1

Date: May 5

Event: Cinco de Mayo

Lesson plan: Students will be able to describe the significance of Cinco de Mayo and to compare this Mexican holiday with the Fourth of July celebration in the United States.

Activity: Display a map of Mexico and locate Puebla, the site of the decisive battle. Students will research the event and write a short journal article explaining the events leading up to the battle. With school policy in mind, perhaps some Mexican foods may be used in the classroom for a festive mood or a piñata may be made.

Questions:

1. Why did the Mexicans fight the war?
2. How do people in Mexico celebrate this holiday?
3. What does "El Cinco de Mayo" mean?
4. What U.S. holiday does Cinco de Mayo resemble?
5. Who was Mexico's "George Washington"?

Skills taught: Reading, writing, analyzing information, and research

Resources: A map of Mexico, encyclopedias, and trade books such as *Fiesta Days of Mexico* by G. E. Fay (University of Northern Colorado, 1970)

Activity 2

Date: Last Monday in May

Event: Memorial Day

May

1	2	3	4	5	6	7
Lei Day in Hawaii First U.S. postcard issued, 1873 First Chicago skyscraper begun, 1884 May Day	Henry Robert (Robert's Rules of Order, b. 1837) French Revolution begun, 1814	Sun Day, celebrated since 1977 Golda Meir (Israeli statesperson, b. 1898)	Invisible ink first used in France, 1776 Nicholai Lenin (b. 1870) China: Youth Day	Japan: Children's Day First train robbery (Bend, OR, 1865) Elizabeth Cochrane Seaman (a.k.a., Nelly Bly, journalist, b. 1867) Cinco de Mayo	First postage stamp with glue issued, 1840 Roger Bannister breaks 4-minute mile, 1954 Robert E. Peary (explorer, b. 1856)	Johannes Brahms (composer, b. 1833) Peter Tchaikovsky (composer, b. 1840) Robert Browning (poet, b. 1812)

8	9	10	11	12	13	14
Harry S. Truman (33rd president, b. 1884) World Red Cross Day Native American Day	Native American Day Smokey Bear Day Sir James Barrie (author, *Peter Pan*, b. 1860)	Transcontinental railroad completed, 1869	Minnesota Admission Day, 32nd state, 1858 Irving Berlin (American composer, b. 1888) Martha Graham (dancer, b. 1894)	Florence Nightingale (nurse, b. 1820) Limerick Day	Astronomy Day Mother's Day Mexican War begun, 1846	Jamestown settled, 1607 Gabriel Fahrenheit (Fahrenheit scale, b. 1686) Thomas Gainsborough (English painter, b. 1727)

15	16	17	18	19	20	21
First baseball stadium opened, Brooklyn, NY, 1862 U.S. returns Okinawa to Japan, 1972 L. Frank Baum (Author of Oz books, b. 1856)	First nickel authorized, 1866 Biographer's Day	*Brown v. Board of Education* (1954) National Defense Transformation Day	Mt. St. Helens erupts, 1980 Armed Forces Day International Museum day	First Ringling Bros. Circus, 1884 Malcolm X (civil rights leader, b. 1925) 27th amendment (1992)	Homestead Act (granted farmers right to settle, 1862) Dolly Madison (wife of President James Madison, b. 1768)	Charles Lindbergh completes solo flight to Paris, 1927 Amelia Earhart completes first female solo flight across Atlantic, 1932

22	23	24	25	26	27	28
Mary Cassatt (artist, b. 1844) Last soldiers killed in American Civil War, 1865 Sir Arthur Conan Doyle (author, *Sherlock Holmes*, b. 1859)	South Carolina Admission Day, 8th state, 1788 Start of Mexican War, 1846	First SST supersonic plane landed in U.S. 1977 Samuel Morse sends first message by telegraph, 1844 Brooklyn Bridge opened, 1883	African Freedom Day Constitutional Convention anniversary, 1787 Bill "Bojangles" Robinson (tap dancer, b. 1878)	Sally Ride (first American woman in space, b. 1951)	Amelia Bloomer (educator, b. 1818) Rachel Carson (American author, b. 1907) Golden Gate Bridge opened, 1937	Jim Thorpe (athlete, b. 1888)

29	30	31				
Rhode Island Admission Day, 13th state, 1848 John F. Kennedy (35th president, b. 1917) Patrick Henry (Patriot, b. 1736)	First auto accident, New York, 1896 Traditional Memorial Day	Walt Whitman (American poet, b. 1819) Union of South Africa proclaimed, 1910 17th amendment, 1913				

Lesson plan: Students will be able to explain why Memorial Day is celebrated and how it has changed slightly from the original idea of honoring the soldiers of our country to remembering all loved ones.

Activity: Ask a member of the local Veterans of Foreign Wars (VFW) organization to speak to the class about the history of the holiday. Each student will make a small 6"x8" flag using white fabric paint to make the blue field and the red stripes to display in the room. Students will bring names of people they know who have died in U.S. wars and conflicts, write the names on cards, and post the cards near the flags.

Questions:

1. Why do we celebrate Memorial Day?
2. How is it different from Veterans' Day?
3. How has the holiday changed in regard to who is remembered?
4. Why is it the last Monday of May?
5. When was Memorial Day first celebrated?

Skills taught: Listening, drawing, and research

Resources: A speaker from the VFW, a world almanac, and encyclopedias

JUNE

The name *June* probably comes from Juno, the Roman goddess of marriage. Some records show that it could also have been a family name, Junius, which was the name of a powerful family in early Roman history.

Some Interesting Facts about June

1. June is the sixth month of the Gregorian calendar.
2. It has 30 days.
3. It is often called the month of roses.
4. It also has been called the wedding month since ancient Roman times.
5. The rose is the official flower for June.
6. The pearl is the gem for June.

Activity 1

Date: June 6

Event: D-Day (Allied Forces invaded Normandy during World War II)

Lesson plan: Students will be able to explain the purpose and describe the complexity of the Allied invasion to retake Europe during World War II.

Activity: Display a large map of Europe. Pinpoint the beaches of Normandy with flags printed with names assigned to the beaches. With an overhead and various colored transparencies, show with colored acetate arrows the different Allied forces involved in the assault. Use a trade book or textbook as a resource and explain the logistics and objectives of the military exercise.

Questions:

1. What are some of the difficulties involved in planning an effort like this?
2. Name the principle Allied countries involved.
3. Why was it necessary to have an amphibious landing in order to retake Europe?
4. On a blank map, locate Normandy, England, the beaches used for the landings, and the various occupied countries.
5. Write a short essay on why the success of the invasion was a turning point in the war.

Skills taught: Observation, analysis, map skills, and writing

Resources: Various history books and maps, encyclopedias, and almanacs

Activity 2

Date: June 14

Event: Flag Day

Lesson plan: Students will be able to state the history and origin of the U.S. flag and describe the code of etiquette for its use.

Activity: Students will select various historical U.S. flags, make paper and paint replicas and display them on the bulletin board. They will read the code of etiquette and the history of the flag from the *World Almanac.*

Questions:

1. What are the different ways that different people salute the flag (e.g., soldiers, nonmilitary men and women)?
2. What uses of the flag are prohibited?
3. Why are there stars and stripes on the flag?
4. Was there really a Betsy Ross, and did she design and make the first flag?
5. Make labels for the flags you have made that give the year they were first flown.

Skills taught: Reading, drawing, writing, and research

Resources: World Almanac (current year)

June

1	2	3	4	5	6	7
Kentucky Admission Day, 15th state, 1792; Tennessee Admission Day, 16th state, 1796	Martha Washington (America's first First Lady, b. 1731)	Jefferson Davis (president of Confederate States of America, b. 1808)	Gemini astronauts "walk in space" for 20 minutes, 1965	Richard Scarry (author, b. 1919); National Trails Day; World Environment Day	D-Day (1944); Korea Memorial Day; Flag Day in Sweden	Boone Day, Kentucky (honors Daniel Boone); Donut Day, Chicago; Paul Gauguin (French painter, b. 1848)

8	9	10	11	12	13	14
Frank Lloyd Wright (architect, b. 1867); Patent granted for vacuum cleaner, 1869	Philadelphia Spelling Book, first book to be copyrighted, 1790; Donald Duck debuts in 1934	Alcoholics Anonymous founded, Akron, OH, 1935	Jacques Cousteau (oceanographer, b. 1910)	First human-powered flight across the English Channel; George Bush (41st president, b. 1924)	*New York Times* runs first installment of Pentagon Papers, 1971; Children's Day	Harriet Beecher Stowe (American author, b. 1811); Flag Day

15	16	17	18	19	20	21
Arkansas Admission Day, 25th state, 1836; Magna Carta Day; Benjamin Franklin's "lightning rod" experiment	Valentine Tereshkova (USSR cosmonaut, first woman in space, 1963)	Father's Day; Battle of Bunker Hill (1775); Watergate Day (1972)	Battle of Waterloo, 1815; Congress declares war on England, 1812	Maximilian, emperor of Mexico, executed, 1867	West Virginia Admission Day, 35th state, 1863; U.S. government adopts the Great Seal, 1782	New Hampshire Admission Day, 9th state, 1788; Summer Solstice

22	23	24	25	26	27	28
U.S. Department of Justice created, 1870	Liberian Independence, 1847	UFOs first sighted, 1947	Virginia Admission Day, 10th state, 1788; George Orwell (author, b. 1903); Battle of Little Big Horn, 1876	United Nations' Charter Day; Pearl Buck (American author, b. 1892)	Helen Keller (educator, b. 1880); Mildren J. Hill (teacher who wrote "Happy Birthday" song, b. 1859)	World War I ends with signing of Treaty of Versailles, 1918; Henry VIII (b. 1491); Queen Victoria crowned, 1838

29	30					
First African-American church established in U.S., 1794	Zaire Independence Day; Margaret Mitchell publishes *Gone With the Wind*, 1936; Charles Brodin walks over Niagara Falls, 1859					

JULY

July's name was originally *quintilis,* which means "fifth" in Latin. It was changed to July by the Romans to honor Julius Caesar when July became the seventh month.

Some Interesting Facts about July

1. July has 31 days.
2. July 2 marks the halfway point of the year.
3. July is known as the hottest month of the year.
4. The Liberty Bell rang for the first time on July 8.
5. The lily is the official flower for July.
6. The ruby is the gem for July.

Activity 1

Date: July 23

Event: Ice cream cones invented

Lesson plan: Students will be able to identify where the ice cream cone was invented and will be able to make ice cream.

Activity: After discussion of the history of the ice cream cone, students will create their own serving of ice cream in a paper cup. Discuss the scientific changes that take place when ice cream is made (the state of matter).

Questions:

1. Where was the ice cream cone invented?
2. How long has the ice cream cone been around?
3. What would we do without ice cream?
4. Where is ice cream most popular?
5. What is ice cream made of?

Skills taught: Research, social, and application skills

Resources: Recipe and ingredients for the production of ice cream

Activity 2

Date: July 11

Event: Cheer Up the Lonely Day

Lesson plan: Students will understand and have compassion for those who are lonely. Further, students will have an understanding of how to help them to feel

July

1 Canada Day; First adhesive postage stamps sold (Franklin, 5 cents; Washington, 10 cents)

2 James A. Garfield shot in Washington, DC, 1881; Thurgood Marshall (Supreme Court Justice, b. 1908); Halfway point of year

3 Idaho Admission Day, 43rd state, 1890; First bank in U.S. opens in New York, 1819

4 U.S. Independence Day; John C. Coolidge (30th president, b. 1872)

5 Washington Irving (author, appointed American ambassador to Spain, b. 1842); Kids' Art Festival, Tacoma, WA, Pt. Defiance Park

6 John Paul Jones (naval officer, b. 1747); International Cherry Pit spitting contest in Michigan

7 Japan Star Festival (Tanabata); Be Nice to New Jersey Week

8 First public reading of Declaration of Independence, 1776; Liberty Bell rung to indicate America's freedom

9 Elias Howe (inventor, b. 1819); 14th amendment (1868); Tom Hanks (actor, b. 1959)

10 Wyoming Admission Day, 44th state, 1890; Bahamas Independence Day

11 John Quincy Adams (6th president, b. 1797)

12 Henry David Thoreau (author, b. 1817); Golden Days, Fairbanks, AK, celebrate discovery of gold

13 Lincoln birthplace, Founders' Day weekend, Hodgenville, KY; Old Fashioned Ice Cream Festival, Rockwood Museum, Wilmington, DE

14 Gerald Ford (38th president, b. 1913); Edward Whymper scaled the Matterhorn, 1865

15 Clement C. Moore (author, b. 1823)

16 Atomic Bomb Day, first explosion of A-bomb, 5:30 A.M., 1945, NM; District of Columbia established, 1790

17 Civil War in Spain begins, 1930

18 Nelson Mandela (South African President, b. 1918); Hot Dog Night in Luverne, MN, 12,000 hot dogs served free of charge

19 First Women's Rights Convention, 1843; Bloomer Day, first introduced as women's clothing

20 Moon Day, Armstrong and Aldrin become first men on the moon, 1969

21 Guam Liberation Day; Ernest Hemingway (American author, b. 1899)

22 William Spooner (b. 1844); Poland: National Holiday

23 Ice cream cones invented, 1904; First U.S. swimming pool opened, Boston, 1927

24 Amelia Earhart (aviator, b. 1898); Detroit's birthday, 1701; Pioneer Day, Utah

25 Walter Payton (football player, b. 1954); First test-tube baby born, 1978

26 New York Admission Day, 11th state, 1788

27 President Nixon impeached by House Judiciary Committee, 1974

28 President Hoover ordered army to drive out World War I vets camped in D.C., 1932; Singing telegram birthday, 1933

29 Benito Mussolini (Italian dictator, b. 1883)

30 Henry Ford (entrepreneur, b. 1863); 26th amendment (1871)

31 Samuel Hopkins receives first U.S. government patent, 1790

Lesson plan: Students will understand and have compassion for those who are lonely. Further, students will have an understanding of how to help them to feel less lonely.

Activity: Discuss loneliness and how it feels to be lonely. Divide the class into groups and have each group "adopt" an elderly person from a nursing home to be their friend. Throughout the year, students will be responsible for doing things for their elderly friend (e.g., writing letters, visiting, making gifts). Tell students to treat their new friend as they would like to be treated.

Questions:

1. What makes you feel good?
2. How does it feel to be lonely?
3. What can we do to make others less lonely?
4. Why are people lonely?
5. Who gets lonely?

Skills taught: Research, social, and analysis skills

Resources: Pen pals from a nursing home

AUGUST

The month of August was originally named *Sextilis,* which means "sixth" in Latin. The Romans renamed this month August to honor the Emperor Augustus.

Some Interesting Facts about August

1. August is the month during which the first picture of the moon was taken from space.
2. August has 31 days.
3. August takes one day away from February, leaving February with 28 days.
4. The first Lincoln penny was issued in August.
5. The poppy and gladiolus are the official flowers for August.
6. The sardonyx and peridat are the gems for August.

Activity 1

Date: August 28, 1963

Event: Dream Day

Lesson plan: Students will be able to recognize the "I Have a Dream" speech and be able to identify their own personal dreams.

Activity: After reading and discussing the "I Have a Dream" speech by Martin Luther King, Jr., students will relate what he said to what is going on today in the United States. Students will be asked to identify their own dreams with respect to their personal lives and the life of the nation. Once dreams have been identified and discussed, students will create a speech and share it among a small group of students.

Questions:

1. Who was Martin Luther King, Jr.?
2. Why is his speech so famous?
3. Why did people listen to Martin Luther King, Jr.'s, dreams?
4. Did King's dream come true?
5. How did he make his dream speech so effective?
6. Where was the "I Have a Dream" speech given?

Skills taught: Research, social, analysis, and creative skills

Resources: "I Have a Dream" speech by Martin Luther King, Jr., August 28, 1963

Activity 2

Date: August 6, 1945

Event: Hiroshima Day

Lesson plan: Students will be able to explain the effects of dropping an atomic bomb.

Activity: Students will read *Hiroshima* and discuss the novel as a class. They will brainstorm and try to think of solutions other than using an atomic bomb to resolve conflict.

Questions:

1. Why was the bomb dropped?
2. How did the bomb affect the United States?
3. How did the bomb affect the rest of the world?
4. Who gave permission to drop the bomb?
5. Are the effects of the bomb permanent?

Skills taught: Research, reading, and interpretive skills

Resources: *Hiroshima* (novel by John Hersey) and maps of Asia

August

1	2	3	4	5	6	7
Colorado Admission Day, 38th state, 1876 Francis Scott Key (*Star-Spangled Banner*, b. 1779)	Friendship Day	Columbus Sailing Day anniversary, 1492 Colorado Day	"Save the Whale" commemorative postage stamps issued, 1988	First English colony in North America founded, 1585 Australia: Picnic Day	Hiroshima Day, 1945 Bolivia Independence Day, 1825 First man executed in electric chair, New York, 1890	First picture of earth from space, 1959 Iran invades Kuwait, 1990 Ralph Bunche (American diplomat/novelist, b. 1904)

8	9	10	11	12	13	14
Jesse Owens wins his fourth Olympic gold medal, 1936	National Hobo Convention, Britt, IA Omak (WA) stampede and suicide race	Missouri Admission Day, 24th state, 1821 Herbert Hoover (31st president, b. 1874)	Herbert Hoover Day in Iowa Presidential Joke Day Alex Haley (author, b. 1921)	USSR National Sports Day First domestic sewing machine made by I. M. Singer, 1851 First trans-Atlantic telegraph cable completed, 1858	National Alcoholism Awareness Day Fidel Castro (Cuban president, b. 1927) Aztec Empire falls to Spain, 1521	Victory Day, last shots fired in World War II, 1945 Liberty Tree Day in Massachusetts

15	16	17	18	19	20	21
Panama Canal opened, 1914 Transcontinental railroad completed, 1870 Napoleon Bonaparte (b. 1769)	Bennington Battle Day, Vermont, 1777	David Crockett (frontiersman, b. 1786) Geology and Astronomy weekend, West Virginia	Marshall Field (b. 1835)	Orville Wright (aviator, b. 1871) Bill Clinton (42nd president, b. 1946) Gail Borden patented condensed milk in the US, 1856	Benjamin Harrison (23rd president, b. 1833)	Hawaii Admission Day, 50th state, 1959 American Bar Association anniversary Mona Lisa stolen from the Louvre, 1911

22	23	24	25	26	27	28
Archibald Willard (Painted *Spirit of '76*, b. 1836)	Romania Liberation Day Rudolph Valentino (actor, dies 1926)	India Amarnath Yarta Italy: Vesuvius Day	Bret Harte (novelist, b. 1836)	Susan B. Anthony Day, Massachusetts 19th amendment (1920)	Lyndon Baines Johnson (36th president, b. 1908) J.A.C. Charles, French physicist, tested first hydrogen balloon Kellog-Briand Pact, 1928	First undersea telegraph cable completed, across English Channel, 1850 Junipero Serra (missionary, died 1784)

29	30	31				
Oliver Wendell Holmes (poet, b. 1809)	Huey P. Long Day, Louisiana	Capital Day				

SEPTEMBER

September's name comes from the Latin *septem*, meaning "seven." It was the seventh month of the year until Julius Caesar changed the calendar to make January 1 the beginning of the year instead of March.

Some Interesting Facts about September

1. September 21 is the equinox, when night and day are the same length.
2. September is cable TV month.
3. September is library card sign-up month.
4. September has 30 days.
5. The morning glory is the official flower for September.
6. The sapphire is the gem for September.

Activity 1

Date: September 20

Event: Rosh Hashanah

Lesson plan: Students will be able to explain what Rosh Hashanah is and what some of its traditions are.

Activity: Read the story "Start with Something Sweet" by Sidney Taylor from *Holiday Storybook*. Once the story has been read and discussion has taken place, the students will predict what might be their fate for the upcoming year.

Questions:

1. Who celebrates Rosh Hashanah?
2. What is a synagogue?
3. What is a shofar? What kind of noise do you think the shofar would make?
4. What are some of the traditional things done on the eve of Rosh Hashanah?
5. How is it decided on what day Rosh Hashanah will fall?
6. What day is (was) it on this year?

Skill taught: Research, reading, and discussion skills

Resources: Holiday Storybook by Sidney Taylor

Activity 2

Date: September 3, 1939

Event: World War II declared

Lesson plan: Students will be able to discuss the significance of World War II and how it affected our country.

September

1 Earthquake destroys Tokyo, 1923 Queen Liliuokalani (Last Hawaiian sovereign, b. 1838) Edgar Rice Burroughs (author, *Tarzan*, b. 1875)	**2** V-J Day, Japanese surrender, 1945 Christa McAuliffe (first teacher in space, b. 1948) Labor Day (Canada and U.S., first Monday)	**3** Prudence Grandall (educator who taught young black females in 1830s) World War II declaration, 1939 Treaty of Paris signed, 1783	**4** Marcus Whitman (doctor, b. 1802) Los Angeles birthday, 1781 Newspaper Carrier Day	**5** Jesse James (outlaw, b. 1847) Terrorism at 1972 Olympic Games in Munich, Germany Louis XIV (French King, b. 1638)	**6** Jane Addams (Chicago's Hull House founder, b. 1860) Boston Bicycle Club began first 100 mile bike trip, 1882	**7** Last holdup by Jesse James, 1881 First Miss America Pageant, 1921 Anna Mary Roberson Moses (Grandma Moses, b. 1860)
8 National Pledge of Allegiance Day	**9** California Admission Day, 31st state, 1850 Beethoven's last public performance, 1825	**10** Elias Howe patents sewing machine, 1846 Swap Ideas Day	**11** First policeman with arresting powers appointed in Los Angeles, 1910	**12** Jesse Owens (track star, b. 1913) Ethiopia National Revolution Day	**13** First pro football game played, 1895 Walter Reed (physician, b. 1851) Milton Hershey (chocolateer, b. 1847)	**14** Gregorian calendar adopted by Great Britain and American colonies, 1752
15 James Fenimore Cooper (novelist, b. 1789) William H. Taft (27th president, b. 1857) Agatha Christie, (Author, b. 1890)	**16** *Mayflower* departs from Plymouth, England, 1620	**17** Andrew "Rube" Foster (founder of Negro baseball league, b. 1879) Citizenship Day	**18** Herman Melville publishes *Moby Dick*, 1851 First edition of *New York Times* printed, 1851 UN Peace Day	**19** George Washington's farewell address, 1796	**20** Aloha Week Festival, celebrates Hawaiian tradition Alexander the Great (b. 356 B.C.)	**21** Sandra Day O'Connor becomes first woman appointed to U.S. Supreme Court, 1981 Autumnal Equinox
22 American Business Women's Day Hobbit Day	**23** Lewis and Clark Expedition ends (1806)	**24** National Hunting and Fishing Day Jim Henson (Muppets creator, b. 1936) Native American Day John Marshall (Chief Justice, b. 1755)	**25** First trans-Atlantic telephone begins operation, 1956 First doubleheader in baseball, 1882	**26** Johnny Appleseed (b. 1774) Good Neighbor Day	**27** Thomas Nast (American political cartoonist, b. 1840) Samuel Adams (American revolutionary, b. 1722)	**28** Confucius (b. 551) Juan Cabrillo becomes first European to see San Diego harbor, 1542
29 Munich Pact, 1958	**30** First annual fair in U.S., 350th anniversary, 1641					

Activity: Have a variety of literature on hand that reflects World War II. Students need to discuss the differences among the books and imagine what it would have been like to live at that time. Students will write down their ideas and then interview a grandparent or someone of that generation to find out what it was like to live during and be a part of World War II. Compare the similarities and differences between the students' ideas and the results of their interviews.

Questions:

1. Where did World War II take place?
2. Which countries were involved in World War II?
3. How did World War II affect the American people?
4. What other countries were greatly affected by World War II?
5. How was World War II resolved?

Skills taught: Research, reading, interviewing, and analytical skills

Resources: Encyclopedias, maps, and source books on World War II

OCTOBER

The name of October comes from the Latin word *octo,* which means "eight." October was the eighth month in the early Roman calendar. It later became the tenth month when the ancient Romans moved the beginning of the year from March 1 to January 1.

Some Interesting Facts about October

1. In the Northern Temperate Zone, the first frost usually occurs in October.
2. Leaves change to brilliant crimson, russet, and gold.
3. The frost kills many insects, and most birds have left for the south, but sparrows are fond of October and stay later.
4. The calendula is the official flower for October.
5. The opal is the gem for October.

Activity 1

Date: October 2

Event: Mohandas Gandhi's birthday

Lesson plan: This activity is designed to introduce students to Mohandas Gandhi and trace his influence on political thought and action.

Activity: Trace the life and times of Mohandas Gandhi and draw parallels between his actions in India and the struggle for racial equality in all lands.

Questions:

1. Who was Mohandas Gandhi and when did he live?
2. Why was he called "Mahatma"?

October

1 Jimmy Carter (39th president, b. 1924) James Meredith becomes first black student admitted to University of Mississippi, 1962	2 Nat Turner (b. 1800) Mohandas Gandhi (spiritual leader, b. 1869) Thurgood Marshall sworn in as first black justice on U.S. Supreme Court, 1967	3 W. H. Felton (first woman senator, b. 1922)	4 Rutherford Hayes (19th president, b. 1822) Frederick Remington (American artist, b. 1861) USSR launches Sputnik, 1957	5 Chester Arthur (21st president, b. 1830) Tecumseh (Shawnee leader, d. 1813)	6 American Library Association's birthday Ballpoint pen patented, 1921 First talking motion picture, New York, 1927	7 Child Health Day Marion Anderson (opera star, b. 1914)
8 Canadian Thanksgiving (first Monday in October) Chicago Fire anniversary Jesse Jackson (civil rights leader, b. 1941)	9 Leif Erikson visited North America, 1000 A.D.	10 Japan Health Sports Day Eleanor Roosevelt (b. 1884) Giuseppi Verdi (composer, b. 1813)	11 Boer War begins in South Africa, 1899 Weems Parson (traveling bookseller, b. 1759)	12 Columbus Day (Columbus sights land, 1492)	13 Alaska Day Celebration Molly Pitcher (Revolutionary War heroine, b. 1754) Margaret Thatcher (former British prime minister, b. 1925)	14 Dwight D. Eisenhower (34th president, b. 1890) e.e. cummings (author, b. 1894) William Penn (Quaker, b. 1644)
15 National Poetry Day Lee Iacocca (b. 1924) National Grouch Day	16 William Douglass (b. 1898) Noah Webster (dictionary, b. 1758) Oscar Wilde (poet, b. 1854)	17 Jupiter Hammon (poet, b. 1711) Black Poetry Day U.S. Constitution adopted, 1787	18 Alaska Day since 1867	19 Sweetest Day	20 Barnum and Bailey Circus opens, 1919 Missouri Day Mickey Mantle (baseball player, b. 1931)	21 Somalia National Day Jamaica National Hero's Day Alfred Nobel (scientist, b. 1833)
22 Cuban Missile Crisis, 1962 Franz Liszt (composer, b. 1811)	23 Sarah Bernhardt (actress, b. 1844) Beirut terrorist attack, 1983	24 United Nations Day Pony Express service ends, 1861 Black Thursday on Wall Street, 1929	25 Pablo Picasso (artist, b. 1881) Johann Strauss, Jr. (composer, b. 1825) Grenada invasion, 1983	26 Erie Canal opens, 1825	27 Teddy Roosevelt (26th president, b. 1858) Dylan Thomas (poet, b. 1914) Navy Day	28 Harvard University founded, 1636 Statue of Liberty dedicated, 1886 James Cook (explorer, b. 1728) Potato Day (Norway)
29 Stock market collapse, 1929	30 John Adams (2nd President, b. 1735) Orson Welles's *War of the Worlds* broadcast, 1938	31 Halloween Nevada Admission Day, 36th state, 1864 Louisiana purchased from France, 1803 National UNICEF Day				

3. How instrumental was he in helping his nation gain independence?
4. What were the basic tenets of his philosophy?
5. How did he influence Dr. Martin Luther King, Jr.?

Skills taught: Reading, comprehension, and critical thinking

Resources: Biographies on Gandhi, newspapers and periodicals of the time in which Gandhi lived

Activity 2

Date: October 28

Event: Statue of Liberty Day

Lesson plan: This activity can be used effectively with all high school students (with some modifications). Its purpose is to educate students about the origin and meaning of the Statue of Liberty. Students will be able to give information about the history of the Statue of Liberty.

Activity: Locate the Statue of Liberty on the map. Discuss with the students why it is located there. Create a scale model of the statue out of papier mâché and paint it.

Questions:

1. How did the Statue of Liberty come to be?
2. What does it symbolize?
3. What other things do we use to symbolize freedom?
4. If you were going to create something as a gift for freedom, what would it be? Why?

Skills taught: Map skills, creative thinking, and research skills

Resources: Pictures of the Statue of Liberty and history books

NOVEMBER

The name for November comes from the Latin word *novem*, which means "nine." November was the ninth month in the early Roman calendar when March 1 was the beginning of the year.

Some Interesting Facts about November

1. November comes between autumn and winter.
2. In the Northern Temperate Zone, the trees are bare in November.
3. The fallen leaves from October have lost their brilliant colors.

4. The soft grays and browns of northern landscapes are sometimes covered with a light snow.
5. The chrysanthemum is the official flower for November.
6. The topaz is the gem for November.

Activity 1

Date: Entire month

Event: Aviation History Month

Lesson plan: This activity is designed for all middle and secondary school students in recognition of aviation. Its purpose is to stress the roles that aviation plays in our lives. Students will understand the importance of aviation in today's world.

Activity: The students will research early transportation methods and read about early attempts at aviation. Construct with them a timeline of aviation.

Questions:

1. How does aviation affect our lives?
2. Who were the pioneers of aviation?
3. What were some types of early flying machines?
4. What are some differences and similarities between early aviation and modern aviation?

Skills taught: Research, reading, and comparing and contrasting

Resources: Aviation literature and old and new photographs

Activity 2

Date: Entire month

Event: Child Safety and Protection Month

Lesson plan: This activity is designed to make all students aware of their rights and of what they can do to help themselves stay safe. Students will become aware of child safety and protection issues.

Activity: Visit a public or school library and check out books centering around the topics of child safety. Make these books available to the students and discuss with them all of the major topics.

Questions:

1. Why do children need to be protected?
2. What are some of the reasons that children may seek help?
3. Where can children seek help?
4. What can be done to improve child safety?

November

1 Worldwide Peace Day National Author's Day *Wizard of Oz*, 1901, by Frank Baum Aviation History Month	2 N. Dakota Admission Day, 39th state, 1889 S. Dakota Admission Day, 40th state, 1889 James Polk (11th president, b. 1795) Warren Harding (29th president, b. 1865)	3 John Mantague (4th Earl of Sandwich, b. 1718) American Revolutionary War ends, 1783	4 Nellie T. Ross became nation's first woman governor, 1924 King Tut's tomb discovered, 1922	5 Florence Nightingale arrived at Barrack Hospital, Turkey during the Crimean War, 1854 FDR only President in U.S. to be elected for 3rd term	6 James Naismith invented basketball, 1891 John Phillip Sousa (composer, b. 1854) Adolphe Sax (Instrument maker, b. 1814)	7 Marie Curie (scientist, b. 1867)
8 Montana Admission Day, 41st state, 1889 Edmund Halley (astronomer, b. 1656) Edward Brooke elected first black U.S. senator in 85 years, 1966	9 Smokey the Bear dies, 1976, age 26 Workers in Berlin walk out on jobs in revolt, 1918	10 Edmund Fitzgerald sank, 1975 Over 30 million Americans and Canadians without power in "The Night the Lights Went Out," 1965	11 Washington Admission Day, 42nd state, 1889 Veteran's Day Remembrance Day (Canada) "God Bless America" introduced, 1939	12 Nadia Comaneci (gymnast, b. 1961) Sun Yat-sen (Chinese statesman, b. 1866) August Rodin (French sculptor, b. 1840)	13 A doctor in St. Louis invented peanut butter, 1890 Robert Lewis Stevenson (Author of *Treasure Island*, b. 1850)	14 Robert Fulton (inventor of steamboat, b. 1815) Claude Monet (Impressionist painter, b. 1840)
15 American Enterprise Day Georgia O'Keefe (American artist, b. 1887)	16 Oklahoma Admission Day, 46th state, 1907	17 Suez Canal opened, 1869 American Education Week Great American Smokeout	18 Mickey Mouse debuted, 1928 Alan Shepard (first American in space, b. 1925) Haiti Army Day	19 James A. Garfield (20th president, b. 1831) Abe Lincoln's Gettysburg Address, 1863	20 First tank battle, Cambrai, France, 1917 Robert Kennedy (U.S. attorney general, NY senator, b. 1925)	21 North Carolina Admission Day, 12th state, 1789 World "Hello" Day
22 John F. Kennedy assassinated, 1963 "China Clipper" anniversary since 1935	23 Billy the Kid (outlaw, b. 1859) First play-by-play football game broadcast, 1919 Franklin Pierce (14th president, b. 1804)	24 Zachary Taylor (12th president, b. 1784) Dale Carnegie (entrepreneur, b. 1888) Scott Joplin (Black musician, b. 1868)	25 Automobile speed reduction from 70 to 55, 1973 Joe Dimaggio (baseball player, b. 1914) National Indian Heritage Day	26 Charles Schulz (cartoonist, b. 1922) Sojourner Truth (Abolitionist, d. 1883)	27 Ginger Bread House competition, Lahaska, PA Buffalo Bob (TV personality, b. 1917)	28 William Blake (Poet, b. 1757)
29 Louisa May Alcott (b. 1832) C. S. Lewis (author, b. 1898) Madeleine L'Engle (author, b. 1918)	30 Mark Twain (novelist, b. 1835) Turkey declares war against Russia, 1914 First softball game played, Chicago 1887, invented by George Hancock					

Skills taught: Research, reading, and discussion

Resources: Literature on safety, school, counselors

DECEMBER

December's name comes from the Latin word *decem,* which means "ten." December was the tenth month in the early Roman calendar when March 1 was the beginning of the year.

Some Interesting Facts about December

1. Winter begins during December in the northern half of the world.
2. December 21 or 22 is the shortest day of the year in the Northern Hemisphere. This is the winter solstice, when the sun appears to have traveled the farthest south.
3. The poinsettia is the official flower for December.
4. The turquoise is the gem for December.

Activity 1

Date: December 15

Event: Bill of Rights Day

Lesson plan: This activity is designed for middle level and high school students. Its purpose is to stress the importance of the Bill of Rights. Students will be able to discuss the importance of the first ten amendments and to list several civil rights given to us in the Constitution of the United States.

Activity: Arrange students in cooperative learning groups and give each group a fictitious nation. Explain that they must decide on a government structure, its rules, and a symbol for their nation. have each group present their "Constitution" to the class. Later, have them improve or make "amendments" to their constitution to make it more effective.

Questions:

1. Who decides what rights we as citizens have?
2. What control over the government do we have?
3. What were the first ten amendments, and who is affected by them?
4. What can we as citizens do to improve our nation?

Skills taught: Cooperative learning, decision making, and critical thinking

Resources: Encyclopedias, books on government, and history books

December

1	2	3	4	5	6	7
Rosa Parks Day, 1955 First drive-in gasoline station opened, Pittsburgh, 1913	Monroe Doctrine, 1823 Napoleon I and Josephine crowned emperor and empress of France, 1804	First heart transplant, by Dr. Barnard, South Africa, 1967 Illinois Admission Day, 21st state, 1818	Manila paper patented, 1843	Martin Van Buren (8th president, b. 1782) Walt Disney (cartoonist, b. 1901) 21st amendment (1933)	Thomas Edison makes first sound recording, 1877 St. Nicholas Day Columbus, first European to land on Haiti, 1492	Delaware Admission Day, 20th state, 1817 Pearl Harbor attacked, 1941
8 Civil Rights Week Eli Whitney (inventor of cotton gin, b. 1765)	**9** Giant Christmas tree lighting at Rockefeller Plaza Emmett Kelly (clown, b. 1898)	**10** Mississippi Admission Day, 20th state, 1817 End of Spanish-American War, 1898 Thomas Gallaudet (established first school for the deaf, 1857)	**11** Indiana Admission Day, 19th state, 1816 Pinckey Pinchback, first black elected governor of Louisiana, 1872	**12** Pennsylvania Admission Day, 2nd state, 1787 W. L. Garrison (b. 1805) Mexico Guadalupe Day	**13** St. Lucia's Day	**14** Alabama Admission Day, 22nd state, 1819 George Washington, d. 1799 South Pole discovered, 1911
15 Sitting Bull, Sioux leader, d. 1890 Bill of Rights Day (1791) National Care and Share Day	**16** Ludwig Van Beethoven (composer, b. 1770) Boston Tea Party, 1773 Battle of the Bulge began, 1944	**17** Aztec Stone Calendar discovery anniversary Wright Brothers' first plane, 1903	**18** New Jersey Admission Day, 3rd state, 1787 First atomic power plant produces 100,000 watts, 1951 13th amendment (1865)	**19** U.S. invasion of Panama, 1989	**20** South Carolina, first state to secede from the Union, 1860 Mudd Day in remembrance of Dr. Samuel Mudd who aided John Wilkes Booth	**21** Forefather's Day, commemorates Pilgrim landing First crossword puzzle in U.S. appeared in *New York World*, 1913
22 Winter begins in Northern Hemisphere	**23** Englebert Humperdinck's opera *Hansel and Gretel* first performed,1843 First nonstop flight around world without refueling, 1987	**24** Kit Carson (b. 1809) First radio program broadcast, Brant Rock, MA, 1906 Christmas Eve	**25** Christmas Day Hirohito becomes the 124th emperor of Japan, 1926	**26** Boxing Day, when those who rendered services (postmen, lamplighters) were given gifts in honor in England Kwanzaa begins	**27** Louis Pasteur (inventor, b. 1822)	**28** Iowa Admission Day, 29th state, 1846 Thomas Woodrow Wilson (28th president, b. 1856)
29 Texas Admission Day, 28th state, 1845 Andrew Jackson (17th president, b. 1808) Anniversary of Wounded Knee Massacre, 1890	**30** John Milne (geologist, first accurate seismograph, b. 1850) John Altgeld (b. 1847) Simon Guggenheim (American philanthropist, b. 1856)	**31** Last day of year Make Up Your Mind Day New Year's Eve				

Activity 2

Date: Before December 31

Event: Reflecting on the past year

Lesson plan: This activity is designed for most grade levels. Its purpose is to reflect on all the changes and advances the students have witnessed or participated in. The importance of this lesson is to ensure that all the information is relevant and meaningful. Students will understand that time past is history.

Activity: Students will collect old newspapers, magazines, photographs, and assignments. Pull out the main topics (politics, national events, local events, etc.) and make a chart. Discuss with them all the events and reflect on all the information.

Questions:

1. What is history?
2. What is the importance of studying history?
3. How can we keep track of historical events?

Skills taught: Research, discussion, analysis, and evaluation

Resources: Old newspapers, magazines, and photographs

CHAPTER SEVEN

The Study of Humankind Is Not a Trivial Matter

"Why shouldn't truth be stranger than fiction?
Fiction, after all, has to make sense."

—Mark Twain

Although history can appear to be a pile of unrelated, useless, irrelevant information, the notion persists that history can be an interesting and enjoyable subject. History bridges time and space and gives us an intimate peek at who we were—our successes, failures, and follies. In essence, those things that humanize the study of history make it interesting and relevant.

How do teachers enliven textbooks filled with apparently mundane, unimportant information? In part, that depends on the teacher's attitude toward social studies and how much value he or she places on teaching it to students. If the subject is approached with enthusiasm and knowledge, the learners can find joy in learning history and geography—not to mention having fun in the process.

Content knowledge is important, but so is methodology. Even the teacher with limited content information can make social studies a viable and exciting subject for his or her students. The secret is to build on a student's natural curiosity and to share historical tidbits about the people, places, or things that make up history. Trivia, as we have seen from the popularity of board games and TV shows, can be an excellent vehicle to stimulate curiosity and interest in the study of history and geography.

The following pages are a compilation of some general information and facts related to the history of humanity. We encourage readers to add to this list with information they may find in newspapers, books, journals, almanacs, or even game shows. Incorporating this kind of information into a classroom is fun and makes studying social studies a bit more palatable for students. The following are some tidbits of history to share with students.

HISTORICAL FACTOIDS

United States of America

- The weekly diet of plantation slaves in the United States consisted of 40 cups of cornmeal and about 3.5 pounds of meat.
- Three U.S. presidents died on July 4: John Adams, Thomas Jefferson, and James Monroe.

- Quincy, Massachusetts, is the only town in the United States to produce two presidents—John Adams and John Quincy Adams.
- During World War II the United States kept 56,000 homing pigeons on duty.
- The first book in the New World was most probably Marco Polo's accounts of his travels. Christopher Columbus took it with him in 1492 when he thought he might reach China.
- American casualties during the bombardment on Fort McHenry consisted of 4 dead and 24 wounded.
- President William Howard Taft once said, "No tendency is quite so strong in human nature as the desire to lay down rules of conduct for other people."
- It is reported that the first man executed in the early American colonies for a capital crime was *Mayflower* passenger John Billington, who shot to death a hunter he found in his part of the woods. Billington was hanged.
- The *USS Monitor* was the first warship to have flushable toilets.
- President Theodore Roosevelt held the first press conference.
- Rhode Island boasts of the nation's oldest Baptist church, the oldest Quaker meeting house, and the oldest Jewish synagogue.
- Barbara Tuchman once noted that "war is the unfolding of miscalculations."
- The southeastern corner of Montana is closer to Texas than it is to the northeastern corner of Montana.
- Five U.S. vice-presidents were named John: Adams, Calhoun, Tyler, Breckenridge, and Gardner.
- Of the 59 original signers of the Declaration of Independence, at least 14 died in American Revolution. Five were captured, then executed, and nine died in combat.
- During the U.S. Civil War, history records that the British sympathized with the confederacy, while Imperial Russia sided with the Union.
- It was Judison Welliver, literary clerk and speech-writer to Presidents Warren G. Harding and Calvin Coolidge, who coined the term "Founding Fathers."
- Mark Spitz won eight gold medals for swimming in the 1972 Olympics. Today, not one of his winning times would even qualify him for the U.S. team.
- In 1800, seven children per couple was the average in the United States.
- Colonial Americans had no potatoes, so their main vegetable was parsnips.
- It was President Lyndon B. Johnson who put speeches into categories: the Mother Hubbard, which covers everything but touches nothing, and the bikini, which covers only the essentials.
- Film star Carole Lombard, who died in a plane crash while selling war bonds in 1942, is listed as the first American killed in World War II.
- Cherokee Bill was a noted trailblazer and feared gun fighter in the old West. Like Mary Hodges and Bill Picket, a rodeo and movie star, Bill was a famous African American who left his marks on our Western history.
- In 1948, the Tucker car's third headlight turned with the steering wheel to show drivers exactly where they were going.
- Nellie Ross Taylor was the first woman to have her name on a federal building cornerstone. Her name appears on the U.S. Depository, Fort

Knox, Tennessee. Ms. Taylor was the first woman elected governor (Wyoming) and served as Franklin D. Roosevelt's director of the U.S. Mint in 1933.

- Pollsters report that 4 out of every 10 Americans know that the Fourth of July has something to do with the American Revolution, but do not know exactly what! For those four: The signing of the Declaration of Independence.
- Robert Frost (1961) and Maya Angelou (1993) are the only poets to have read their respective works at a presidential inauguration.
- The caricature of Uncle Sam was first depicted by cartoonist Thomas Nast. Dan Rice, a circus clown, was the model.
- Abraham Lincoln and George Washington were circus buffs.
- John Howard Payne, a lonely and destitute wanderer most of his life, wrote the song "Home Sweet Home."
- These U.S. presidents wrote the most books (of 36 or more pages):

  1. Theodore Roosevelt (39 books)
  2. John Quincy Adams (24 books)
  3. Herbert Hoover (16 books)
  4. Woodrow Wilson (14 books)
  5. Thomas Jefferson (11 books)
  6. Grover Cleveland (10 books)

- The United States of America has had nine capitals:

  1. Philadelphia (1774–1776; 1777; 1778–1783)
  2. Baltimore (1776–1777)
  3. Lancaster, Pennsylvania (1777)
  4. York, Pennsylvania (1777–1778)
  5. Princeton, New Jersey (1783)
  6. Annapolis, Maryland (1783–1784)
  7. Trenton, New Jersey (1784)
  8. New York City/Philadelphia (1785–1800)
  9. Washington, D.C. (1800–present)

- George Washington's favorite activities were:

  1. Shopping
  2. Betting on cockfights
  3. Betting on horses
  4. Fox hunting
  5. Attending the theater
  6. Duck shooting
  7. Dancing
  8. Playing cards

- Food firsts

  1. Canned food (Napoleon's army), 1808
  2. Peanut butter (St. Louis doctor), 1890
  3. Canned soup (Campbell's), 1897
  4. Ice cream cone (St. Louis World's Fair), 1904
  5. Frozen foods (Bird's Eye), 1930

- About 4 million slaves were officially freed after the American Civil War ended in 1865.
- Rebecca Felton was the first female U.S. senator (appointed in October 1922).
- Hattie Carroway was the first woman elected to the U.S. Senate (1932).
- Benjamin Franklin invented suspenders in 1736.
- The three most popular natural attractions in the United States are:

  1. The Grand Canyon (Arizona)
  2. Yellowstone National Park (Wyoming)
  3. Niagara Falls (New York)

- George Washington's favorite soup was made from peanuts.
- The Labor Day holiday was probably created by either Peter McGuire or Matthew McGuire. The argument has never really been resolved.
- Elizabeth Hisington was the first female general in the U.S. Army (appointed in 1970).
- The first American zoo was the Philadelphia Zoological Gardens, which opened in 1874. It still exists on the same grounds.
- Benjamin O. Davis in 1940 became the first African American general in the U.S. Army.
- Ben Nighthorse Campbell of Colorado was the first Native American to be elected to the U.S. Senate (1992).
- Francis Perkins was the first woman to become a cabinet member. She served as Secretary of Labor in the Roosevelt administration from 1933 to 1945.
- Martha Washington was the first woman to appear on a U.S. postage stamp (1918).
- Herbert Hoover was the first U.S. president born west of the Mississippi River (August 10, 1874, in Iowa).
- Carol Moseley Braun was the first African American woman to be elected to the U.S. Senate (1992).
- *Park* is the most common street name in the United States.
- Since 1899, it has been illegal for a factory to dump waste into any body of U.S. water.
- Youngest presidents at death:

  1. John F. Kennedy (46 years, 177 days)
  2. James Garfield (49 years, 304 days)
  3. James Polk (53 years, 225 days)
  4. Abraham Lincoln (56 years, 62 days)
  5. Chester Arthur (57 years, 44 days)
  6. Warren Harding (57 years, 273 days)
  7. William McKinley (58 years, 228 days)
  8. Theodore Roosevelt (60 years, 71 days)

- Presidential facts:

  1. The youngest person to *become* president was Theodore Roosevelt (43 years old).
  2. The youngest person to be *elected* to the presidency was John F. Kennedy (43 years old).

3. The oldest to be elected to the presidency was Ronald Reagan (69 years old).
4. The tallest presidents were Abraham Lincoln and Lyndon Johnson (6′4″).
5. The shortest president was James Madison (5′3″).
6. The most obese president was William Howard Taft (300+ pounds).
7. The longest tenured president was Franklin Delano Roosevelt (13 years).
8. The shortest tenured president was William Henry Harrison (1 month).

- States with smaller populations than Washington, D.C. (620,000) are:

  1. Wyoming (471,000)
  2. Alaska (513,000)
  3. Vermont (556,000)

- The only elected U.S. presidents to succeed the president they served as vice-president were:

  1. John Adams (succeeded George Washington, 1797)
  2. Thomas Jefferson (succeeded John Adams, 1801)
  3. Martin Van Buren (succeeded Andrew Jackson, 1837)
  4. George Bush (succeeded Ronald Reagan, 1989)

- What's in a name?

  1. Michigan ("great water")
  2. Connecticut ("long river place")
  3. Oklahoma ("red man")
  4. Wisconsin ("grassy place")
  5. Minnesota ("cloudy water")

- The three faces originally scheduled to be carved on Mount Rushmore were:

  1. Kit Carson
  2. Jim Bridger
  3. John Colter

- The most common surnames in the United States are:

  1. Smith
  2. Johnson
  3. Williams
  4. Jones
  5. Brown
  6. Miller
  7. Davis
  8. Martin
  9. Anderson
  10. Wilson

- "Blues" music started in Memphis, Tennessee.
- The most recognizable U.S. brand names worldwide are:

  1. Coca-Cola
  2. Campbell's Soup
  3. Pepsi
  4. AT&T
  5. McDonald's
  6. American Express
  7. Kellogg's
  8. IBM
  9. Levi's
  10. Sears

- Weather extremes in the continental United States:

  1. Warmest is Key West, Florida (average 77.7 degrees)
  2. Coldest is International Falls, Minnesota (average 36.4 degrees)
  3. Driest is Yuma, Arizona (average 2.65 inches of rain)
  4. Wettest is Quillayute, Washington (average 104.5 inches of rain)
  5. Sunniest is Yuma, Arizona (average 17 days of rain)

- William Wirtz was the only military person executed for war crimes at the conclusion of the Civil War. He was the commandant of the famous Andersonville prison, where thousands died.
- The popular and familiar American version of Santa Claus was created by a Coca-Cola magazine ad in the early 1930s.
- In 1874 the elephant first appeared as a Republican Party symbol in a cartoon by Thomas Nast in *Harper's Weekly.* Nast used the elephant several times as the symbol and it soon caught on for the Republican Party.
- The donkey was used as a political symbol by Andrew Jackson after his opponents called him a "jackass" during the 1828 election campaign. Later, Thomas Nast, as he had done with the elephant for the Republican party, used the donkey to represent the Democratic party in his political cartoons, and it too became the official symbol for the 1880s.
- "I only regret that I have but one life to give for my country." Who said that? Evidently, not Nathan Hale. Recently discovered eyewitness accounts indicate that his last words were: "It's the duty of every good officer to obey any orders given to him by his commander-in-chief."
- William McKinley is the only U.S. president who has no personal residence still standing.
- *Time, People, Sports Illustrated, TV Guide,* and *Newsweek* were the magazines with the highest advertising revenue in the 1990s.
- At latest count, four former U.S. presidents were schoolteachers: Millard Fillmore, Chester A. Arthur, William McKinley and Lyndon B. Johnson.
- The first four U.S. presidents had no middle name.
- Sergeant William Carney was the first African American to win the Congressional Medal of Honor. He was a soldier with the 54th Massachusetts Regiment during the Civil War.
- Some notable African Americans who were early Western trailblazers and personalities:

1. York—Lewis and Clark Expedition
2. Beckwith—trailblazer
3. Mary Hodges—trailblazer, settler
4. Cherokee Bill—gunfighter
5. Bill Pickett—rodeo and movie star

- Only five U.S. cities have "The" as the official first word in the city's name:

  1. The Dalles, Oregon
  2. The Village, Oklahoma
  3. The Village of Indian Hills, Ohio
  4. The Plains, Ohio
  5. The Meadows, Illinois

- President Thomas Jefferson predicted it would take 40 generations to conquer the American wilderness. *It took only about four generations!*
- State capitals with "City" in their names:

  1. Salt Lake City, Utah
  2. Jefferson City, Missouri
  3. Carson City, Nevada
  4. Oklahoma City, Oklahoma

- Some famous people born on the Fourth of July:

  1. Calvin Coolidge
  2. Stephen Foster
  3. Nathaniel Hawthorne
  4. Louis Armstrong
  5. Neil Simon
  6. Ann Landers and Abagail Van Buren (twins)

- In 1890, President Millard Fillmore brought into the White House a kitchen stove, thereby ending the practice of cooking meals over fireplaces. All the cooks quit in protest.
- The first uniformed policewoman with full powers of arrest in the United States was Alice Stebbins Wells, who had been a social worker. Ms. Stebbins began her career on September 12, 1940, in Los Angeles.
- Half of all U.S. farmers do not live on their farms.
- Key West, Florida, is closer to Havana, Cuba, than to Miami in its own state.
- Thomas Paine coined the name "United States of America."
- The person behind the city:

  1. Orlando, Florida (Orlando Reeves, Indian runner)
  2. Cleveland, Ohio (Moses Cleveland, Connecticut surveyor)
  3. Dallas, Texas (George Dallas, U.S. vice-president)
  4. Denver, Colorado (James Denver, governor of Kansas Territory)
  5. Gary, Indiana (Judge Elbert Gary)
  6. Reno, Nevada (General J. L. Reno, Civil War)
  7. Seattle, Washington (Seattle, Duwamish chief)

- Peter Cooper invented Jell-O, ran for U.S. president, made hats, brewed beer, designed the first commercial American steam locomotive (the "Tom Thumb"), helped lay the first Atlantic cable, and founded Cooper Union (a free school of higher education in the arts and sciences). He was a true Renaissance man!
- Rugby, North Dakota, is the geographical center of North America.
- U.S. casualties in major conflicts:

  1. Revolutionary War, 1775–1783 (4,435 deaths)
  2. War of 1812, 1812–1815 (2,260 deaths)
  3. Mexican War, 1846–1848 (1,733 deaths)
  4. Civil War, 1861–1865 (498,332 deaths; 677,392 casualties)
  5. Spanish-American War, 1898 (385 deaths; 4,108 casualties)
  6. World War I, 1917–1918 (53,402 deaths; 320,518 casualties)
  7. World War II, 1941–1945 (291,557 deaths; 1,076,245 casualties)
  8. Korean War, 1950–1953 (33,629 deaths; 157,530 casualties)
  9. War in Southeast Asia, 1964–1975 (47,382 deaths; 211,438 casualties)

- About 80,000 Americans are injured yearly in gun-related incidents.
- Andrew Jackson is credited with being the first president to kiss a baby during an election campaign.
- The most valuable matchbook cover is the Charles Lindbergh trans-Atlantic flight commemorative (1927). Only two are known to exist.
- In 1849, Elizabeth Blackwell became the first woman in the United States to earn a medical degree.
- Virginia Dare was the first child born to English parents in the New World, at the Roanoke Island Colony in 1587. The colony and all of its settlers mysteriously disappeared without a trace.
- The first surviving colonial child born in the New World was named Peregrine White. He was born aboard the Mayflower as the ship lay at anchor. The name Peregrine is Latin for "pilgrim" or a person in a foreign land. Peregrine White lived to be 83 years old.
- The Democratic party, founded by Thomas Jefferson, is the oldest continuing political party in the world.
- The Pilgrims rarely drank water before they came to the New World because of the poor quality of water where they had previously lived.
- It is believed that the most stressful jobs in the United States are:

  1. Inner-city high school teacher
  2. Police officer
  3. Miner
  4. Air-traffic controller
  5. Medical intern
  6. Stockbroker
  7. Journalist
  8. Customer service employee
  9. Waitress
  10. Secretary

- Charles Lubin of Chicago was the first baker to have supermarkets sell his baked goods. He was also the father of Sara Lee, whose bakery products are popular today.

- In 1863, President Lincoln called for Americans to celebrate the *last* Thursday of November as the official Thanksgiving holiday. In 1931, Thanksgiving became a national holiday. In 1941, Franklin D. Roosevelt changed Thanksgiving to the *fourth* Thursday in November.
- Christmas has been an official holiday only since about 1891.
- In Benjamin Franklin's day, people powdered their wigs, wiped their teeth, and scraped their tongues. "Toilet" kits of well-to-do colonials often included silver tongue scrapers.
- Abraham Lincoln was the first full-bearded U.S. president, and Benjamin Harrison was the last.
- William Howard Taft was the first U.S. president to play golf.
- In 1789, at the first session of Congress, lack of a quorum forced the Congress to adjourn:

  1. Senators—8 of 22 attended.
  2. Representatives—13 of 59 attended.

- It was Abraham Lincoln who first said "government of the people, by the people, and for the people."
- The South has been called "Dixie" since about 1850. Credit the Citizens Bank of New Orleans, Louisiana, for that. Before the Civil War, it produced reliable $10 bills, accepted nationwide. Printed partly in English and partly in French, the bill showed *dix*, meaning "ten" on it. The word *dixie* came to stand for "good currency," and then came to be a nickname for the South.
- Sonan is the oldest surviving family name in the United States; descendants go back to 1565 in St. Augustine, Florida.
- What is in a name and how is it named?

  1. Parker House Rolls (Parker House Hotel, Boston)
  2. Dr. Pepper (owner of drugstore where it was developed)
  3. Noxzema (from the words *knocks eczema*)
  4. Worcestershire sauce (from Worcester, England)
  5. Murine (chemical formula muriate of berberine)
  6. Avon products (founder loved the works of William Shakespeare)

- General George Armstrong Custer was a hero at the Battle of Gettysburg.
- President Rutherford B. Hayes's favorite sport was croquet.
- Woodrow Wilson was so sick with migraine headaches as a child that he did not learn to read until he was 11 years old. He later became a university president and then president of the United States.
- "Lemonade" Lucy Rutherford was so named because she would not allow alcoholic beverages to be served in the White House during her husband's term of office.
- Thomas Jefferson invented the folding chair.
- In Benjamin Franklin's day, if you had a rug in your house you were considered rich.
- Youngest first ladies:

  1. Frances Cleveland—21 years, 226 days
  2. Julia Tyler—24 years, 53 days

3. Jacqueline Kennedy—31 years, 176 days
4. Edith Roosevelt—40 years, 39 days
5. Edith Wilson—40 years, 140 days
6. Dolly Madison—40 years, 288 days
7. Sarah Polk—41 years, 181 days
8. Mary Lincoln—42 years, 81 days

- The last American Civil War veteran died in 1959.
- The "Star-Spangled Banner" became our official national anthem in 1931.
- Thomas Edison failed 24,999 times before successfully inventing a storage battery.
- There are about half a million words in the American-English language.
- Phoenix (Arizona) and Indianapolis (Indiana) are the two largest (by population) capital cities. Montpelier (Vermont) and Pierre (South Dakota) are the two smallest.
- Americans love to munch and snack all day long:

1. Chicago, per capita, consumes the most Twinkies.
2. Dallas loves Fritos.
3. New York City devours Hershey's Kisses.
4. Pikeville (Kentucky) has the biggest per capita consumption of Pepsi Cola.
5. Miami is tops in Perrier and prune juice consumption.
6. Portland (Oregon) loves Grapenuts.
7. Salt Lake City has the biggest per capita consumption of Cracker Jacks.
8. Hartford and New Haven (Connecticut) and Springfield (Massachusetts) are the pasta centers of the U.S.
9. Chicago's O'Hare International Airport sells more hot dogs than any other concession in the United States.
10. Seattle has the most Hershey bar eaters.
11. Midwesterners are the biggest per capita consumers of lunch meat.

- The oldest one-family farm in the U.S. is the Tuttle vegetable farm in Dover, New Hampshire, dating back to 1632.
- The first pay phone was installed in Hartford, Connecticut, in 1889.
- Anne Bradstreet is considered by some to be the first significant U.S. poet.
- Kit Carson, American frontiersman and explorer, reportedly had these dying words: "I'm gone, good-bye, doctor. Adios, compadre."
- Iowa raises the most pigs, California the most eggs, Georgia the most peanuts, and Arkansas the most rice.
- The typewriter revolutionized U.S. business when it came on the market in 1888.
- No U.S. president ever won a majority vote of all registered voters. Lyndon Johnson came the closest with 38% of all registered voters.
- President Taft, in 1910, reported that cocaine posed the greatest threat to the United States of America.
- California was the first state to elect two women to serve concurrently in the Senate (1992).
- Benjamin Franklin invented the spelling bee.
- The states with the largest population of retired people:

1. Florida
2. Pennsylvania
3. Iowa
4. Rhode Island
5. West Virginia
6. Arkansas

- The Navajo reservation is larger than West Virginia.
- The first U.S. Thanksgiving took place in mid-October of 1621. Ninety-one Native Americans and 56 Pilgrims dined on venison (brought by the Native Americans), eel pie, duck, goose, lobster, clams, bass, cornbread, and fresh fruit.
- The Cherokee are the only Native American tribe to have a written language.
- At least 189 people perished while defending the Alamo in 1836. Interestingly, at least 31 of those defenders came from nations other than the United States, such as Denmark, Great Britain, Ireland, Scotland, Germany, and Mexico.
- The first Peace Corps volunteer went to Ghana, Africa, in 1961.
- Charles Curtis, vice-president under Herbert Hoover, was the first Native American to serve in that office. His mother was a member of the Kaw tribe.
- Extremes—USA style:

1. Northernmost point—Point Barrow, Alaska
2. Southernmost point—Ka Lae, Hawaii
3. Easternmost point—West Quoddy Head, Maine
4. Westernmost point—Cape Wrangel, Alaska

- The first leg of any trip out of Hawaii is at least 2,200 miles.
- A black man from Haiti named Jean Baptiste Pointe du Sable founded a settlement in 1772 and called it Eschikagou. Today we call it Chicago.
- There are 132 Hawaiian Islands. The Hawaiian Islands are only one of many archipelagoes in the world. Others are the Philippines, Japan, Micronesia, and the Marshall Islands.
- Hawaii is the state with the least fresh lake water.
- The Sioux call themselves "Lakota."
- Reportedly, the first person to set foot on Plymouth Rock in 1620 was a woman.
- Thomas Nast, the political cartoonist, prompted the coinage of a word because of his terse political cartoons: *nasty*.
- In 1956 the polio vaccine developed by Dr. Jonas Salk was given to children for the first time. Dr. Salk worked for nearly twenty years developing the vaccine.
- Campbell soup cans have red and white labels because the decision maker in 1898 admired the Cornell football team.
- Juliette Low, founder of the Girl Scouts of America, was deaf.
- L. Frank Baum, who wrote *The Wonderful Wizard of Oz*, also wrote *The Art of Decorating Dry Goods, Windows and Interiors*.
- Sandra Berenson, Abbot of Smith College, is considered by many to have been the first person to write the rules for women's basketball.
- Latest count of languages spoken in the U.S. stands at 329.

- Thus far, John Adams, James Madison, Herbert Hoover, and Ronald Reagan are the only former U.S. presidents to celebrate their 85th birthday.
- The first broadcast of a real trial was the radio rendition of the Scopes trial ("Monkey Trial") in 1925. A sportscaster did the play-by-play report.
- How big are the Great Lakes?

  1. Lake Ontario is the size of Hawaii and Rhode Island together.
  2. Lake Erie is the size of Vermont.
  3. Lake Michigan is the size of Delaware, Vermont, Rhode Island, and New Hampshire.
  4. Lake Huron is the size of Missouri, New Jersey, and Connecticut.
  5. Lake Superior is the size of South Carolina and Rhode Island.

- "Walk softly and carry a big stick" was a well-known proverb in West Africa long before Theodore Roosevelt borrowed it.
- Contaminated meat, not warfare, killed the greatest number of troops in the Spanish–American War (1898).

International

- The seven sins, according to Mohandas Gandhi, were:

  1. Wealth without work
  2. Pleasure without conscience
  3. Knowledge without character
  4. Commerce without morality
  5. Science without humanity
  6. Worship without sacrifice
  7. Politics without principle

- The name native people call their own country:

  1. Iceland—Lydveldid Island
  2. Iran—Keshvare Shahanshahiueiran
  3. China—Chung-hua Jen-min Kung-ho Kuo
  4. Taiwan—Chung-hua Mink-Kuo
  5. Ceylon—Sri Lanka
  6. South Korea—Daehan-Minkuk
  7. Tibet—Po

- Canadian Thanksgiving is celebrated on the second Monday of October.
- The first telephone operators in Connecticut in 1878 answered with "Ahoy" instead of "Hello." Today other countries answer this way:

  1. Greece—"Come in"
  2. Russia—"I am listening"
  3. Spain—"Tell me"
  4. Mexico—"Well?"
  5. India—"Greetings"

6. Iran—"Yes"
7. Germany—"Hello, who is speaking?"
8. Italy—"Ready, with whom am I speaking?"
9. Japan—"Excuse, excuse"

- The Spanish conquistadors recorded that all Aztec boys had to go to school. Perhaps the Aztecs were the first people to make education compulsory.
- It was the Muslims who, in the ninth century, opened public drugstores.
- *Gobi* means sand.
- The American Navajo "Night Chant" is a ritual song that lasts nine days.
- Ancient Egyptians worshipped cats because they ate rats thus saving warehoused grain for the population.
- Sudan's Rashaida's interpretation of Islamic law requires females to wear veils from age 5.
- Phoenicians put wheels on their boats and paraded them through the streets in their many Mediterranean colonies. The Romans called them *carre naval*—"naval carriages"—hence our word *carnival*. The Spanish called them *flotas*—hence our word *floats*.
- The Roman alphabet was all capital letters. It was Charlemagne's monks who invented lower-case letters.
- The Nambiguara Indians in west central Brazil have a language that contains no numbers!
- Unlike most Americans, who pump once or twice when they shake hands, Europeans tend to pump hands five to six times.
- When Cristobal Colon (Christopher Columbus) first showed up in the Western Hemisphere, an estimated 2,200 languages were spoken here— far outnumbering all the known languages of Europe and Asia combined.
- Heinrich Himmler of Nazi Germany tried to replace the Christian Christmas with a nationalistic holiday called Julfest and ordered SS troops to celebrate it on December 21st.
- Traditional Greek mourning lasts five years.
- English may be the current universal language and Chinese is probably spoken by more persons than any other language, but Spanish is also a dominant language on the globe. The following nations have large Spanish-speaking populations:

1. Spain
2. Mexico
3. Argentina
4. Chile
5. Peru
6. Ecuador
7. Colombia
8. Cuba
9. Uruguay
10. Paraguay
11. Bolivia
12. Venezuela
13. Honduras
14. Nicaragua
15. Guatemala
16. Costa Rica
17. Panama
18. Guinea
19. United States

- The Incas were most probably the first New World highway builders. One of their roads went from Colombia to Chile—about 2,500 miles.

- The Tsaatan, Mongolian Gypsies, are probably the smallest ethnic group on earth. Only about 80 survive.
- The United States granted women the right to vote in 1920. The first countries to grant women the right to vote were:

  1. New Zealand (1893)
  2. Australia (1902)
  3. Finland (1906)
  4. Norway (1913)
  5. Denmark (1915)
  6. Greenland (1915)
  7. Iceland (1915)
  8. USSR (1917)

- Dogs were probably first domesticated in Persia (present-day Iran) some 2,000 years ago.
- In Great Britain, Valentine's Day is celebrated by:

  1. Sending cards signed with dots
  2. Receiving gifts of fruit and money
  3. Singing special Valentine songs
  4. Baking buns with seeds or raisins
  5. Women waiting by a window for a man to pass (the old custom said that the first man by the window would become your husband)

- To date, the five Africans to win a Nobel Peace Prize are: Anwar Sadat, Bishop Desmond Tutu, Albert Luthuli, F. W. de Klerk, and Nelson Mandela.
- Besides Oskar Schindler and Raoul Wallenberg, who saved thousands of Jewish people, other, less famous, also provided visas for Jews trying to escape the terror of Nazi Germany. They included Jan Zwartendijk of the Netherlands, who provided passage to the Dutch West Indies, and Chiune Sugihara, the Japanese consul-general, who saved hundreds in Lithuania before World War II.
- Buddhist Monks in India developed karate about 2,500 years ago.
- Checkers originated as a game of war strategy in Egypt.
- Costa Rica in Central America contains more plant species than all the rest of North America combined.
- Guyana is the only nation in South America where English is the official language.
- Every sixth Canadian was born somewhere else.
- Iceland boasts it has the highest literacy rate in the world—100%. Australia and New Zealand also lay claim to this title.
- Top ten nations where 75% (or more) of the total population lives in urban areas:

  1. United Kingdom: 91.5%
  2. Denmark: 88.9%
  3. Netherlands: 88.4%
  4. Qatar: 88.0%
  5. Venezuela: 86.6%
  6. Malta: 85.3%

7. Argentina: 84.6%
8. Uruguay: 84.6%
9. New Zealand: 83.7%
10. Chile: 83.6%

- The United States of America has approximately 73.9% of its population living in urban areas.
- The Philippines is a mountain chain.
- The St. Lawrence Seaway between the U.S. and Canada is the longest ship canal in the world (2400 miles long).
- Murmansk, Russia (population 468,000), is the world's largest city north of the Arctic Circle.
- Names on the map do change:

1. Uganda was once Buganda.
2. Bermuda was Somers Island.
3. Ecuador was Quito.
4. Ghana was Gold Coast.
5. Cameroon was German Kamerun.
6. Mexico was New Spain.
7. Indonesia was Netherlands East Indies.
8. Crete was Candia.
9. Myanmar was Burma.
10. Saudi Arabia was Arabia.
11. The Commonwealth of Independent States was the Union of Soviet Socialist Republics.

- Two years before Christopher Columbus sailed to the New World, a German mapmaker named Martin Behaim made the first geographical globe and called it Earth Apple. Columbus never saw it, but he, like many educated Europeans, knew the world was round.
- Even explorers do not always know what they have found or how to get there:

1. Columbus thought Cuba was China.
2. Ponce de Leon thought Florida was an island.
3. John Cabot thought that Newfoundland was China.

- Half the baseball caps worn in America are made in Asia.
- In 1992, Singapore banned chewing gum. For those caught importing it, the first-offense penalty is a $6173 fine and a year in jail.
- Most common surnames:

Ireland: Murphy
Japan: Suzuki
France: Martin
Russia: Kuznetsky
Poland: Kowalski
China: Wang
Spain: Gomez
U.S.:   Smith

- It has been estimated that at the beginning of the next century, 40% of the world's population will be living in cities. It is predicted that at least 83% of the population growth through the 1990s will occur in urban areas in Asia, Africa, and Latin America. Here are the megacities with projected population for the year 2000:

  1. Mexico City: 25.6 million
  2. Sao Paulo: 22.1 million
  3. Tokyo: 19 million
  4. Shanghai: 17 million
  5. New York: 16.8 million
  6. Calcutta: 15.7 million
  7. Bombay: 15.4 million
  8. Beijing: 14 million
  9. Los Angeles: 13.5 million
  10. Jakarta: 13.7 million

- Note that seven of these cities are in Third World countries—just the opposite of 1950 statistics on the world's largest cities.
- Marie and Pierre Curie recorded in their notebooks their experiments with radium in the early twentieth century. *Their notebooks are still radioactive!*
- Iceland had an armed robbery—once!
- Gaya, a city near Calcutta, India, is identified by Buddhists as the holiest city.
- How long did it take the world to reach 1 billion people? It was 1800 when the world's population reached 1 billion. In 1930 it was at 2 billion, at 3.3 billion by 1965, and about 5.2 billion as of 1996.
- Mexico City grew from 3 million people in 1950 to 20 million in 1990.
- The largest continents (in land size) are north of the Equator.
- Christopher Columbus made four voyages to the New World:

  1. 1492: He explored San Salvador, northern Cuba, and Hispaniola with three ships.
  2. 1493–1496: With 17 ships, he explored southern Cuba and Puerto Rico.
  3. 1498–1500: He explored the eastern coast of South America.
  4. 1502–1504: He explored the Central American coast and the northern coast of South America.

- Columbus died in 1506 after years of ill health and essentially without recognition from the Spanish Crown. No one knows with absolute certainty where he is buried.
- Six nations are smaller than Washington, DC (63 square miles):

  1. Vatican City (.17 square mile)
  2. Monaco (.73 square mile)
  3. Nauru (8 square miles)
  4. Tuvalu (10 square miles)
  5. San Marino (24 square miles)
  6. Liechtenstein (61 square miles)

- The wildest river in North America is probably the Yukon in northern British Columbia, Canada.
- The U.S.–Canadian border is 3,987 miles long; the U.S.–Mexican border is 1933 miles long.
- There are eight time zones in North America.
- Madrid, Spain, at 2150 feet above sea level, is the highest capital city in Europe.
- Reykjavik, Iceland, is the westernmost capital city of Europe.
- The Federal Republic of Mexico contains 31 states and one federal district.
- Santa Fe, New Mexico, is the U.S. capital city with the highest elevation at about 7000 feet above sea level.
- Meaning of capital city names:

  1. Jerusalem, Israel: "city of peace"
  2. Beirut, Lebanon: "well"
  3. Bangkok, Thailand: "forest village"
  4. Madrid, Spain: "timber"
  5. Warsaw, Poland: "castle"
  6. Seoul, South Korea: "capital"
  7. Beijing, China: "northern capital"
  8. Ottawa, Canada: "to trade"

- Size comparisons:

  1. Romania is slightly smaller than Oregon.
  2. Hungary is slightly smaller than Indiana.
  3. Luxembourg is slightly smaller than Rhode Island.
  4. Poland is slightly larger than New Mexico.

- Colombia, South America, exports the most fresh-cut flowers to the United States. The Netherlands ranks second.
- Approximate size of eight Mideast countries:

  1. Iraq is more than twice the size of Idaho.
  2. Kuwait is smaller than New Jersey.
  3. Iran is larger than Alaska.
  4. Saudi Arabia is less than one-fourth the size of the United States.
  5. Ethiopia is less than twice the size of Texas.
  6. Syria is larger than North Dakota.
  7. Jordan is smaller than Indiana.
  8. Egypt is more than three times the size of New Mexico.

- There are thirty countries in the world with no coastline.
- The five largest metropolitan areas in the world in the 1990s are:

  1. Tokyo–Yokohama, Japan
  2. Mexico City, Mexico
  3. Saõ Paulo, Brazil
  4. Seoul, Korea
  5. New York, U.S.

- China raises more horses than the entire U.S.
- There are no native trees in Antarctica.
- The poorest nation in the world is probably Bhutan, where people earn on average less than $100/year.
- The *Fiji Times* claims that it is "the first newspaper published in the world today." (The International Dateline is very close to Fiji.)
- The only walled metropolis in North America is in Quebec City, Canada.
- The shortest transcontinental railroad (Atlantic to Pacific) is located at the Panama Canal.
- Canada is a really big country! Vancouver, British Columbia, is closer to Tokyo, Japan, than it is to Nova Scotia's Halifax on Canada's east coast.
- Before Christopher Columbus came to the New World, a squirrel, if so inclined, could go by treetop from the Atlantic Ocean to the Mississippi River. Where have all the trees gone?
- Population growth in the world's five largest countries, predicted for the next thirty years (1990–2020):

  1. China—34,400 persons per day
  2. India—47,600 persons per day
  3. CIS—5,900 persons per day
  4. U.S.—3,900 persons per day
  5. Indonesia—8,900 persons per day

- The population under age 15 in the world's most populous countries:

  1. Nigeria—45% under age 15
  2. Pakistan—45%
  3. Bangladesh—44%
  4. Indonesia—40%
  5. India—38%
  6. Brazil—36%
  7. China—28%
  8. CIS—26%
  9. Japan—22%
  10. U.S.—22%

- Illiteracy rate in ten of the world's 11 largest countries (by population) (persons age 15 or older):

  1. Bangladesh—74%
  2. Pakistan—74%
  3. Nigeria—66%
  4. India—64%
  5. Indonesia—33%
  6. Brazil—24%
  7. China—23%
  8. Japan—less than 1%
  9. Australia—less than 1%
  10. New Zealand—less than 1%
  11. Russia—less than 1%

- Female life expectancy is lower than male life expectancy in the following countries:

1. Afghanistan
2. Bangladesh
3. India
4. Iran
5. Nepal
6. Pakistan

- Female life expectancy in the United States is 78. Male life expectancy in the United States is 71.
- Names of the days:

English	Russian	Hebrew	French
Sunday	Voskresenje	Yom rishon	Dimanche
Monday	Ponedeljinc	Yom sheni	Lundi
Tuesday	Vtornik	Yom shlishi	Mardi
Wednesday	Sreda	Yom ravii	Mercredi
Thursday	Chetverg	Yom hamishi	Jeudi
Friday	Pjatnitsa	Yom shishi	Vendredi
Saturday	Subbota	Shabbat	Samedi

Italian	Spanish	German	Japanese
Domenica	Domingo	Sonntag	Nichiyobi
Lunedi	Lunes	Montag	Getsuyobi
Martedi	Martes	Dienstag	Kayobi
Mercoledi	Miercoles	Mittwoch	Suiyobi
Giovedi	Jueves	Donnerstag	Mokuyobi
Venerdi	Viernes	Freitag	Kin-yobi
Sabato	Sabado	Samstag	Doyobi

- Queen Mary II of England, Scotland, and Ireland died in 1694. Her lands' judges, who had worn colors, put on black robes to mourn. They never switched back, and black robes became the costume of judges in many nations—including the U.S.
- What is a supercity? A megacity? A supercity has 2 to 8 million people. A megacity has 8 million and up. *The world currently has 101 supercities and 28 megacities!*
- Astrid Lindgren, a Swedish housewife living in Nazi-occupied Sweden in 1944 wrote *Pippi Longstocking,* which has become the most widely translated children's book ever. It is still sold widely in more than 60 languages.
- The blue blazer, standard wearing apparel today, originated in the British Navy when the commanding officer of the *HMS Blaze* ordered his crew to wear blue serge jackets with navy buttons about a century ago.
- Kissing has been around for a very long time. Poets from ancient India, Greece, and Persia all wrote about kissing some 4,000 years ago.
- *Subaru* is the Japanese name for the constellation known as the Pleiades, or "seven sisters." Check out the Subaru car emblem!
- The oldest letter of any alphabet is *O.*
- In World War I, Germany was first to equip its pilots with parachutes.
- Sir Arthur Conan Doyle, who created Sherlock Holmes, named his character after the American judge Oliver Wendell Holmes, whom he greatly admired.

- The world's biggest employer is India's railways—some 1.5 million people on the payroll.
- The world's super rich live mostly in Japan, Germany, Mexico, and the U.S.
- Saskatchewan's capital was not always called Regina. It started out as "Pile o' Bones."
- Mexican historians point out that more than half of their original territory was taken over by the United States.
- In 1876, Lord Gormley Whiffle missed a four-inch putt on the St. Andrews old golf course, which cost him a silver medal, hence the modern term *whiff*.
- British-born explorer David Thompson spent 28 years exploring much of the same territory later traversed by the Lewis and Clark party.
- Approximately 15 tons of gold a year reportedly go into class rings.
- In Germany, the game of Monopoly is called "Wienerstrasse."
- It was Thomas Arnold, an English public headmaster, who promoted the notion that sports build character in the early 1800s.
- A woman named Christian Bowman, convicted of making counterfeit coins in Great Britain, was the last woman there to be executed by burning. In that same year (1789), Ben Franklin wrote, "Nothing is certain but death and taxes."
- Leonardo da Vinci was intimidated by crowds, so he avoided them.
- Two out of every three people in the shoemaking business are women.
- Of all ball games still being played, polo is the oldest.
- It was Europeans who introduced fishing with earthworms as bait to the Native American population.
- The year dividing *ancient* and *medieval* times is 476 A.D.
- The most popular colors for flags around the world are red, white, and blue.
- The Humber Suspension Bridge near Hull, England, is the longest bridge in the world. It is 4626 feet long and was completed in 1981.
- Trygve Lie of Norway was the first secretary-general of the United Nations (1946–1952).
- Marie Curie was the first woman to win a Nobel Prize. She did so twice, in 1903 for physics and in 1911 for chemistry.
- Arthur de Lulli was originally listed as the composer of "Chopsticks" in 1877. In truth, it was a 16-year-old girl named Euphemia Allen who used the name of "de Lulli."
- Authors most frequently translated into other languages:

  1. Agatha Christie
  2. Leonid Brezhnev
  3. Karl Marx
  4. Vladimir Lenin
  5. Jules Verne
  6. The Brothers Grimm
  7. Hans Christian Andersen
  8. Jack London

- Leonardo da Vinci is credited with inventing scissors.
- How long have the following items been around?

1. Needle (prehistoric times)
2. Button (300 B.C.)
3. Pin (1817)
4. Trouser fly (mid-1800s)
5. Hatpin (1832)
6. Safety pin (1849)
7. Snap-fastener (1855)
8. Zipper (1890)

- Wilhelm Roentgen won the first Nobel Prize for Physics with his invention of the X-ray.
- From Neanderthal times, human teeth have been getting smaller.
- It is said that storytelling is the oldest art form. Supposedly, no human society with a language did not tell stories.
- Ages when musicians began to play instruments:

1. Wolfgang Mozart (harpsichord), age 3
2. Ludwig van Beethoven (piano), age 3
3. Johann Sebastian Bach (violin), age 4
4. Peter Tchaikovsky (piano), age 4
5. Johannes Brahms (viola and violin), age 5
6. Frederic Chopin (piano), age 5 (played original melodies without any lessons)

- The largest animal in the history of the world is currently alive—the blue whale.
- By his twentieth birthday, Mozart had composed 30 symphonies, 12 masses, 8 operas, 12 sonatas, and 13 string quartets. He also wrote several serenades, dances, marches, vocal works, and concertos.
- "Twinkle, Twinkle Little Star" was written by Mozart before he was 5 years old.
- The expression "bite the dust" is not from an old cowboy movie. It comes from the *Iliad* by Homer.
- Victorious foot racers in ancient Greece received a celery stalk rather than a gold medal.
- Shoelaces were invented in England four years before the United States came into being.
- Christmas and May Day always fall on the same day of the week.
- Queen Elizabeth I is given credit for inventing the "gingerbread man" (the royal chef probably invented it).
- The first jigsaw puzzle was a map of Europe that was divided into national boundaries as they were in 1766.
- Giovanni Caboto is explorer John Cabot's real name.
- Brazil proudly reports that it has the world's largest snakes, biggest spiders, biggest rodents, and biggest ants.
- Most English-speaking nations base their legal system on English common law—all except the Scots, who built theirs on Roman law.
- Japan's national anthem has only four lines of lyrics.

CHAPTER EIGHT

Conclusion

"Education is not filling a bucket but lighting a fire."

—William Butler Yeats

This book was created to serve middle and secondary school educators in a multitude of ways. First, it provides basic information about the current state of both history and geography education as well as a preview of how those subject areas will probably be affected as we move into the twenty-first century. Second, it has the best qualities of encyclopedias, atlases, and almanacs which allow the user a quick, at-a-glance reference when seeking content information. Along with this, it also provides the user with a number of classroom-tested activities that are intended to assist the teacher in helping students learn the data and apply it to their personal life and times. It is in that sense a pragmatic resource for the teacher and learner alike. Third, the book, while presenting baseline data in history and geography, also tries to present those subject areas in a more personalized way. Too often, history and geography are presented as a matter-of-fact compilation of names, places, and events. Rarely do we humanize the people or events that make up the collective history of humankind. By doing so, we contend, we will make history and geography more relevant and meaningful to students and a greater pleasure to teach.

The record of history is much more than a chronicle of events. It records not only what we have done but also what we have tried to do—our motivations and the hopes that drive us to strive for something better. History is a repository of human values and attitudes, the accumulation of efforts, experiences, dreams, and accomplishments that have slowly civilized humankind. It is, however, paramount that we teach both history and geography in an objective and honest manner, recognizing that historical perspective is essential if we are to comprehend why people did what they did or why events happened as they did—when they did. The great danger here is that we too often apply today's morals and values to the past and condemn people and their actions by applying standards of conduct we currently consider acceptable. Just remember the old cliché that hindsight is 20/20.

The story of human progress is awe-inspiring, especially when one reflects on the fact that it is neither inevitable nor preordained. Our march through the millennia has been successful as a result of human effort—often short-sighted, often frustrated, and rarely mindful of either the past or the present, but nonetheless a steady progress to where we are today. The human adventure has been a fantastic one, and there is no limit to what we may yet achieve in the future.

What is important is that we who love history and geography must not only make our students aware of our historical journey to the present but also prepare them for the journey into the future on which they have embarked.

References

Abramowitz, J. (1975). *World history.* Chicago: Follette.

American Heritage dictionary. (1979). New York: Houghton Mifflin.

Baker, P. (1991). *Fashions of a decade: The 1950s.* New York: Facts on File.

Barbeau, Arthur E., & Floretti, Henri. *The Unknown Soldier: Black American Troops in World War I.* Philadelphia: Temple University Press, 1974.

Bartz, B. S. (1970). Maps in the classroom. *Journal of Geography, 69.* 18–24.

Beal, M. (1963). *"I will fight no more forever"; Chief Joseph and the Nez Perce War.* Seattle: University of Washington Press.

Benson, K., & Haskins, J. (1988). *The 60's reader.* New York: Viking Kestrel.

Bernard, R. N. (1983). Integrating literature and history in universities and secondary schools. *History Teacher, 16*(4), 505–516.

Boyce, A. N. (1983). *Europe and South Africa.* Johannesburg: Juta and Company.

Bradley Commission on History in Schools. (1988). *Building a history curriculum: Guidelines for teaching history in the schools.* Washington, DC: Educational Excellence Network.

Brook, C. (1990). *Best editorial cartoons of the year.* Getra: Pelican.

Brooks, T., & March, E. (1992). *The complete directory to prime time network TV shows, 1946–present* (p. 1009). New York: Ballantine Books.

Brownstone, David, & Franck, Irene. (1994). *Timelines of the arts and literature,* New York: HarperCollins.

Burne, J. (Ed.). (1989). *Chronicle of the world* (pp. 1118–1136). Harlow, Essex, UK: Longman Press.

Carey, J. (1990). *Eyewitness to history.* New York: Avon Books.

Carruth, G. (Ed.). (1993). *The encyclopedia of American facts and dates,* 9th ed. (pp. 506–545). New York: HarperCollins.

Cartooning Washington: 100 Years of Cartoon Art. (1990).

Cavallini, D. (1985). Are history textbooks killing the past? *History Teacher, 18.* 599–662.

Chapin, T. (1989). Picnic of the world. On *Mother Earth* [medium of recording]. Hollywood: A&M Records.

Clark, E. (1953). *Indian legends of the Pacific Northwest.* Berkeley: University of California Press.

Connelly, O. (1972). *The epoch of Napoleon.* Florida: R. E. Krieger.

Craig, G. A. (1972). *Europe since 1914.* New York: Holt, Rinehart and Winston.

Demko, G. T. (1992). *Why in the world? Adventures in geography.* New York: Doubleday.

Downey, M. J. (1985). *History in the schools.* National Council for the Social Studies (Bulletin 74). (ERIC Document Reproduction Service No. ED 254 477).

Ehrhart, W. D. (Ed.). (1985). *Carrying the darkness: American Indochina: The poetry of the Vietnam War.* New York: Avon Books.

Fadiman, C. (1985). *The Little, Brown Book of Anecdotes.* Boston: Little, Brown.

Feder, B. (1968). *Viewpoints in world history.* New York: American Book Company.

Ferrell, R. (Ed.). (1983). A letter from Harry Truman to Bess, Berlin, July 20, 1945. In *Letters to Bess.* New York: Norton.

Filipovic, Z. (1994). *Zlata's diary—A child's life in Sarajevo* (Christina Pribichevich-Zoric, Trans.). New York: Viking/Penguin.

Fisher, J. (1974). *The Elysian Fields.* London: Chaucer Press.

Forma, M., et al. (Eds.). (1989). *Cartooning Washington: 100 years of cartoon art in the Evergreen State.*

Forsyth, A. S. (1988). How we learn place location: Bringing theory and practice together. *Social Education,* November–December, pp. 500–502.

Frank, Anne. *Anne Frank: The diary of a young girl.* (1958). New York: Pocket Books/Washington Square Press.

Gabriel, P. (1990). Biko. On *Shaking the tree* [Compact Disc]. Virgin Records.

Gagnon, P. (Ed.) (1989). *Historical literacy. The case for history in American education.* New York: Macmillan.

Gerassi, J. (1968). *North Vietnam: A documentary.* New York: Bobbs-Merrill.

Gradwohl, R., & Greenber, R. (1988). *Saving the tropical rain forests.* Washington, DC: Ireland Press.

Grammer, R. (1986). Places in the world. On *Teaching peace* [medium of recording]. New York: Smilin' Attcha Music.

Gross, Ernie. (1990). *This day in American history.* New York: Neal Schuman.

Grun, B. (Ed.). (1975). *The timetables of history: A horizontal linkage of people and events* (pp. 516–531). New York: Simon & Schuster.

Gundlach, S. (1986). Putting the story back into history. *Curriculum Review, 25,* 77–80.

Harvey, E. (1994). *Our glorious century.* Pleasantville, NY: Reader's Digest Association.

Hasluck, T. (1969). *Teaching history.* London: Oxford University Press.

Higgins, E. L. (1949). *The French Revolution as told by contemporaries.* Boston: Houghton Mifflin.

History/social science framework for California public schools, kindergarten through grade 12. (1988). Sacramento, CA: History Social Science Unit State Department of Education.

Hoffman, F. W., & Bailey, W. G. (Eds.). (1990). *Arts and entertainment fads* (pp. 129–130). New York: Haworth Press.

Honig, B. (1987). The challenge of making history come alive. *Social Studies Review, 28*(2), 3–6.

Horton, J. (1989). The sinking of the Bismarck. On *American Originals.* [Compact Disc]. Columbia Records.

Jackdaw series. (1976). London: Jackdaw Publications.

Joel, B. (1985). Goodnight Saigon. On *Billy Joel: Greatest Hits Vol. II.* [Compact Disc]. Columbia Records.

Johnson, O. (Ed.). (1994). *The 1994 information please almanac: The ultimate browser's reference.* New York: Houghton Mifflin.

Johnson, O., Dailey, V., Bruno, W., Lyons, D., & Reed, A. (Eds.). (1991). *The 1991 information please almanac.* Boston: Houghton Mifflin.

Johnson, O., Dailey, V., Janice, E., Johnson, K., Lyons, D., Nemeth, T., & Reed, A. (Eds.). (1992). *The 1992 information please almanac.* Boston: Houghton Mifflin.

Johnson, O., Dailey, V., Kenny, J., Johnson, E., Lyons, D., Nemeth, T., & Reed, A. (Eds.). (1993). *The 1993 information please almanac.* Boston: Houghton Mifflin.

Johnson, O., Dailey, V., Scalza, R. A. T., Lyons, D., Nemeth, T., & Reed, A. (1994). *The 1994 information please almanac.* Boston: Houghton Mifflin.

Jones, M. W. (1975). *The cartoon history of the American Revolution.* New York: G. P. Putnam's Sons.

Kennan, G. *Memoirs.* New York: Little, Brown.

King, D. C. (1990). *Literature and the social studies. "People, not events, make history."* (City): MA: Sundance.

King, M. L. (1986). *I have a dream* [MPI Video]. ISBN 1-55607-247-3.

Kniep, W. M. (1985). Global education in the eighties. *Curriculum Review, 25 (2).* 16–18.

Lefebrye, G. (1947). *The coming of the French Revolution.* Princeton, NJ: Princeton University Press.

Levertov, D. (1991). What were they like? In J. P. Hunter (Ed.), *The Norton introduction to poetry.* New York: W. W. Norton.

Lewis, C. L. (1969). *Famous old world sea fighters.* Freeport, NY: Books for Libraries Press.

Long, L. H. (Ed.). *The world almanac and book of facts (1960–1969).* New York: Newspaper Enterprise Association.

Longfellow, H. W. (1988). Paul Revere's ride (the landlord's tale). In C. Sullivan (Ed.), *America in poetry.* Harry N. Abrams Publisher.

Lowe, N. (1969). *Mastering world history.* London: Hamlyn.

Luce, D., & Sommer, J. (1969). *Vietnam: The unheard voices.* Ithaca, NY: Cornell University Press.

MacGlobe. Broderbund Educational Marketing, 500 Redwood Boulevard, Novato, CA 94947.

MacTimeliner. Tom Snyder Productions, Inc., 80 Coolidge Hill Road. Wateron, MA 02172.

Markowitz, R., & Rosner, R. (Eds.). (1987). A letter from an American mother, Detroit, November 27, 1939. In *Slaves of the Depression: Workers' letters.* New York: Cornell University Press.

Marshall, S. L. (1978). *World War I.* Boston: Houghton Mifflin.

McCarthy, G. (1977). *War story: Vietnam war poems.* New York: Crossing Press.

Mehlinger, H. D. (1988). The reform of social studies and the role of the National Commission for the Social Studies. *History Teacher, 21*(2), 195–206.

Meneval, C. L. (1894). *Memoirs illustrating the history of Napoleon I from 1802 to 1815.* London: Hutchinson.

Mersmann, J. F. (1974). *Out of the Vietnam vortex; A study of poets and poetry against the war.* Lawrence: University of Kansas.

Milliken transparencies. (1973). London: Milliken.

Muir, S. P. (1985). Understanding and improving students' map reading skills. *Elementary School Journal, 86,* 207–216.

National Council for Geographic Education. (1991). *Directions in geography: A guide for teachers.* Washington, DC: Author.

National Council for the Social Studies (1989). *Charting a course.* Washington, DC: Social Studies for the 21st Century.

National Geographic Society, Geography Education Program, 17th and M Streets, N.W., Washington, DC 20036.

National Geographic Standards 1994: Geography for Life. American Geographical Society, Association of American Geographers, National Council for Geographic Education, National Geographic Society, Washington, DC.

National Standards, United States History Grades 5–12. (1994). National Center for History in the Schools, University of California.

Neli, E. (1985). Mirror of a people: Folktales and social studies. *Social Education, 49.*

The New Grolier Electronic Encyclopedia on CD-ROM. Grolier Electronic Publishing, Sherman Turnpike, Danbury, CT 06816.

Noakes, G., & Pridham, G. (Eds.). (1990). A letter from Helene to her father, 1939. In *Nazism, Vol II: A history in documents and eyewitness accounts, 1919–1945*. New York: Schocken Books/Random House.

Northwest Comic News. (1992). Editorial cartoons from the USA and abroad. No. 94.

Obst, L. R. (Ed.). (date) *The sixties*. New York: Random House/Rolling Stone Press.

Overly, N. V., & Kimpston, R. D. (1976). *Global studies: Problems and promises for elementary teachers*. Washington, DC: Association for Supervision and Curriculum Development.

Oxford dictionary of quotations. (1980). Oxford: Oxford University Press.

Palmer, R. R. (1969). *A source book for modern history*. London: McGraw-Hill.

Press, C. (1981). *The political cartoon*. Rutherford, NJ: Fairleigh Dickinson United Press.

Ravitch, D., & Finn, C. (1987). *What do our 17-year-olds know? A report on the first national assessment of history and literature*. New York: Harper & Row.

Reader's Digest. (1977). *The Readers Digest book of strange stories, amazing facts. Stories that are bizarre, unusual, odd, astonishing, incredible, but true.* (2nd ed.) London: Reader's Digest.

Richards, D. (1968). *Early modern Europe*. London: Oxford University Press.

Rottman, L., Barry, J., & Paquet, B. (Eds.). (1972). *Winning hearts and minds; War poems by Vietnam veterans*. New York: First Casualty Press.

Rowe, J., & Berg, R. (1991). *The Vietnam war and American culture*. New York: Columbia University Press.

Sann, Paul. (1979). *The angry decade: The sixties*. New York: Crown Publishers.

Schubert, D. (Writer, Director), Glinski, F. (Editor), & Gerber, J. (Narrator). (1990). *Ode to joy and freedom–The fall of the Berlin Wall* [Video], Rian TV, Berlin.

Silver, J. (1992) *Ready-to-use world geography activities for grades 5–12*. New York: Simon & Schuster; Center for Applied Research in Education.

Simon, P. (1990). 7 o'clock news. On *Simon & Garfunkel collected works* [Compact Disc]. Columbia Records.

Simon, P. (1990). Silent night. On *Simon & Garfunkel collected works* [Compact Disc]. Columbia Records.

Snyder, L. (Ed.). (1981). An eyewitness account by Kurt Ludecke on first hearing Hitler speak. In *Hitler's Third Reich: A documentary history*. Chicago: Nelson-Hall.

Taylor, A. J. (1970). *History of the twentieth century*. London: Purnell.

Terkel, S. (1970). *An oral history of the Great Depression*. New York: Pantheon Books.

Thompson, D. (1966). *Europe since Napoleon*. London: Penguin Books Limited.

Thompson, J. M. (1964). *Napoleon's letters*. London: Everyman's Library.

Tye, K. (1991). *Global education from thought into action*. Alexandria, VA: Edwards Brothers.

West, P. (1990). *Portable people*. Library of Congress Cataloging-in-Publication Data ISBN 945167-35-0.

World almanac book of facts. (1995). New York: Pharos Books.

"In the long run of history, the censor and the inquisitor have always lost. The only sure weapon against bad ideas is better ideas. The source of better ideas is wisdom. The surest path to wisdom is a liberal education."

—A. Whitney Griswold

Index